Empire and Slavery
in American Literature
1820–1865

W9-CYB-172

Empire and Slavery in American Literature 1820–1865

Eric J. Sundquist

University Press of Mississippi / *Jackson*

www.upress.state.ms.us

The University Press of Mississippi is a member of the
Association of American University Presses.

Published 2006 by University Press of Mississippi by
arrangement with Cambridge University Press
All rights reserved
Manufactured in the United States of America

© Cambridge University Press 1995
Reprinted with permission.

∞

Library of Congress Cataloging-in-Publication Data

Sundquist, Eric J.
    Empire and slavery in American literature, 1820–1865 / Eric J. Sundquist.
    p. cm.
    Originally published as: The Cambridge history of American literature,
volume 2, 1820–1865. Cambridge [England] : Cambridge University Press,
1994–<2004>
    Includes bibliographical references and index.
    ISBN 1-57806-863-0 (pbk. : alk. paper) 1. American literature—19th
century—History and criticism. 2. Slavery in literature. 3. African Americans
in literature. 4. Indians in literature. I. Cambridge history of
American literature. II. Title.
    PS201S86 2006
    810.9'358—dc22   2006001043

British Library Cataloging-in-Publication Data available

Contents

Empire and Slavery
in American Literature
1820–1865

Introduction

"Escaped from the house of bondage," wrote Herman Melville in a well-known statement of the nation's post-revolutionary mission in *White-Jacket* (1850), America is "the Israel of our time." Bearing "the ark of liberties" for the world, the new nation appeared to be the long-awaited "political Messiah," to whom God had given "the broad domains of the political pagans, that shall yet come and lie down under the shade of our ark, without bloody hands being lifted." Elected to liberate the world in fulfillment of scripture, according to one strain of Protestant millennialist theory, Americans absorbed biblical typology into national history and envisioned an empire extending not just to the borders of the current United States but beyond the far reaches of the New World.

In view of his sustained inquiry into the risks of empire-building in *Moby-Dick* (1852) and elsewhere, Melville's paean to manifest destiny may be judged ironic, but it mirrored the grandiloquent prose found in idealizations such as Charles W. Dana's emigration guide *The Garden of the World; Or, the Great West* (1856): "The Land of Promise, and the Canaan of our time . . . broadens over the vast prairies and mighty rivers, over queenly lakes and lofty mountains, until the ebb and flow of the Pacific tide kisses the golden shores of the El Dorado. . . . O, the soul kindles at the thought of what a magnificent empire the West is but the germ, which, blessed with liberty and guaranteeing equal rights to all, shall go on conquering . . . until the whole earth shall resound with its fame and glory."

With no less enthusiasm, Senator William Seward, later responsible for the purchase of Alaska, which enlarged the nation by some 600,000 square miles, found comparable prophecy in the 1848 Treaty of Guadalupe Hidalgo, which concluded the Mexican War and enlarged the nation by 1.2 million square miles. If only North and South could remain united, Seward argued, the westward march that began when European nations sent explorers in search of trade routes to Asia would be completed. "The ripening civilization of the West" will soon "mingle with the declining civilization of the East on our own free soil," at which point "a new and more perfect civilization will arise to bless the earth, under the sway of our own cherished and beneficent democratic institutions." Like the wars waged against one after another tribe of American Indians, war with Mexico was but a step along the way to hemispheric conquest in natural fulfillment of the American Revolution. To this people "nursed into full vigor, by long and bloody Indian wars," declared George Lippard in *Legends of Mexico* (1847), "God Almighty has given the destiny of the entire American continent. . . . As the Aztec people crumbled before the Spaniard, so will the mongrel race, molded of Indian and Spanish blood, melt into, and be ruled by, the Iron Race of the North."

Nor were such romantic visions necessarily contradicted by the practice of slavery. As Edward Pollard wrote in *Black Diamonds Gathered in the Darkey Homes of the South* (1861), the expansion of the section's slave-based economy was a matter involving "the world's progress," and he foresaw American cotton and sugar production extending throughout the Caribbean and Central America. Territory once the home of "flashing cities and great temples," but "now covered with mute ruins and trampled over by half-savages," would thus be restored as the new seat of an American empire "controlling the commerce of the world, impregnable in its position, and representing in its internal structure the most harmonious of all systems of modern civilization."

In the event, slavery did not spread, and North and South were reunited at the cost of terrible bloodshed; but in the aftermath of the Civil War Walt Whitman found renewed energy in the nation's westward advance. Invoking the voyages of Christopher Columbus and forecasting what would now be termed globalization, Whitman marveled in "Passage to India" (1871) at promised blessings both material and transcendental:

> Passage to India!
> Lo, soul, seest thou not God's purpose from the first?
> The earth to be spann'd, connected by network,
> The races, neighbors, to marry, and be given in marriage,
> The oceans to be cross'd, the distant brought near,
> The lands to be welded together.

Such sentiments may seem incredible today—even when measured against contemporary announcements of America's obligation to bring democracy to tyrannized peoples and benighted lands. Both in fact and in persistent mythology, however, the belief of Americans that they are the "redeemer nation" (to cite the evocative title of Ernest Tuveson's classic study), the "iron race" of people chosen by God or motivated by some deep-seated psychic impulse to enlighten and to master the world, has been periodically interrupted and transformed but seldom diminished. Analyzing the mission of Apollo 11 in *Of a Fire on the Moon* (1970), Norman Mailer thought the rush of wind through the Cape Canaveral launch towers resonated "across two thousand miles to the grain elevators by the side of railroad tracks in the mournful empty windings of the West" and wondered if "the ghosts of old Indians [were] awakening in the prairies and the swamps." In the "iron of astronauts" selected for the moon landing, Mailer found "the core of some magnetic human force called Americanism, patriotism, or Waspitude." Perhaps, he speculated, the Wasp—the white, Anglo-Saxon Protestant—"had emerged from human history in order to take us to the stars. How else account for that strong, severe, Christian, missionary, hell-raising, hypocritical, ideologically simple, patriotic, stingy, greedy, God-fearing, nature-despoiling, sense-destroying, logic-making, technology-deploying, brave human machine of a Wasp?"

Illustrative of the leftwing critique of American imperialism that reached a fever pitch in the late 1960s, Mailer's catalogue of traits was bombastic. But blithe confidence that America bears the "ark of liberties" for the world has never lacked voices of opposition, and the nation's expansive ambitions have assuredly been seen in different terms by the people who felt the effects of such hubris, whether naïve or malicious. "Born in genocide" in its wars against American Indians and further "disfigured" by slavery, wrote Martin Luther King, Jr., in *Why We Can't Wait* (1964), the United States had betrayed, rather than fulfilled, the blessings of liberty. Taking inspiration from Third World revolutionary movements, more militant race nationalists of the civil rights era frequently defined themselves as participants in anticolonial struggle. "From the beginning," contended Harold Cruse in a 1962 essay entitled "Revolutionary Nationalism and the Afro-American," the enslavement of black Americans "coincided with the colonial expansion of European powers and was nothing more or less than a condition of domestic colonialism." Brown Power, the power of *La Raza*, echoed Black Power. "El Plan Espiritual de Aztlán," a manifesto of Chicano self-determination written in 1969, was predicated on the recovery of mythic tribal lands alienated by successive waves of Euro-American conquest and capped by the Mexican Cession of 1848. "Our search for Chicano roots led to Mesoamerica and Aztec legend," the novelist Rudolfo Anaya later observed, "and there we found Aztlán; put another way, Aztlán was waiting for us."

In the case of American Indians, their rejoinders to invasion and subjugation have typically had both political and ecological dimensions. Whereas nineteenth-century advocates of Indian Removal insisted that people guided by "true philanthropy" could not possibly "prefer a country covered with forests and ranged by a few thousand savages to our extensive Republic, studded with cities, towns, and prosperous farms," in the 1830 words of President Andrew Jackson, Native Americans perceived that such philanthropy required the sacrifice not just of their own customs and lives but also of the natural world with which they once existed in harmonious balance. The white man's insatiable vocation of conquest, according to Leslie Marmon Silko in *Storyteller* (1981), might best be imagined as a contest among witches that led to the destruction of the Indians' world and would issue one day in the uranium-fueled annihilation of the whole planet:

They will take this world from ocean to ocean
they will turn on each other
they will destroy each other
Up here
in these hills
they will find the rocks,
rocks with veins of green and yellow and black.
They will lay the pattern with these rocks
they will lay it across the world
and explode everything.

To put it another way, the literature of colonization and empire provoked a corresponding literature of anticolonial resistance, one that arose from a more tragically acute knowledge of America as the land of promise. Richard Wright thus saw the twentieth-century migration of blacks from South to North as a modern extension of slavery's radical dislocation of Africans and their culture to the Americas. In just three hundred years, he argued in *12 Million Black Voices*

(1941), blacks had "traversed through swift compulsion" a historical terrain equivalent to two thousand years of European history. "Hurled from our native African homes into the very center of the most complex and highly industrialized civilization the world has ever known," said Wright, "we stand today with a consciousness and memory such as few people possess." Who, indeed, was the exemplary American? "The white man does not understand the Indian for the reason that he does not understand America," wrote Luther Standing Bear in *Land of the Spotted Eagle* (1933). "The white man is still troubled with primitive fears; he still has in his consciousness the perils of this frontier continent, some of its fastnesses not yet having yielded to his questing footsteps and inquiring eyes. . . . The man from Europe is still a foreigner and an alien. And he still hates the man who questioned his path across the continent."

Such oppositional voices belong to the panoramic multiculturalism now taken for granted in academic and popular culture. Both literature and the scholarly study of it have in recent decades become multiethnic and implicitly postcolonial to a fault. Just as generic and topical boundaries have been eroded through the introduction of new paradigms drawn from fields such as critical race studies, political theory, anthropology, and environmental studies, so the emergence of globalization as a guiding rubric of literary criticism, as well as contemporary economic, social, and cultural analysis, is the latest stage in the study of literature as an expression of nationalism and its attempted subversion. Although postcolonial theory may provide a more accurate lens for reinterpreting European literatures in their clash and merger with the literatures of Africa, Asia, and the Middle East, its strategies have been brought increasingly to bear upon American literature for the simple reason that the paradoxical entanglement between liberty and oppression, freedom and its denial, lies at the heart of antebellum literature, no less with respect to American Indians and Mexicans (or other Latinos) than with respect to African Americans.

One can point to any number of later authors to demonstrate that the roots of modern-day multiculturalism lie in the history and literature of the early national period. When she formulated her influential theory of a new "*mestiza* consciousness . . . a consciousness of the Borderlands" in *Borderlands / La Frontera* (1987), for example, Gloria Anzaldúa looked back at a "racial, ideological, cultural and biological cross-pollenization" that had been underway for hundreds of years prior to the border being drawn between the United States and Mexico. When she created her maroon slave rebel, Cuffee Ned, in

The Chosen Place, the Timeless People (1969), Paule Marshall memorialized
historical figures such as Nat Turner and Gabriel Prosser while joining in the
reconstruction of slave culture—its African inheritances, its kinship structures,
its hunger for freedom—documented first in slave narratives. When he wrote
in "The Man Made of Words" (1970) that "our whole experience as a nation
in this century has been a repudiation of the pastoral ideal which informs so
much of the art and literature of the nineteenth century," that "we may be
perfectly sure of where we are in relation to the supermarket and the next cof-
fee break, but I doubt that any of us knows where he is in relation to the stars
and to the solstices," N. Scott Momaday described not just a Native American
ethic and epistemology but a way of relating to the land, for all peoples of the
nation, that had been radically transformed by capitalism and technology.

Paying tribute to California as the temporary limit of the American frontier in *The Land of Gold* (1850), Walter Colton predicted that "the tide of
Anglo-Saxon blood" will "yet flow the globe round, and beat in every nation's
pulse." For better and for worse, Colton was to be proved correct. Even when
America's territorial ambitions were checked, the reach of its political, economic, and cultural power remained extensive and in many cases irresistible—
but with the consequence, moreover, that its own culture long ago ceased to
be a homogenous expression of white, Anglo-Saxon Protestantism. In the
nation's expansion "the globe round," benevolence and arrogance, generos-
ity and exploitation, have been commingled, but what constitutes "American"
culture has also continued to grow more complex and invigorating. Through
its propensity for constant economic and cultural expansion, combined with its
capacity to provide haven to millions of the world's emigrants, the "blood" of
other nations and cultures—whether those of the continent, the Americas at
large, or those beyond—came to beat ever more strongly in the nation's pulse
as well.

Each generation writes literary history in terms of its own ideals and pre-
occupations. In telling part of the story for this generation, my aim has been
to recover, in sufficient detail, an array of material that makes it possible to
understand American literature in its formative period in more inclusive ways.
Empire and Slavery in American Literature, 1820–1865 originated as a contribution to Volume Two of the *Cambridge History of American Literature*, edited
by Sacvan Bercovitch and published in 1995, and its organization and quasi-
encyclopedic argument are in keeping with that purpose. Some corrections

have been made, and chapter titles and section subtitles, as well as some para-graph breaks, have been added, but the text of this new edition is otherwise unchanged. Insofar as other contributors to the original volume dealt with more canonical prose and poetry, as well as popular fiction and literary mar-kets, my section meant to tell the story of writing much of which had been little noticed for a century—the literature of exploration and expansion, of American Indians and the frontier, and of slavery and African Americans. Some of the writers included here were well regarded and widely read in their own day and later—James Fenimore Cooper, for example, or Harriet Beecher Stowe—while others have only recently been included in accounts of "major" American writers, Frederick Douglass being the most obvious. By the same token, vernacular art such as the slave spirituals and stereotypical figures such as the frontier gunslinger, both of which took on their definitive contours in the early national period, are so ingrained in American culture as to seem vir-tually timeless, while other works such as Native American chants or Mexican-American *corridos* were rediscovered and made integral to modern literary practice in the twentieth century.

Although scholarly attention to non-canonical works and alternative con-structions of literary history have burgeoned in recent years—as one may judge by some of the recent titles now added to the bibliography—a good deal of the literature surveyed here remains relatively unstudied, if it is known at all, except by specialists in one or another field. Not all texts are of equal value, of course, and a number of those cited have greater significance as documents of cultural history than as literature. But it is one purpose of this volume to pro-vide a context for thinking more carefully about Melville, Cooper, Whitman, Stowe, and other writers traditionally regarded as canonical, another to insist that literary history is a turmoil of voices, both major and minor, arranged into explanatory patterns bound to be conflicted, provisional, and reflective of one's own era. We are now likely to find, for instance, that Melville was in quest not of a white whale alone but of white ideology—that is, the assump-tions governing the imperial venture that, in its contradictory combination of virtue and vice, asserted and sought to extend European and American empire. *Moby-Dick* showed the Euro-American world in contention with others—the world of enslaved Africans, the diverse world of American Indians, and not least the entire ecological world that was being harnessed to new machines of industry. Melville, in other words, has to be understood in terms of Charles

Wilkes's *Narrative of the United States Exploring Expedition* (1845), and in terms of Martin Delany's novel of trans-Caribbean slave resistance, *Blake* (1859), and in terms of the letter sent by Dwamish chief Seathl (Seattle) to President Franklin Pierce in 1855: "What is man without the beasts? If all the beasts were gone, men would die from great loneliness of spirit, for whatever happens to the beast also happens to man. All things are connected. Whatever befalls the earth befalls the sons of the earth." And so, too, should Wilkes, Delany, and Seathl be understood in terms of Melville.

In 1963 Malcolm X, with his canny appreciation of racial inversions, could turn cultural color codes upside down by proclaiming a rainbow coalition from which whites would be excluded: "Black, brown, red, yellow, all are brothers, all are one family. The white one is a stranger. He's the odd fellow." Today, however, we are far closer to a multinational, multiethnic norm—so much so that it is yet another purpose of this volume to suggest that the great variety of contemporary American writing and criticism makes concepts such as "canonical" and "minority" less and less stable, or at least less and less easily assigned according to ethnicity, gender, and other such attributes. Those who wished to keep the culture and the canon uncontaminated—"KEEP AMERICA PURE WITH LIBERTY PAINTS," begins a sequence burlesquing white supremacy in Ralph Ellison's *Invisible Man* (1952)—were doomed to fail, but so are those who have argued for a contrary kind of purity. As Ellison speculated in "The Little Man at Chehaw Station" (1977), it could be hoped that "the call for a new social order based upon the glorification of ancestral blood and ethnic background" would lead not to chaos, one plausible result, but instead to dynamic heterogeneity: "Where there's a melting pot there's smoke, and where there's smoke it is not simply optimistic to expect fire, it's imperative to watch for the phoenix's vernacular, but transcendent, rising."

The Land of Promise
Exploration and Empire

Looking back on the years following the U.S. conquest of the territories of northern Mexico in 1848, the former Mexican military commander Mariano Vallejo concluded his five-volume *Recuerdos históricos y personales tocante a la Alta California*, completed in 1875, with an illuminating but unusual critique. Despite the Treaty of Guadalupe Hidalgo, he wrote,

the Americans have treated the Californians as a conquered people and not as citizens who willingly became part of that great family which, under the protection of that glorious flag that proudly waved at Bunker Hill, defied the attacks of European monarchs, those who, seated upon their tottering thrones, were casting envious eyes toward California and the other regions embraced within the great federation of the sons of liberty.

Vallejo's assessment, marked as it is by his consent to the ideology of American empire, has to be read in the context of his own highly nationalistic narrative, and his views were by no means representative of the newly colonized Mexican people of the Southwest and California. Yet his memoir sums up the important paradoxes generated during nineteenth-century American expansion by the clash between the liberating ideals of democracy and the drive toward territorial acquisition, just as his own life symbolically reflected the ambiguities of national allegiance and power in the contested lands of the American continent.

Vallejo's career, in fact, followed a pattern not entirely unlike that of famous Anglo-American political leaders or advocates of western expansion such as Andrew Jackson. By the time of Mexico's war with the United States, Vallejo was an eminent figure in California history. He had led Mexican troops in a bloody battle against an 1829 uprising of Indians at Mission San José; had commanded the northern frontier of California against the fear of Russian and European encroachment and in warfare against other American Indian tribes; had created for his family a vast feudal barony in the area north of San Francisco Bay; had, with his nephew Governor Juan Batista Alvarado, briefly proclaimed an independent state of California in 1836; and had gradually become a proponent of the annexation of California by the United States, which he thought preferable to the disorganization of local governments and distant Mexican rule. Whatever the importance of Vallejo's adopted patriotism, his view that the Mexican War was fought primarily to protect America's national interests from foreign threat and to rescue a willing native population from despotic rule was clearly not accepted by many Mexicans, or even by all Anglo-Americans, in 1848. But his remarks drew upon long-standing arguments about the destined expansion of America as a democratic nation free from tyranny—arguments that, since the outset of colonial settlement, had typically remained untroubled by the fact that the economic and political greatness of the United States would be achieved at the expense of American Indians and other nonwhite groups. Vallejo's own appropriation of the rhetoric of the American Revolution, as crucial to the U.S. war against Mexico as it was in the sectional conflict over African American slavery that led to the Civil War, indicates the confluence of ideological forces that gave complex meaning to the territory coveted by the "sons of liberty."

To extend America's "area of freedom," as Andrew Jackson called it, necessitated the absorption or the subjugation of American Indian tribes and Mexicans. In this respect, however, American expansion in the nineteenth century was not unique. A common argument closely linked to Enlightenment ideas of progress based on scientific inquiry was that the exploration of unknown lands and the conversion of alien peoples through political and economic expansion took place according to organic laws of growth. Throughout the world, the nineteenth century was a great age for exploration, as the limits of the seas from pole to pole were probed, and the interiors of previously uncharted continents in both hemispheres revealed. Although American explorers and settlers, like their European counterparts, usually believed their quests to be scientifically progressive and culturally beneficial, they frequently remained blind to the integrity and achievements of the peoples they encountered. While European powers established colonies in Africa, Asia, and Latin America, the United States in the four decades before the Civil War enveloped an enormous contiguous territory between the eastern seaboard and the Pacific coast. Roughly twice the size of the former U.S. holdings, this territory might also be thought of as "colonial" in that it was originally occupied by politically and militarily less powerful peoples. Its literature is the narrative of a relentless conquest in which the march of one civilization destroyed or utterly changed many others through dispossession and absorption.

Treaties with Great Britain in 1818 and 1846 gave the United States the upper Great Plains and the Pacific Northwest to the Forty-ninth Parallel; the Mexican Cession of 1848 and the Gadsden Purchase of 1853 established the southern border along the Rio Grande in Texas, then west through the New Mexican territory and southern California to the Pacific. The literal mapping of the United States was accompanied by a vast written record that established the psychological and political boundaries of the nation—a territory that existed as an act of prophetic vision even before poets and novelists expanded its horizons. Written in the form of diaries, journals, formal reports, travel narratives, and fiction, and composed by trappers, adventurers, scientists, common pioneers, soldiers, and professional writers, the literature detailing the exploration of the territories opened to conquest by the American Revolution and the Louisiana Purchase, and later by treaty and war with Great Britain and Mexico, may claim to be the new republic's first national literature. The writing about actual exploration often borrowed the imperial rhetoric of expansionism produced by politicians and journalists who had little contact with the vast wilderness but who foresaw its economic and social significance and coveted its wealth of natural resources. The prevailing idea of America's "manifest destiny"—its mission to conquer and regenerate the North American continent, the western hemisphere, or even the entire world—picked up strains of perfectionism from Puritan discourse and, guided by the imagined fulfillment of America's democratic promise unleashed by the Age of Revolution, made the mapping of the United States coincident with an eschatological idealism. The extension of American boundaries, it was argued, would mean the extension of democracy; the opening of a "virgin land" to settlement would release boundless energies of creativity and industry; the discovery and cultivation of material abundance would benefit the whole world by giving America the means to make itself an asylum for the oppressed of foreign nations.

Throughout the antebellum period poetic and political visions often shared the belief that the civilizations of the past were to be telescoped into the future of America and made a function of its limitless vistas of space. A number of important American writers of the antebellum period—James Fenimore Cooper, William Cullen Bryant, Mary Jemison, Washington Irving, Herman Melville, Henry David Thoreau, Francis Parkman, Black Hawk, Frederick Douglass, and Edgar Allan Poe among them—explored the theme of expansion. The issue found perhaps its most representative voice in Walt Whitman, who wrote in "Starting From Paumanok" (1860):

> See revolving the globe,
> The ancestor-continents away group'd together,
> The present and future continents north and south, with the isthmus between.
> See, vast trackless spaces,
> As in a dream they change, they swiftly fill,
> Countless masses debouch upon them,
> They are now cover'd with the foremost people, arts, institutions, known. . . .
>
> Americanos! conquerors! marches humanitarian!
> Foremost! century marches! Libertad! masses!
> For you a programme of chants.

Whitman's use of the Indian name for Long Island (Paumanok) and the Spanish word for "liberty" suggest the ironies latent in American expansion. American Indians seldom belonged, except symbolically, to the envisioned greatness of American futurity, at best offering a special problem of assimilation for the "nation of nations." In addition, the settlement of the Southwest and the Mexican War were justified by many on the principle that the United States would democratically "regenerate" backward and slavish Mexicans. Moreover, only civil war, not a "programme of chants," brought the semblance of freedom to black American slaves. Although the question of slavery's extension was important to settlement and boundary questions in the Plains and southwestern territories, it sometimes seemed to have little effect on inspired proclamations of America's destiny. Like other social problems, slavery appeared to many to be an example of human tyranny that would be eradicated upon the realization of democratic perfection. Class, racial, and gender inequities, claimed important proponents of American expansion, would disappear if only the highest ideals were kept in view. Catharine Beecher, for example, writing on the role of women and the necessity of a domestic model to the realization of democratic ideals in her *Treatise on Domestic Economy* (1841), placed herself securely in the tradition of America's millennial evolution. Women engaged in "renovat[ing] degraded man," she argued, "are agents in accomplishing the greatest work that was ever committed to human responsibility. It is the building of a glorious temple, whose base shall be co-extensive with the bounds of the earth, whose summit shall pierce the skies, whose splendor shall beam on all lands."

Conceived of as organic, predestined, or necessitated by the claims of political morality, expansion was authorized on a variety of grounds: territorial security; the development of resources, navigation, and trade; the guarantee of individual liberty and self-sufficiency; and notions of predestination and futurity. Nonetheless, the idea of America's exceptional mission was so clearly a function of the great wealth of new territories open for exploration, marketing, and development that the concept of millennial destiny explains less than some of its most vocal advocates thought. The "passage to India," whether overland, upriver, or by transcontinental railroad, was possible only because the land was there to be opened to Euro-American progress. However culpable the United States might come to seem in its treatment of American Indians and Mexicans over the next century and beyond, nineteenth-century observers argued that the social organization and land use of the two groups were a hindrance to progress as it was defined according to the standards of Euro-American civilization. The literature of exploration, like the claims of manifest destiny, played a significant role in the construction of the frontier ideology by which both Indians and Mexicans were categorized in the white mind. Many accounts by explorers and settlers were very sympathetic to native inhabitants, but much of the writing was imbued with fatalistic notions of the inevitable demise of "savage" life or the corruption and degeneration of Hispanic culture.

The concept of the primitive (or the savage) split off in several directions that were important for ideas about the western expansion. The wilderness could be portrayed as an Edenic abode for the realization of man's true primordial instincts (suppressed in complex society); it could seem the refuge of renegades and "mountain men" who sought an arena for dissipation; or it could be imagined as a source of sublime inspiration, which would liberate the American mind from its enslavement to corrupting or decaying Old World ideas and institutions. Until well into the 1850s, moreover, "the West" could refer to virtually any territory beyond the Allegheny Mountains. The argument between Old World antiquity and New World virginity, central to rising calls for a nationalistic culture and literature from the 1820s on through the 1860s, was thus played out in successive stages in America's westward development. The differentiations provided by narratives of exploration did not so much modify claims of national destiny as give them an ever more magnificent natural stage setting.

America's vast and complex geography prompted a multitude of political and literary responses ranging from ecstatic celebrations of its sublime beauty to utilitarian proposals for its industrial and agricultural use, all of them grounded in a sense of America's special destiny among the nations of the world. The vast American West imposed upon the Euro-American mind a landscape that was alternately splendorous, terrifying, and anarchic precisely because it seemed as yet uncontaminated by extensive human presence. What are "the towers in which feudal oppression has fortified itself," with its "despotic superstitions," asked Charles F. Hoffman (1806–84) in *A Winter in the West* (1835), compared "to the deep forests which the eye of God has alone pervaded, and where Nature, in her unviolated sanctuary, has for ages laid her fruits and flowers on His altar!" Similarly, journalist and man of letters Nathaniel Parker Willis (1806–67), in an Emersonian moment, wrote in *American Scenery* (1840) that Americans look "upon all external objects as exponents of [their own] future." Instead of finding himself surrounded by unchanging names, landmarks, and modes of culture, as in Europe, the American's first thought when looking over an untouched valley "is of the villages that will soon sparkle on the hill-sides, the axes that will ring from the woodlands, and the mills, bridges, canals, and railroads that will span and border the streams that now rush through sedges and wild flowers."

Writing about the West, whether documentary or fictional, fed the enthusiasm for Romantic primitivism that permeated much American literature in the antebellum period and that provoked echoes of revolutionary rhetoric about breaking the constraints of British and European custom. A writer for the *United States Magazine and Democratic Review*, for example, offered a strong challenge in 1841:

We look to see yet in the West a bolder and manlier action of the American mind, which will scorn that emasculate imitativeness of England and English things that yet holds us in an unworthy thraldom, which will surrender itself more freely to the guidance of the genius of American democracy, and will find an inspiration stimulating it to achievements worthy of itself, in all those vast sublimities of nature, ever young in her most hoary age, that are there spread out before it as though for this very purpose.

The ideas of liberty, originality, wilderness, moral health, and national mission became intertwined, not always exactly equivalent but nonetheless provoking constant associations with one another. Reflected in various writings about the West, as well as in the grand landscapes of nineteenth-century American painters, the sublime in America became at once an aesthetic, a metaphysical, and a political force at the heart of the country's new spirit of nationalism—a spirit that deliberately conceived of the "heart" of America as its interior or western regions.

As early as 1815, Daniel Drake, writing of Ohio, had declared that the inhabitants of the West, secluded from inordinate contact with "foreign luxuries," were "destined to an unrivaled excellence in agriculture, manufactures, and internal commerce; in literature and the arts; in public virtue; and in national strength." Perhaps the fullest early expression of the western promise appeared in Edward Everett's 1824 Phi Beta Kappa oration, "The Circumstances Favorable to the Progress of Literature in America." In Everett's conception, the democratic institutions of the United States, its apparently limitless space, and its rapidity of development had combined to create a remarkable commonality of governmental purpose and linguistic energy. In terms that were soon used by others to describe the land beyond the Rocky Mountains, Everett argued that Providence had provided America as a "last refuge" to men "flying westward from civil and religious thraldom." Quoting with admiration Bishop Berkeley's famous stanza beginning "Westward the course of Empire takes its way," Everett called upon patriots and scholars alike to realize the ancient prophecies of "a land of equal laws and happy men," a Golden Age in the West:

We are summoned to new energy and zeal, by the high nature of the experiment we are appointed [by] providence to make, and the grandeur of the theatre on which it is to be performed. . . . Here must these bright fancies [of a Golden Age] be turned to truth; here must these high visions be realized, in which the seers and sages of the elder world took refuge from the calamities of the days in which they lived. There are no more continents to be revealed; Atlantis hath arisen from the ocean; the farthest Thule is reached; there are no more retreats beyond the sea, no more discoveries, no more hopes.

The rhetoric of Drake and Everett became commonplace in arguments for expansion during the first half of the nineteenth century. As Whitman wrote in his final preface to *Leaves of Grass*, America and its poets were to have leading parts in the unfolding of history, "as if in some colossal drama, acted again like those of old, under the open sun, the Nations of our time, and all the characteristics of Civilization, seem hurrying, stalking across, flitting from wing to wing, gathering, closing up, toward some long-prepared, most tremendous, denouement." The American geography was to embody the destiny of a new democratic nation that now more than ever imagined itself as a "city upon a hill," a moral example for the rest of the world. John L. O'Sullivan (1813–95), editor of the *New York Morning News* and the *Democratic Review*, would become famous for coining the term "manifest destiny" in an 1845 essay calling for the admission of Texas into the Union. But the concept was hardly new, and O'Sullivan himself had used a variation of the idea in an 1838 essay entitled "The Great Nation of Futurity," which expressed the prevailing view of America's "boundless future":

> In its magnificent domain of space and time, that nation of many nations is destined to manifest to mankind the excellence of divine principles; to establish on earth the noblest temple ever dedicated to the worship of the Most High—the Sacred and the True. Its floor shall be a hemisphere—its roof the firmament of the star-studded heavens, and its congregation a Union of many Republics, comprising hundreds of happy millions, calling, owning no man master, but governed by God's natural and moral law of equality.

The secular literature of exploration and expansion was in this sense a natural continuation of the colonial literature of Christian self-examination and prophecy. The Puritan goal of inspiring religious freedom in Europe was transfigured into the postrevolutionary purpose of inspiring further democratic revolutions in Europe. As Catharine Beecher's father, Lyman Beecher, wrote in *A Plea for the West* (1835), the inspirational example of the American West should rouse "from the sleep of ages and the apathy of despair" the oppressed of Europe, throwing the light of freedom into "their dark prison house" and "sending [an] earthquake under the foundations of their [rulers'] thrones." Even before it was inhabited or adequately explored, the West acted, paradoxically, as a line of division between the New World and the Old, less a geographical area than an imagined sphere collapsing present time and future space. As Thoreau would write in his late essay "Walking" (1862):

We go eastward to realize history and study the works of art and literature, retracing the steps of the race; we go westward as into the future, with a spirit of enterprise and adventure. The Atlantic is a Lethean stream, in our passage over which we have had an opportunity to forget the Old World and its institutions. . . . The West of which I speak is but another name for the Wild; and what I have been preparing to say is, that in Wildness is the preservation of the World. Every tree sends its fibres forth in search of the Wild. The cities support it at any price. Men plow and sail for it. . . . The West is preparing to add its fables to those of the East. The valleys of the Ganges, the Nile, and the Rhine having yielded their crop, it remains to be seen what the valleys of the Amazon, the Platte, the Orinoco, the St. Lawrence, and the Mississippi will produce. Perchance, when, in the course of ages, American liberty has become a fiction of the past—as it is to some extent a fiction of the present— the poets of the world will be inspired by American mythology.

More frequently than Thoreau, Melville tempered his view of the western frontier, the terrain of the future, with skepticism about such fictive promises of American liberty. In *Moby-Dick* (1851), to cite the most famous example, the symbolic white whale is "a most imperial and archangelical apparition of the unfallen western world," an American emblem of "those primeval times when Adam walked majestic as a god, bluff-bowed and fearless." It is also a sign of annihilation and atheism, the abundance of nature painted "like a harlot, whose allurements cover nothing but the charnel-house within." The duplicitous mirage of the West in *Moby-Dick*, in pursuit of which the mad captain Ahab sacrifices his entire ship of state, is a territory not of promise but of alienation and destruction. In fact, the American West frequently united Edenic possibility and demonic desire; its mythology, created largely in advance of its history, provided a simultaneously geographical and psychological stage on which Americans' dreams of liberty, prosperity, and world leadership could be enacted.

A Grand Outlet for Our Empire

In the aftermath of Meriwether Lewis and William Clark's achievement of a Northwest Passage in their journey of 1804–6 (made famous in Nicholas

Biddle's 1814 *History of the Expedition Under the Command of Captains Lewis and Clark to the Sources of the Missouri, Thence Across the Rocky Mountains and Down the River Columbia to the Pacific Ocean*) and Zebulon Pike's survey of the southern Rocky Mountains and northern New Mexico in 1805–7 (recounted in his 1810 volume *Account of Expeditions to the Sources of the Mississippi and Through the Western Parts of Louisiana*), the future shape of the United States had begun to be defined. The overland route out of St. Louis and up the Missouri River to Oregon and northern California, and the Santa Fe Trail into the Southwest, became the most traveled in the country. The two expeditions served to frame the penetration of the West, in both cases because they detailed not only the geographical features of their respective regions but also the prospects for establishing trading posts and routes. Commerce and scientific or military inquiry were tied together in the expeditions, as they would be in all the important surveys of the West and the narratives of its settlement. Capped by the Gold Rush of the late 1840s and early 1850s, the advances of Euro-American explorers and pioneers alike in the decades following the 1820s usually had in view several goals: freedom from social and political constraint, the discovery of untrammeled landscape, the cultivation of fresh agricultural or mineral resources, and the means of marketing in the East the new wealth of the West. The trade routes to the Southwest, the Northwest, into the Rocky Mountains, and finally across the Sierra Nevada were the weblike lines of America's immense expansion, later echoed in roads and railroads, and the narratives that accompany them told the story of nationalism so fervently advocated by politicians and literary intellectuals in the already established states of the Union. Although the vast majority of settlers and explorers left no lasting record of their journeys, those who did write their stories composed in effect the nation's first and most influential nationalistic literature.

The 1820s were an especially important period for the establishment of an American empire. In the aftermath of the War of 1812, penetration south by the British fur trade declined and American activity haltingly accelerated; in the Southwest, the Mexican Revolution of 1821 left the territory of New Mexico much more vulnerable to incursion and settlement. The euphoric sense of national security that followed the War of 1812 was driven by technological developments in transportation and industrial and agricultural machinery which augmented the spiritual and material romance of America. In the postrevolutionary period and especially after 1815, exploration of the continental territory implied profitable contact with territories beyond. Missouri senator Thomas Hart Benton, a vocal expansionist throughout the coming decades, predicted in an editorial of 1818 that significant trade with Asia would be opened by settlement of Oregon: "In a few years, the Rocky Mountains will be passed, and the 'children of Adam' will have completed the circumambulation of the globe, by marching to the west until they arrive at the Pacific ocean, in sight of the eastern shore of that Asia in which their parents were originally planted." Elaborated by Thoreau and Whitman, among others, the idea that the destiny of the "children of Adam" lay in Asia capitalized upon an existing trade with China that would be dramatically increased by the development of efficient overland routes to the Pacific. The route East by way of the West aroused conflict on all sides. The contest with Great Britain over Oregon would not be resolved until the treaty of 1846, which divided the United States and Canada at the Forty-ninth Parallel and was signed by President James K. Polk on the eve of war with Mexico over territory in the Southwest and California. By then, however, the success of Lewis and Clark had long since opened the way to traders and, more important, to agricultural pioneers.

Although Manuel Lisa, George Drouillard, and John Colter preceded him in the Euro-American exploration of the upper Missouri and Yellowstone, it was John Jacob Astor who was most responsible for opening the Northwest to trade. A German immigrant who organized the Pacific Fur Company to compete with existing outfits such as the Hudson's Bay Company, Astor sent a ship around Cape Horn to build Fort Astoria on the Columbia River and at the same time launched overland expeditions in 1811 led by Wilson Price Hunt and Robert Stuart. Fort Astoria and Astor's trading company fell victim to the War of 1812, but the Hunt and Stuart expeditions established the main lines of what would come to be known as the Oregon Trail. Both wrote diaries that record their daily hardships; yet the major literary record of the Astor enterprise would have to wait more than two decades until Washington Irving (1783–1859) was persuaded by Astor to set down the story in *Astoria; or, Anecdotes of an Enterprise Beyond the Rocky Mountains* (1836). In the period between the explorations sponsored by Astor and Irving's account, a great deal of territory had been opened and written about, often in documents less popular but more reliable than Irving's.

The "Yellowstone Expedition" of Stephen Long, which set out in 1819 on a military and scientific survey, never reached the upper Missouri (the unique assault by steamboat failed), and the intention of finding a suitable location for the military outpost desired by Secretary of War John Calhoun therefore came to naught. Ordered to turn south, Long's group proceeded along the east range of the Rocky Mountains (where they were the first to climb Pike's Peak), then split into two groups that followed river routes back to Arkansas. The expedition itself was not a striking success: Long was stigmatized with having mapped and immortalized the seemingly useless "Great American Desert" of the southwestern Plains and having wasted the technological resources of his topographical engineers. Yet the main source of information about the expedition, botanist Edwin James's *Account of an Expedition from Pittsburgh to the Rocky Mountains* (1823), is a significant report on the country's flora and geological formations, the ethnology of the Kansas and Omaha tribes (with, typically, particular attention to intertribal warfare), and the vast, mysterious region of the Plains. James (1797–1861) echoed Long's own report to Calhoun, which declared that the region was "almost wholly unfit for cultivation, and of course uninhabitable by a people dependent upon agriculture for their subsistence." James's volume foreshadowed the tremendous influence of later reports by topographical engineers attached to military and mercantile expeditions, and it established a paradigm for Euro-American frontier attitudes and character when little was known of the middle Plains. The *Account* was a primary source, for example, for James Fenimore Cooper's conception of the landscape in *The Prairie* (1827), and the popularization of the theory that the central Plains regions were uninhabitable was instrumental in President James Monroe's advocacy of a policy of Indian Removal.

The failure of the Long expedition to penetrate the Northwest did not deter William Henry Ashley from placing a famous advertisement in a St. Louis newspaper in 1822 calling for "Enterprising Young Men" to spend several years developing routes to the Pacific. Like the most successful of the "mountain men" who would follow after him, Ashley, the lieutenant governor of Missouri, was both a businessman and an adventurer, and his establishment of a fur trade on the upper Missouri took precedence over the romance of exploration. His initial company nevertheless included some of the men who would become best known as western explorers: Jedediah Smith, William Sublette, James Clyman, and James Beckwourth. Their several expeditions from 1822 through 1826, followed by further advances into the Far West by Smith over the next few years, opened the entire central Rockies to the fur trade and established the South Pass as the key feature of the route followed by future settlers along the Oregon Trail into the Northwest. The journals and diaries of Ashley, Clyman, and Smith, like those of many other mountain men, were published in the twentieth century. Smith, however, became a particularly popular figure in his own day. His forays beyond the Green River and the Great Salt Lake on into California by way of the Mohave Desert were signs of a country opened not just to fur trading but to immigration, and his map of the western Rockies, partially incorporated into Albert Gallatin's *Map of the Indian Tribes of North America* (1836), remained the standard ethnographic map until the 1850s. Maps, like the taxonomy of natural phenomena and Indian tribes, were classifying representations of the West that codified the superimposition of an inherently imperialistic scientific paradigm upon the Romantic literary imagination.

As Edwin James's account of the Long expedition indicated, the opening of the Far West coincided with two related phenomena: an increase in the sophistication of scientific investigations of western lands and a growing pressure for exploration that would eventually reach beyond the territory of North America. Both the new interest in minerological and biological information about the country and the quest into unknown regions at the far ends of the hemisphere promoted the energies of manifest destiny and signaled the beginning of an imperial drive that would soon bring Texas, the New Mexican Southwest, and California into the U.S. orbit. In 1838 the government made the Army Corps of Topographical Engineers a separate branch of the military under the command of Colonel John James Abert. Its express purpose was to explore and develop the West for settlement, transportation, and production.

Some of the most important writing to come from nineteenth-century expeditions was done by talented scientists, whether in private enterprise or employed by the Army Corps. Stephen Long's expedition produced not only James's 1823 report but also the collections and observations that would appear in Thomas Say's *American Entomology* (1824–8). The Bostonian Nathaniel Wyeth's second expedition to Oregon included the botanist Thomas Nuttall and the zoologist and ornithologist John Kirk Townsend, who provided a full account of the trip in his dramatic and well-written *Narrative of a Journey Across the Rocky Mountains to the Columbia River* (1839). The enormous wealth of scientific materials collected by those who accompanied the explorations of the West, rendered in volumes such as John James Audubon's famous

The Birds of America (1840–4), coincided with the similarly staggering wealth of data about American Indians collected by ethnologists like Henry Rowe Schoolcraft, Thomas McKenney, and George Catlin. The classifying of vast quantities of both natural phenomena and alien human customs thus often tended to blur into a combined scientific, diplomatic, and economic enterprise that worked in service of political and cultural hegemony. For example, Samuel Morton's influential study of racial traits based on skull size and other physiological data, *Crania Americana* (1839), was modeled on Alexander Wilson's nine-volume *American Ornithology* (1808–14). On the Long expedition, Say investigated the racist hypothesis that Indians, blacks, and simian animals were related species but found he could not place American Indians in a workable zoological context. As ethnology and zoological classification became more and more entangled, white people's propensity to view Indians as part of "savage nature" was increased and the ease of linking political conquest to scientific progress heightened. Whereas personal journals often recorded the mundane, frequently harsh details of the journey west, public documents, typically uniting scientific observation and imaginative projection, better revealed national identity.

The figure of the explorer as hero, derived from Biddle's account of Lewis and Clark and given new significance by the expeditions of Long, Ashley, and others served a variety of nationalistic purposes that were well established before Irving published *Astoria* in 1836. Because of his fame as an expatriate interpreter of America and a historian of world events, Irving's authorship of western narratives was itself symbolic of the new penchant for national literature sweeping the United States. Upon his return from residence in Europe to the United States, Irving undertook a trip into Oklahoma with a military company that resulted in a very popular narrative of camp scenes, hunting, and Indian life entitled *A Tour of the Prairies*, part of *The Crayon Miscellany* (1835). Given the significant volumes of history Irving had already produced up to this point in his career—for example, *The History of the Life and Voyages of Christopher Columbus* (1828), *A Chronicle of the Conquest of Granada* (1828–9), and even the burlesque *History of New York* (1809)—it is no surprise that he turned again to his native country and portrayed it in terms that placed it on the same stage with great epic events of world history. Allusions and comparisons to Europe appear throughout *A Tour of the Prairies*, but the volume also advocates the pastoral reflection that such a tour made possible for the member of a democratic society: "We send our youth abroad to grow luxurious and effeminate in Europe; it appears to me that a previous tour on the prairies would be more likely to produce that manliness, simplicity, and self-dependence, most in union with our political institutions."

Astoria was an even more pronounced instance of such nationalistic intentions. Although some historians have doubted the book's authenticity, it was based on the diaries of Hunt and Stuart, the letters and reports of Astor, and a variety of other primary materials, and it is an important expression of the American enthusiasm for expansion in the decades after Astor's initial expedition. The biographical sections devoted to Astor and his fur trade minimize the economic failure of the enterprise not only in order to glorify Astor himself as an exponent of Jacksonian capitalist energy but also to signal the coming American dominion over the continent. In the context of Irving's works, the portrait of Astor links him to other heroic figures like George Washington and Andrew Jackson, men in whom Irving located the masculine power necessary to open and command the American wilderness. The hero thus imagined had to combine traits of unharnessed energy and clear-sighted organization. Irving joined commonplace conceptions of frontiersmen as rugged outlaws to the theory that the central plains were uninhabitable—a "Great American Desert," in the image first elaborated by Zebulon Pike—and predicted the rise there of "new and mongrel races, like new formations in geology, the amalgamation of the 'debris' and 'abrasions' of former races . . . [the descendants of] deperadoes of every class and country yearly ejected from the bosom of society into the wilderness." At the same time, however, he was confident that the course of American economic destiny, and thus its political interests, lay in the West. The volume concludes with Irving's regret that the federal government had not seized the disputed Oregon territory, which was now so clearly within its necessary sphere: "As one wave of emigration after another rolls into the vast regions of the west, and our settlements stretch towards the Rocky Mountains, the eager eyes of our pioneers will pry beyond, and they will become impatient of any barrier or impediment in the way of what they consider a grand outlet of our empire."

Astoria supports Irving's claims of empire with an enormous variety of material, including Astor's representative life, a detailed story of the expeditions, accounts of the Indian tribes of the Missouri River and Northwest, and brilliantly drawn landscapes that pictured for readers, usually for the first time, the immense spaces of their country's future. Irving helped popularize the idea that a vast part of the central Plains was a virtual wasteland, but his sublime descriptions sometimes betrayed a corresponding fascination with the empty terrain and its wildlife, as in his account of the Stuart party's return along the Missouri and Platte rivers:

> They continued on for upwards of a hundred miles; with vast prairies extending before them as they advanced; sometimes diversified by undulating hills, but destitute of trees. In one place they saw a gang of sixty five wild horses, but as to the buffalos they seemed absolutely to cover the country. Wild geese abounded, and they passed extensive swamps that were alive with innumerable flocks of water fowl, among which were a few swans, but an endless variety of ducks.
>
> The river continued a widening course to the east northeast, nearly a mile in width, but too shallow to float even an empty canoe.
>
> The country spread out into a vast level plain, bounded by the horizon alone, excepting to the north, where a line of hills seemed like a long promontory stretching into the bosom of the ocean. The dreary sameness of the prairie wastes began to grow extremely irksome. The travellers longed for the sight of a forest, or grove, or single tree to break the level uniformity and began to notice every object that gave reason to hope they were drawing towards the end of this weary wilderness. . . . Thus they went on, like sailors at sea, who perceive in every floating weed and wandering bird, harbingers of the wished for land.

Irving's description of the prairie, like other renderings of landscape in the volume, outlines the human drama of exploration at the same time it indicates the Euro-American conception of the West's unrealized potential. The enterprise of Astor and his explorers can be conceived of in both physical and unintentionally self-reflexive psychological terms, as they penetrate "to the heart of savage continents: laying open the hidden secrets of the wilderness."

Irving's next volume on the American West, *The Adventures of Captain Bonneville in the Rocky Mountains and Far West* (1837), extended his celebration of the pioneer spirit to embrace a larger territory and the larger group of mountain men and fur traders who followed in the wake of William Ashley and Jedediah Smith. One of them, Benjamin Bonneville, in 1832 headed an expedition less important for his own accomplishments than for those of his subordinate, Joseph Walker, who led a reconnaissance of the western shores of the Great Salt Lake and then made his way into California, down the Humboldt River, and eventually to Monterey. Bonneville himself turned

north to follow the Astorian route to Oregon. Information about the territory recorded in his journals would appear first in Irving's *Astoria* and then in
Captain Bonneville, along with maps of the Rocky Mountain West and Great
Basin region by Bonneville that were the most detailed of the day. Irving's
treatment of Bonneville as hero is less inspired than his account of the explorers in *Astoria*, and his theorizing about the literary value of his material became
self-consciously intrusive: "all this romance of savage life," he notes, will soon
"seem like the fictions of chivalry or fairy tale." But his portrait of the heroic
age of mountain fur trappers is valuable in its own right and as an indication
that the work of exploration had reached a point where it could be romanticized and its gradual displacement by more permanent settlement foreseen.

As Irving's volumes proved, the exploration of the American West brought
forth rugged individuals whose achievements were easily shaped into myth.
The mountain men were significant not just for their role in the fur trade but
also for their popular fame as rough men of opportunity willing to strike
out into a dangerous life in the hope of wealth and exotic adventure. As one
of them, George Ruxton, wrote in his *Adventures in Mexico and the Rocky
Mountains* (1847), there is "not a hole or corner [that has not] been ransacked
by these hardy men. From the Mississippi to the mouth of the Colorado of the
West, from the frozen regions of the north to the Gila in Mexico, the beaver-
hunter has set his traps in every creek and stream. All this vast country, but for
the daring and enterprise of these men, would be even now a *terra incognita* to
geographers." Responsible for the earliest and often the most reliable maps, the
mountain men also produced some of the best literary accounts of the Euro-
American exploration of the West. Joseph Walker's pioneering 1834 penetration of the Sierra Nevada to San Francisco Bay, down through San Joaquin
Valley, and back across the Sierra through Walker's Pass (which would become
a popular route to California) was recorded in his own report on the journey,
in a later narrative dictated to George Nidever, and most famously in Zenas
Leonard's *Narrative of the Adventures of Zenas Leonard, Fur Trader* (1839).

Leonard's exhilarating account, which covers his trapping career from 1831
to 1835, offered a model later followed by Alexander Ross, Warren Ferris, James
Beckwourth, and others. Leonard gave a more authentic view of Walker's
expedition than that found in Irving's *Captain Bonneville* and, like other advocates of expansion, he praised the economic potential of the West. More important, he saw the issue of the West in terms of the conjunction of domestic and

foreign policy and warned of inroads being made by the Spanish, British, and the Russians:

Even in this remote part of the Great West before many years will these hills and valleys be greeted with the enlivening sound of the workman's hammer, and the merry whistle of the ploughboy. . . . Our government should be vigilant. She should assert her claim by taking possession of the whole territory as soon as possible—for we have good reason to suppose that the territory *west* of the mountains will some day be equally as important to the nation as that [to] the east.

James Beckwourth's *Life and Adventures* (1856) is notable for its material on the fur trade, its western tall tales, and its unorthodox account of Beckwourth's life among the Crow, with whom he lived intimately but continued to reject as barbaric people who might best be expeditiously exterminated. Narratives such as Beckwourth's suggest that the factual account of exploration and the frontier novel of Indian conflict were equally responsible for creating the mythic image of the mountain man as a figure who lived among "savages" without succumbing to savage life. David Coyner's *The Lost Trappers* (1847) crossed fact and fiction in that its largely fabricated account of life in the fur trade was supposedly based on the journal of Ezekial Williams, a member of the first trapping expedition after Lewis and Clark. Like Beckwourth, Coyner wrote at a time when the continent was mapped and its history could be written with the expectation that the increasing emigration to California in the 1840s would lead to complete possession. Caught in the same irony as James Fenimore Cooper, who respected the advance of "enlightened" society but created its most magnificent outcast in Natty Bumppo, Coyner advocated the destined rise of American civilization on the shores of the Pacific even as he celebrated the trapper as a man who "despises the dull uniformity and monotony of civilized life" and rejects "the galling restrictions of organized society."

Closest among living figures to Cooper's mythic hero was the trapper, scout, and Indian agent Christopher ("Kit") Carson, the best known of mountain men. His autobiography, published in the next century, showed a frontier hero somewhat less flamboyant and isolated than the one who had appeared in the popular volumes *Life and Adventures of Kit Carson*, by DeWitt C. Peters (1858), *Life of Kit Carson: The Great Western Hunter and Guide* (1862), by Charles Burdett, and the earlier novel by Charles Averill, *Kit Carson, The Prince of the Gold Hunters* (1849). The Kit Carson of popular literature overshadowed the real man and accentuated all those characteristics the mountain men claimed for themselves and which their mythologizers assigned them in any event: extraordinary courage, melodramatic skills in woodcraft and combat, and a visionary belief in American destiny. Because Carson's fame rested in large part on his role in John Frémont's western explorations and the events of the Mexican War, he additionally gave expression to those characteristics of the popular masculine dream of western empire—virility, independence, and daring—that were implicit in the heroes created by Cooper and Irving, as well as in the lives of the mountain men themselves.

Even though he did not qualify as a mountain man and his journey into the Rocky Mountain West took him by steamboat and horseback only as far as Fort Laramie, Wyoming, the historian Francis Parkman (1823–93) wrote one of the most popular nineteenth-century narratives of western life. First serialized in the *Knickerbocker Magazine* in 1847, *The California and Oregon Trail* (1849) recorded brilliantly detailed, often breathtaking depictions of the region and of the Sioux and Pawnee hunting culture of the Platte River. Parkman's reflections on Indian life, more so than those found in the journals of more experienced trappers and explorers, were marked by both tendentious romanticism and racialist notions of savagism, and his observations of life along the emigrant trail paradoxically offered little aid for the many emigrants by then eagerly seeking a route west. Even so, Parkman in some passages ranks with Melville in his ability to capture the turbulence of man's appropriation of the natural world—perhaps most eloquently in his many descriptions of the decimation of buffalo herds, which were also implicitly descriptions of the demise of the western Indian tribes:

While we were charging on one side, our companions attacked the bewildered and panic-stricken herd on the other. The uproar and confusion lasted but a moment. The dust cleared away, and the buffalo could be seen scattering as from a common centre, flying over the plain singly, or in long files and small compact bodies, while behind them followed the Indians, riding at furious speed, and yelling as they launched arrow after arrow into their sides. The carcasses were strewn thickly over the ground. Here and there stood wounded buffalo, their bleeding sides feathered with arrows; and as I rode by them their eyes would glare, they would bristle like gigantic cats, and feebly attempt to rush up and gore my horse.

Like his later classic statement of the "doom" of the American Indian in *The Conspiracy of Pontiac* (1851), Parkman's account of life on the Plains elevates into a metaphoric, elegiac vision comparable to Melville's in *Moby-Dick* his own essential understanding of the irreversible course of American empire. Indeed, the book's significance as a literary treatment of frontier life was best described by Parkman himself when he reflected on the change in the American West in a preface to *The California and Oregon Trail* written in 1892: "The buffalo is gone, and of all his millions nothing is left but bones. Tame cattle and barbed wire have supplanted his vast herds and boundless grazing lands. . . . The slow cavalcade of horsemen armed to the teeth has disappeared before parlor cars and the effeminate comforts of modern travel."

The transfiguration of the West witnessed by Parkman, however, did not have to wait until the end of the century. The advance of the agricultural frontier across the Midwest from the 1820s through the 1860s, accelerated by innovations in production and transportation, quickly modified conceptions of western territory even as it destroyed American Indian cultures and drove the mountain men toward the Pacific. Space became functional and commercial before its mythic allure had fully dissipated. Ralph Waldo Emerson's 1844 essay on expansion, "The Young American," asserted that the mystic power of the land would have an "Americanizing influence, which promises to disclose new virtues for ages to come." Americans, he added, who "have grown up in the bowers of a paradise," in "the country of the Future," must therefore be educated in the arts of engineering, architecture, scientific agriculture, and minerology. Like Melville's Ahab, he envisioned the paradisal garden of America vitalized by mechanical technology: "Railroad iron is a magician's rod, in its power to evoke the sleeping energies of land and water."

Emerson's characteristic location of the idealistic abstraction within the realm of commerce philosophically broke down distinctions between mind and nature. Much commonplace literature of the western landscape did so pragmatically, and none more so than the emigrant guide, which by 1840 had become a literary genre in its own right. In the emigrant guide, factual information, dramatized stories, and autobiographic reflection were often combined. Space, the promise of a boundless future, was translated into time, supplies, profit and loss, and was set in a moral framework in which self-discovery and national character were synonymous. A staunch advocate for the West who ranks with Ashley as a promoter of expansion, the New England merchant Hall J. Kelley issued pamphlets such as "A General Circular to All Persons of Good Character Who Wish to Emigrate to the Oregon Territory" (1831), which helped to set in motion the settlement of Oregon and California. In a variety of publications and petitions to Congress, Kelley called for the swift American colonization of the Pacific Northwest. One of his followers was Nathaniel Wyeth, a Boston ice merchant whose enterprises were later alluded to in *Walden* when Thoreau contemplated the way in which the waters of Walden Pond become mingled with those of the Ganges River. Wyeth organized his own expeditions to Oregon in the 1830s, which included Christian missionaries, a distinguished array of scientists, and veteran mountain men like William Sublette, who discovered that more money was to be made in outfitting and guiding western caravans than in fur trading.

The most important emigrant guides were documents that not only offered practical advice but also carefully endorsed prevailing ideas of manifest destiny. One of the most influential handbooks of the day, Lansford Hastings's *The Emigrant's Guide to Oregon and California* (1845), celebrated the rich resources of the area and their potential for economic development while characteristically playing upon anti-Mexican, anti-Indian, and anti-Catholic sentiments to glorify faith in Anglo-American progress and "promote the unbounded happiness and prosperity, of civilized and enlightened man." The eschatological character of the emigrant guides would reach a new pitch once the Mexican War had opened California to Anglo-American settlement. In journalist Charles Dana's *The Garden of the World; Or, the Great West* (1856), the several hundred pages of information on all the middle and western territories were preceded by introductory passages demonstrating the continuity between Puritan thought and the ideals of manifest destiny:

The *Land of Promise*, and the *Canaan* of our time, is the region which, commencing on the slope of the Alleghenies, broadens grandly over the vast prairies and mighty rivers, over queenly lakes and lofty mountains, until the ebb and flow of the Pacific tide kisses the golden shores of the El Dorado. . . . O, the soul kindles at the thought of what a magnificent empire the West is but the germ, which, blessed with liberty and guaranteeing equal rights to all, shall go on conquering and to conquer, until the whole earth shall resound with its fame and glory.

Although they followed Hastings's model in offering the wisdom of their own experiences to would-be emigrants to the Northwest, both Overton Johnson, in *Route Across the Rocky Mountains* (1846), and Joel Palmer (1810–81), in *Journal of Travels Over the Rocky Mountains* (1847), presented the territory not as a magic Eden but as a place where hard work and a difficult life could lead to independence and success. Similarly pragmatic in their assessments were Rufus B. Sage, whose *Scenes in the Rocky Mountains* (1846) provided a wide range of detailed information on territories from Texas to Oregon to a public agitating for expansion, and the German immigrant F. A. Wislizenus (1810–89), whose *Journey to the Rocky Mountains in the Year* 1839 (1840) employed a common metaphor (one that reached its apotheosis in Frederick Jackson Turner's work at the end of the century) in speaking of the "waves of civilization" that now "cast their spray on the feet of the Rockies." The rush to capitalize upon the West could be so powerful that pretense alone would serve: thus, the journalist and poet Edmund Flagg (1815–90) published a work entitled *The Far West: Or, A Tour Beyond the Rocky Mountains* (1838), which is in fact concerned almost exclusively with Ohio, Illinois, and the Mississippi Valley.

At the extremity of speculative depictions of the West is Edgar Allan Poe's fictional work *The Journal of Julius Rodman, Being an Account of the First Passage Across the Rocky Mountains of North America Ever Achieved by Civilized Man* (1840), which illuminated the lure of the fantastic latent in most exploration narratives. Based on his readings in Biddle's volume on Lewis and Clark, as well as in Irving, Flagg, Robert Townsend, Samuel Parker, and others, Poe's uncompleted farce, as its title suggests, claimed in setting its action in the 1790s to record an adventure in the Far West that preceded all others, a tactic he had already pursued much more successfully in *The Narrative of Arthur Gordon Pym of Nantucket* (1838). Poe's temporal dislocation of the narrative of Julius Rodman into the past has a multiple significance. In addition to burlesquing its genre and the frequently exaggerated claims made by explorers, it corresponded to contemporary efforts by Parkman and others to displace the conquest of the continent and the "doom" of the American Indian into an earlier century. At the same time, it accentuated Poe's own obsession with America's futurity as expressed in his short science fiction tales or in the philosophical dream tract *Eureka* (1848), in which boundless cosmic space appears in part as a figure for the unfolding destiny of the nation. Along with Emerson in *Nature* (1836) and Whitman in numerous poems and prose works, Poe pushed the vision of hemispheric conquest and the establishment of a limitless new Canaan past literal geographical boundaries.

Against the backdrop of American political opinion, however, Poe's vision was not illegitimate. American horizons appeared capable of expanding far beyond what would later come to be the nation's borders. James G. Bennett, the editor of the *New York Herald*, wrote a column in 1845 that hardly seemed extravagant at the time. No longer bounded by the limits that restrained the last generation, "the pioneers of Anglo-Saxon civilization and Anglo-Saxon free institutions now seek distant territories, stretching even to the shores of the Pacific; and the arms of the republic, it is clear to all men of sober discernment, must soon embrace the whole hemisphere, from the icy wilderness of the North to the most prolific regions of the smiling and prolific South." The idea of America's mission in the hemisphere became crystallized during the Mexican War, but terms as comprehensive as Bennett's were plausible in part because of the extracontinental exploration that had taken place in the previous decades. The possibility of America's eventual extension into the far corners of the hemisphere grew from an idealistic belief that the United States would soon be in a position to bring Christianity, republican government, and commercial trade to an enormous part of the globe, after first claiming as wide a territorial base as possible. Bennett's projection aside, the drive toward the Arctic would not take place for several years, and the British and the Russians dominated the early exploration of the North Pole. Although the United States launched few important ventures to this area in the 1850s and 1860s (interest in the Arctic increased after Secretary of State William Seward, foreseeing geological wealth and a possible gateway to American control of Canada and parts of Asia, negotiated the purchase of Alaska from Russia in 1867), a handful of significant volumes on the region appeared: William Snelling's early *The Polar Regions* (1831), firsthand reports such as Elisha Kane's *The U.S. Grinnell Expedition in Search of Sir John Franklin* (1854) and his extremely popular *Arctic Explorations* (1856), Charles Francis Hall's *Arctic Researches* and *Life with the Esquimaux* (both 1864), and the Eskimo Hans Hendrik's *Memoirs*, translated in 1878 at a time of heightened interest in polar exploration.

In the era of manifest destiny, however, the South Pole commanded the most attention in the United States because of interest in Latin America and sea routes to the Pacific. The most significant chapter in this part of antebellum history was a venture that encompassed all of these interests, the United States Exploring Expedition of 1838–42, commanded by Charles Wilkes (1798–1877) and recorded in great detail in the massive five-volume *Narrative of the United States Exploring Expedition* (1845). Conceived by Jeremiah Reynolds, the author of "Mocha-Dick" (1839), one source of Melville's *Moby-Dick*, the expedition

originated with his desire to explore the landmass of the Antarctic and the islands of the South Pacific but eventually was extended to include a survey of the Oregon coast. One of Reynold's inspirations was the theory, propounded by John Symmes (1780–1829), that the earth was hollow and could be entered through vortices at the poles. The theory had received fanciful treatment in a novel by Adam Seaborn (Symmes's pseudonym) entitled *Symzonia: Voyage of Discovery* (1820), which imagined the discovery of a perfectly rational race living in tropical comfort inside the South Pole. Because the Symzonians rejected all appetites and desires as gross and depraved and possessed perfect white features, along with a disgust for darker peoples, the book implicitly argued for a conjunction of white racial superiority and rational perfection, just the features that often underlay the analogy between scientific progress and manifest destiny. These theories, brought to public attention by the Wilkes expedition, offered a great opportunity for the master of hoax Poe, whose *Narrative of Arthur Gordon Pym* described a voyage to the South Pole occurring in 1828 (thus, as in his narrative of Julius Rodman, antedating the actual expedition, which had just begun) and featured wild, parodic flights of fantasy, episodes of cannibalism, the total breakdown of rationality, and a ferocious antagonism between white and darker races. Poe's strikingly imagined narrative superimposed nightmares about southern slavery and slave rebellion upon the public fascination with exotic exploration to parody both and caricature the Wilkes expedition before its own reports could be brought in.

In the event, Poe's version was not quite as absurd as it appeared. For one thing, his interest in the expedition was genuine. In his 1837 essay on Reynolds's belief in a hollow earth—one of several essays by Poe devoted to Lewis and Clark, Irving's *Astoria*, and other accounts of American exploration—he applauded the seamen of the United States who aspired to circle the globe and reach the Pole so as "to cast anchor on that point where all the meridians terminate, where our eagle and star-spangled banner may be unfurled and planted, and left to wave on the axis of the earth itself!" The comedy of the *Narrative of Arthur Gordon Pym* did not so much undermine this apparently genuine patriotic view as it comprehended the contradictory impulses and near chaos of intelligent energies that motivated an expedition as grand as that led by Wilkes. Indeed, Wilkes's *Narrative* itself was a massive, often bizarre report on the geography and ethnology of South American countries, South Pacific islands, Australia, Hawaii (the Sandwich Islands), Asia, and the western coast of North America. Altogether, the work by 1874 ran to twenty-three volumes written by various hands (including, e.g., Titian Peale's *Mammology and Ornithology*, based on hundreds of collected specimens; Charles Pickering's *Races of Man*, a taxonomy of human species; and Horatio Hale's *Ethnography and Philology*, a study of Polynesian and Northwest American Indian languages). Besides recording a great quantity of data relevant to nautical routes, trading practices, and foreign customs and terrain, the narrative also promoted reforms in the whaling trade, in the treatment of both crew and natives, in order to "promote the great cause of morality, religion, and temperance" abroad. Wilkes's *Narrative* verified the existence of the Antarctic landmass and rendered enchanting descriptions of its wildlife and ice fields, some echoing Poe's invented landscapes ("blindfolded as it were by an impenetrable fog"). And in discussing the cannibalism of the Fiji Islanders, Wilkes outdid Poe's demonizing romanticism: he reports that one crew member negotiated with the natives to purchase a "skull yet warm from the fire, much scorched, and marked with the teeth of those who had eaten of it," from which the brain had just been devoured and from which a remaining eye had to be eaten before it could be traded.

The Pacific had become a magnetic territory both because of the many commercial and missionary enterprises that had spread throughout the islands by the 1830s and because it was a logical extension of the drive toward Asia, the "passage to India." Jeremiah Reynolds, for example, had written an exploration narrative and brief for a strong navy in *Voyage of the U.S. Frigate Potomac* (1835); Edmund Fanning's *Voyages to the South Seas* (1833), an account of nineteenth-century expeditions, was in its fifth edition by 1838, the year Wilkes set out; and there appeared such narratives of whaling adventure as Owen Chase's *Narrative of the Most Extraordinary and Distressing Shipwreck of the Whale-Ship Essex* (1821)—another source of *Moby-Dick*—and Francis A. Olmsted's *Incidents of a Whaling Voyage* (1841), before Melville's work one of the best accounts of whaling and the South Pacific available. Officially sanctioned trade with China was begun in 1844 (American ships had actually traded with China since the late eighteenth century), and the popular travel writer Bayard Taylor (1825–78), among others, recorded his trans-Pacific journey in *A Visit to India, China, and Japan in 1853* (1855). But the most significant such volume about Asia in historical, if not literary, terms may be Francis Hawks's *Narrative of the Expedition of an American Squadron to the China Seas and*

Japan (1856), which gives an account of the expedition under Matthew Perry in 1852–4 to open Japan by force to American trade. Hawks (1798–1866) used much of Perry's correspondence and journals verbatim; and although two of the three volumes were given over to reports by the crew on scientific materials brought back, maps, nautical charts, and astronomical phenomena, one illustrated volume brought Asia dramatically into American consciousness in its detailed descriptions of Japanese history, religion, geography, ethnology, trading information, and artistic and scientific achievements.

It was not the Asian continent, however, but the islands of the Pacific that most clearly represented the imperial achievement of America's westward drive in the antebellum years. Calls throughout the period for the annexation of Hawaii were based on the strategic importance of the islands in the routes to Asia, and the islands were written about in volumes such as William Ellis's *A Journal of a Tour Around Hawaii* (1825) and the Reverend Hiram Bingham's *A Residence of Twenty-One Years in the Sandwich Islands* (1847). James Jarves's *History of the Hawaiian Islands* (1847) had a large audience, as did his *Kiana: A Tradition of Hawaii* (1857), which was based on the legend that during Cortés's journey to California a Spanish vessel was wrecked on the islands, stranding a white priest and a white woman, through whom the mitigating effects of Christianity and civilization on the islanders' purported superstition and savagery were first felt. In two volumes devoted to his mission to Hawaii—*A Residence in the Sandwich Islands* (1828) and *A Visit to the South Seas* (1831)—the Reverend Charles Stewart espoused the millennial theory that the advance of Christian civilization would "scatter the spiritual darkness resting on the land, like the vapors of the morning before the rising sun." To many writers, the Pacific islands and Hawaii were at once a realization of the promised American Eden and the site where the battle between American technology and native primitivism would be engaged. Early in the century, David Porter's *Journal of a Cruise Made to the Pacific Ocean* (1815)—a military venture to protect American whalers—recounted his forceful establishment of a new social order on the Marquesas island of Nuku Hiva but left a melancholy description of his march through the Typee valley, where "a long line of smoking ruins now marked our traces from one end to the other."

One of the most penetrating treatments of Hawaii and Tahiti under American imperial incursion, Edward T. Perkins's *Na Motu: Or, Reef-Rovings in the South Seas* (1854), attacked European colonialism but praised the prosperity brought about by American advances in the region. "To kingdoms and tribes we have bequeathed indelible impressions of our national worth and disinterested philanthropy," Perkins argued. With less withering irony than one finds in Melville's *Typee* (1846), Perkins's volume highlighted the analogy between Polynesian Islanders and American Indians in the Euro-American mind, both of them subject to idealistic, if deluded, claims of salvation and disinterested benevolence. Hawaii was a virtual emblem of the New World unencumbered by Old World antiquities: "Though we discover no hiero-glyphics of mystic import to conjure up gloomy reveries, we are ever opening a new page in the Book of Nature, fresh and glowing with the intelligible sym-bols of beauty and sublimity." Popularly uniting Romantic contemplation with America's own imperial design, Perkins's *Na Motu* perfectly represented the expansionist vision whose potentially corrosive internal mechanisms Poe and Melville attempted to expose to view, but whose cultural politics were destined to prevail for decades to come.

The El Dorado of the New World

Analogous problems of cultural interpretation were played out at the same time in the U.S. expansion into regions of Latin America. Just as the literature of the American frontier can only be understood in counterpoint to Native American culture and traditions, however, the U.S. empire in the greater South-west and Latin America requires one to see the Anglo-American literature of that region in relation to the rise of a Mexican American literature, written mostly in Spanish but sometimes in English, which would form the ground-work for modern Latino and Chicano cultural identity. As in the case of American Indians, Mexicans in the colonized regions of the Southwest and California were not simply assimilated into the dominant culture but also pre-served autonomous cultural forms that were transfigured though by no means destroyed by the Anglo-American conquest.

Most of the numerous travel accounts of Mexico more properly belong to the border literature of the New Mexican Southwest and the Mexican War, but South and Central America were also of crucial importance to U.S. national-ism from the 1840s through the 1860s. James Jarves, for example, had turned to Hawaii only after publishing his *Scenes and Scenery in the Sandwich Islands and a Trip Through Central America* (1844). Irving's friend George Washington Montgomery translated his *Granada* into Spanish and wrote *Narrative of a Journey to Guatemala* (1839); E. G. Squier published *Nicaragua* (1856) and *The States of Central America* (1858); and works on the Panama route to California included Joseph W. Fabens's *A Story of Life on the Isthmus* (1853) and the western writer Theodore Winthrop's *Isthmiana* (1863). Among the most influential American travel books of the period were John Lloyd Stephens's *Incidents of Travel in Central America, Chiapas, and Yucatan* (1841) and *Incidents of Travel in the Yucatan* (1843), accounts of his explorations during 1839–43 of the magnificent ruins that would later be established as Mayan. Stephens's descriptions of the structures, idols, artwork, hieroglyphs, and geography, accompanied by Frederick Catherwood's excellent illustrations of the antiquities and the Mayan communities, gained the volumes a wide audience in a country often paradoxically eager to discover its own antiquity even as it insisted that it was unhindered by Old World burdens. As will be noted below, however, Stephens's monumental works cannot be disconnected from the imperial vision that put historical research in the service of contemporary political power.

Equally popular and, like Wilkes's *Narrative* and others, intertwined with the politics of empire, William Louis Herndon's *Exploration of the Valley of the Amazon* (1854) records the first Anglo-American descent of the Amazon from Peru to its mouth in 1851 in a compelling narrative. Set in motion by Lieutenant Matthew Maury, a pioneer in oceanography at the United States Naval Observatory, Herndon's trip sprang from a desire to open the Amazon to navigation and trade (not achieved until 1867). More important, it sprang from Maury's plan, after the Compromise of 1850 had blocked the continental expansion of slavery, to open the territory for the importation of American slaves, a project Maury outlined in *The Amazon and the Atlantic Slopes of South America* (1853). Because the potential for establishing a slave empire in Latin America appealed to many southerners, the Caribbean, Yucatan, and Central America became the focus of dreams of a "Golden Circle" of commerce centered on the Gulf of Mexico and sustained by slave labor. The most volatile pronouncement of slaveholding expansionism appeared in *The War in Nicaragua* (1860) by the adventurer William Walker, who led a renegade guerrilla band first in Mexico and then in a brief conquest of Nicaragua. His narrative offers a complete account of his filibustering activities and a rationale for the extension of slavery based on the white man's supposedly benevolent improvement of the degraded African's lot: "Africa [was] permitted to lie idle until America [was] discovered, in order that she [might] conduce to the formation of a new society in the New World. [Therefore] the true field for the exertion of slavery is in tropical America; there it finds its natural seat of empire and thither it can spread if it will but make the effort."

As Walker's argument indicates, the heart of the American West, if one shared the widespread conception of the West as an arena of Anglo-American triumph, could lie entirely outside the present latitudes of the Union and could involve an even more complex and extensive version of conquest and race mastery. The wealth of the West itself was considered fuel for the engine of American expansion. California gold, the most potent symbol of expansion after 1848, would soon so enrich the nation, claimed *De Bow's Review* in 1854, that no possible investment would be equal to it but the cultivation of the entire western hemisphere. Lying between the two great valleys of the world, the Mississippi and the Amazon, the Gulf of Mexico would link the most productive regions of the earth and, by unlocking trading access to the wealth of the Pacific Basin, make the Atlantic in the modern world what the Mediterranean had been "under the reign of the Antonies in Rome." Given the continued dissolution of European political power, combined with possession of Cuba, Santo Domingo, and Haiti, the United States might control the Gulf and through it the world: "Guided by our genius and enterprise, a new world would rise there, as it did before under the genius of Columbus." But this new Columbian vision had a price. As the author argued, "slavery and war have [always] been the two great forerunners of civilization."

American expansion into Central or South America only made sense if the territories that are now the southwestern United States and Mexico could be brought under American dominion. In the 1830s and 1840s such an extension of democracy's "area of freedom" (in Andrew Jackson's phrase) was often advocated. The annexation of the Republic of Texas in 1845 and victory in the Mexican War, by which the New Mexican territory and California were acquired, proved, however, to draw the limits of the Anglo-American march. Further calls to take possession of "All Mexico" were sounded for another twenty years, but with the exception of the Gadsden Purchase of 1853, which added a strip of land in southern Arizona, the southwestern United States was now complete. Although much of its land was less suited to settlement and sustained cultivation than that of the Northwest, early in the century New

Mexico and the southern deserts were recognized as important areas of trade and avenues to the rich lands of California. Many accounts, especially popular ones such as Richard Henry Dana's *Two Years Before the Mast*, viewed Spanish California as the most important object of American destiny, and the narratives of a number of explorers (e.g., those of Jedediah Smith, Zenas Leonard, George Ruxton, and James Pattie) recount expeditions that embraced almost the whole of the Far West, from Arkansas to the central and southern Rockies to the Pacific coast. Central to all the major narratives are the promise of Mexico's holdings and the question of America's moral or political right to settle and cultivate what was for the most part a commercially undeveloped, but hardly an uninhabited, territory.

Not only did Native Americans precede white settlers in these areas, but Mexican settlements and Mexican culture had long been established. The modern period witnessed the wide settlement of Nueva México, a process documented in ways that have yet to be studied in requisite detail. In 1776, for example, while American colonists were revolting against British rule, Juan Bautista de Anza established a Spanish colony on San Francisco Bay. In the same year a Spanish sea captain reached the mouth of the Columbia River, and Francisco Silvestre Vélez de Escalante set out from Santa Fe to explore Colorado, the Green River, and the Great Basin, territory that Anglo-Americans would not begin to chart for another forty years. Santa Fe itself had been settled in 1609, and by the end of the eighteenth century missions and presidios ran from Texas across New Mexico and Arizona through much of California, principally as a line of defense against the encroachment of France, Russia, and Great Britain upon Spain's control of Latin American commerce and maritime trade. The revolt against Spain and the establishment of the Republic of Mexico in 1821 were followed in the northern provinces of New Mexico and California by intermittent local rebellions and dissatisfaction with national Mexican government. For the most part, however, life in the territories soon to be engulfed by American pioneers was independent of governmental control and comparatively tranquil. The liberal Mexican Colonization Act of 1824 and the secularization of mission lands in 1831 led to easy and widespread ownership of large ranches, especially in California, most of which continued to be worked by Indian laborers who were often virtual slaves. In the province of New Mexico, however, corruption and a stagnant economy were greater problems and led the government to acquiesce to American settlement in Texas and to open the region to American trade in 1822. By 1830, "Texas fever" had created a large American colony that would become the wedge opening the entire region to eventual American domination and military conquest.

By the time Mexico opened its territories to trade, the expeditions of Zebulon Pike, Stephen Long, and others had penetrated New Mexico. Within a few years a regular trade between Santa Fe and the Mississippi Valley had grown up, and the Santa Fe Trail from Independence, Missouri, to Santa Fe (advocated by Senator Thomas Hart Benton and authorized by President Monroe) was established by 1827. Both Americans and some Mexicans in the region argued that the extension of U.S. dominion was in many ways preferable to the distant and often inadequate legal and military protection offered by the Mexican government. The increasing flow of immigrants followed the lead of pioneer explorer-traders such as William Becknell, Thomas James, and Jacob Fowler, who had set out on expeditions to Santa Fe in 1821. James and Fowler left journals of their ventures and residence in Mexico—respectively, *Three Years Among the Indians and Mexicans* (1846) and *Journal of Jacob Fowler* (1898)—as did Susan Shelley Magoffin, the wife of a trader (and secret agent) who kept an excellent diary during the 1840s that was later published under the title *Down the Santa Fe and Into Mexico* (1926). She reported her views of American military victories in the war but gave more attention to the mechanisms of trade and to the political and domestic life of New Mexico. A comparable autobiographical work by David Meriwether, governor of New Mexico in the 1850s, was discovered and published in the next century as *My Life on the Mountains and on the Plains* (1965).

Easily the most impressive narrative of early southwestern exploration belongs to James O. Pattie (1804?–50?), who with his father and others surveyed an incredible territory in New Mexico, southern California (he was preceded among Anglo-American explorers to Los Angeles only by Jedediah Smith), and the central Rockies in several nearly catastrophic years before he reached the age of twenty-six. His *Personal Narrative*, dictated to Timothy Flint and published in 1831, often verges on a tall tale, but much of it has been authenticated. As Flint's introduction points out, however, its value lies in the "moral sublimity [found] in the contemplation of the adventures and daring of such men" as Pattie—even though such moral sublimity was often purchased by obliviousness to existing Native American and Mexican culture or a denial of the racialist foundations of America's new empire.

More reliable and surpassing Pattie's narrative as a statement of growing American interest in the acquisition of Mexican territory is the account by Josiah Gregg (1806–50) of several trading caravans to Santa Fe between 1831 and 1840. *Commerce of the Prairies; or, The Journal of a Santa Fé Trader* (1844) provides a superior history of the trail and the development of trade; despite its own emblematic denigration of many aspects of Indian and New Mexican life, it offers a picture of Gregg's own career and character somewhat at odds with the implied mercenary designs on Mexico. His "passion for Prairie life," he says, created in him a need for solitude and wildness. He had no greater desire than "to spread my bed with the mustang and the buffalo, under the broad canopy of heaven—there to seek to maintain undisturbed my confidence in men, by fraternizing with the little prairie dogs and wild colts, and the still wilder Indians—the *unconquered Sabaeans* of the Great American Deserts." What the successes of Gregg and others proved, however, was that neither the so-called Great American Desert nor the Indian territories of Oklahoma and Arkansas would stand in the way of American prosperity in Texas and New Mexico. The mountain man's solitude had poetic value, yet in practical terms it symbolized but a phase in the absorption of one people and their land by another more commercially and militarily powerful.

Before the era of the Mexican War, the question of Texas, the trial ground for the eventual victory of the United States over Mexico, brought forth several significant documents that expressed that colony's own nationalistic ambitions. The first book published in Texas, Stephen Austin's *Establishing Austin's Colony* (1829), was a brief chronicle of colonization and a compendium of Mexican laws relevant to new settlers. Austin's cousin, Mary Austin Holley, soon after wrote a historical survey, including domestic advice for prospective middle-class settlers on the prairie, entitled *Texas: Observations, Historical, Geographical, and Descriptive* (1833). The rhetoric of the two books suggests how clear was the assumption that Texas, whether by independence, annexation, or both, would eventually enter the U.S. orbit. Joseph Field's *Three Years in Texas* (1836) offers a firsthand view of the "Texas Revolution" for independence in 1836. Some of Sam Houston's voluminous letters, speeches, and proclamations appeared in Charles Edwards Lester's popular *Life of Sam Houston* (1855); but a full picture of Houston's epic life as the heroic antagonist of Santa Anna in the battle of San Jacinto, as president of the Republic of Texas, and as governor and senator following statehood in 1845 would have to await modern scholars. Popular views of Texas history generally were in accord with the image of pioneering heroics that Houston projected. Dedicated to Houston, Anthony Ganilh's novel *Mexico Versus Texas* (1838) followed the argument of many politicians in forecasting the "regeneration" of Mexico. Comparing the country to a prisoner released from a dungeon into sunlight, Ganilh wrote that "Mexico, emerging from the darkness into which the policy of Spain had plunged her, as yet supports with difficulty the brilliancy of modern civilization." Likewise, James W. Dallam contended in his novel *The Lone Star* (1845) that Texas, by the time it joined the Union, had come to seem the nation's newest "city upon a hill." It was "the outpost, the resting place, of Freedom, on its march, and, as such, the gaze of the civilized world is fastened, anxiously and inquiringly, upon her."

The numerous accounts of expeditions and settlement in New Mexico and California that survive from the 1840s and later can be divided generally into three groups: those appearing before the outbreak of war (and thus in some cases contributing to it); those written by Americans as a result of their experiences in the war; and those published in following years from the perspective of pride taken in victory and the magnificent abundance of resources now opened to American use. Of the central works that molded Anglo-American perceptions of California and its Mexican population, none is as important as Richard Henry Dana's *Two Years Before the Mast* (1840). Later known as a prominent Boston attorney and advocate on behalf of American slaves, Dana (1815–82) left Harvard in 1834 to undertake a sea voyage that was to restore his failing eyesight. The volume that described his voyage around the Cape and his work as a hide gatherer on the California coast was extremely popular and fixed in the mind of the eastern public an image of California as a land of potential abundance going to waste because of what was portrayed as Mexican indolence. *Two Years Before the Mast* is neither a work of deep philosophical reflection like *Walden* nor one of complex allegory like *Moby-Dick*; but its detailed treatment of Mexican California's history and customs, along with the superb rendering of Dana's hazardous and grueling life as a sailor, makes it an indispensable work of the period. Like Dana's next volume, *The Seaman's Friend* (1841), a handbook on sailors' rights, the continual meditation in *Two Years Before the Mast* on the questions of labor and individual rights, either aboard ship or on shore, anticipates Melville's *White-Jacket* (1850) in its concern with the role of workers in an industrialized but republican society. The values of Dana's New England are set against the rigidity of ship discipline on the one hand and the carefree luxury of California life on the other. In the wake of independence, Mexican California, in Dana's presentation, is burdened by corruption, arbitrary justice, constant revolution, and domestic immorality, despite the fact that the people inhabit a land with extraordinary natural riches and a five-hundred-mile coastline with excellent harbors. At the same time, Dana's skepticism about the rigidities of Protestant New England often makes his depiction of California a foil for his criticism of the materialist, expansionist spirit of his own culture. "In the hands of an enterprising people," Dana argues with double-edged language, "what a country this might be!" The book's complex treatment of the question of labor is thus linked to the growing myth of the golden possibilities of the American West and, underlined by Dana's irony, to Protestant America's contempt for purported Mexican inefficiency and superstition: "There's no danger of Catholicism's spreading in New England; Yankees can't afford the time to be Catholics."

Because it superimposed the clash between a rising technological society in need of labor and a Romantic vision of "natural" independence upon the era's representative genre, the western travel narrative, *Two Years Before the Mast* signaled a new direction in the ideology of western adventure. Within a matter of years it was joined by a flood of volumes devoted to California and the methods to be employed in getting there. Lansford Hastings's 1845 *Emigrant's Guide*, mentioned above, was preceded by Alexander Forbes's *California* (1839), John Bidwell's *A Journey to California* (1843), and Thomas Jefferson Farnham's *Travels in the Great Western Prairies* (1841) and *Life and Adventures in California* (1844), the last of which appeared in several editions and detailed Farnham's wagon train to Oregon and his travels to Hawaii, California, and Mexico. Although he warned of the hardships to be encountered in the West, Farnham also maintained without irony that California, as its history of Spanish settlement proved, was an "incomparable wilderness" as yet undeveloped by a race driven by the "love of wealth, power, and faith." Alfred Robinson, employed like Dana in the California hide and tallow trade, provided one of the best descriptive histories and geographies of the region during the period before the Gold Rush in *Life in California* (1846), in which he took note of the people's readiness to break with the Mexican government and predicted an imminent American conquest. It is no surprise, then, that one of the most widely read narratives of all was Edwin Bryant's *What I Saw in California* (1848), which included an account of his participation in Frémont's

Bear Flag Revolt and forecast the day when San Francisco would be "one of the largest and most opulent commercial cities in the world." The books by Robinson and Bryant were in harmony with the impulses of the U.S. government under Polk and the general mood of America's perceived destiny to liberate the Mexicans from "the profound darkness of their vassal existence," as an 1847 editorial put it. A writer for the *Boston Times* in the same year could not characterize the war with Mexico as a matter of conquest, because in this case it "must necessarily be a great blessing to the conquered. It is a work worthy of a great people who are about to regenerate the world by asserting the supremacy of humanity over the accidents of birth and fortune."

Given the mood and circumstances of the 1840s, John Frémont (1813–90), explorer, soldier, and politician, was a likely hero. Frémont's exact mission in California remains mysterious. Was he instructed, on secret orders from Polk, to initiate a revolt, or did he simply decide to take on the role of Sam Houston in California? The son-in-law of Senator Thomas Hart Benton, a staunch advocate of western advance, Frémont was on his third official exploring expedition in 1845 when he led the Bear Flag Revolt, which culminated in his capture of northern California for the United States, with southern California falling to regular military forces following outbreak of the Mexican War. His trial for mutiny (after he refused to recognize the authority of Brigadier General Stephen Kearny in California), his success in the Gold Rush, and his later political and military careers made him one of the most intriguing and controversial western figures in the decades before and after the Civil War. His official *Reports* on the expeditions, published in 1843 and 1845, and his unfinished *Memoirs of My Life* (1887) give a wealth of detail about the western territories he explored on surveys whose primary public purpose was to encourage overland emigration. Recalling Irving's depiction of Astor as the incipient hero of capitalist energy, Frémont's writings, widely read by politicians and common emigrants alike, portray him as a model expansionist who was the first to recognize and articulate California's great agricultural value.

War with Mexico in 1846 was rationalized on several premises: the actual desire of some inhabitants of both New Mexico and California to be annexed, grievances over violence against Americans (often provoked by aggressive, unlawful American settlers), the Mexican government's impediments to open trade, and simple land hunger among American pioneers and their official representatives in Washington. The volatile question of slavery also played an immense part in the controversy. In the speeches of political leaders like Thomas Hart Benton and Daniel Webster, the orations of abolitionists such as Theodore Parker, and the fiction of writers like Melville and Martin Delany, slavery determined the nature of the rhetoric and the shape of the debate over Mexico and the Southwest by linking the issue to widespread anti-Catholicism (as when antislavery polemicists depicted Catholicism as a religion of bondage and feudal subjugation) and to the commercial subjugation of the Caribbean and Latin America.

Journalistic and political expressions of America's manifest destiny in Mexico, as evidenced in editorials and proclamations, were supported as well by the Anglo-American travel narratives and fiction devoted more specifically to the Southwest and to the politics of the war. Much interest in the conquest of Mexico was aroused by George Wilkins Kendall's *Narrative of the Texas Santa Fe Expedition* (1844), an account of the ill-fated attempt of a group of Texans to capture Santa Fe. The Santa Fe Trail itself continued to be the primary route of the mountain men and adventurers, but their writings increasingly voiced anti-Mexican sentiments and invited political and military action on behalf of resident Americans. One of the best writers among southwestern travelers, the British adventurer George F. Ruxton (1820–48), occupied a middle ground on the question of American conquest. Although he maintained that an American attack was not justified, his *Adventures in Mexico and the Rocky Mountains* (1847) nevertheless portrayed the Mexicans as degraded and incapable of advanced civilization. Waddy Thompson's *Recollections of Mexico* (1846) gave a full picture of the history, geography, and resources of Mexico but argued that whereas the comparatively sterile environment of Massachusetts had produced prosperity, the rich landscape of Mexico appeared to have been wasted. If Mexico was not ready to be a republic, he maintained, it ought to be sheltered by American occupation from the constant revolutionary tumult in which it now existed. Because its sketches of life along the Santa Fe Trail emphasized that men and women in nature were "stripped of the disguises of civilized life" and existed without "the protection of the social state," Benjamin Taylor's *Short Ravelings From a Long Yarn* (1847) could likewise be seen to promote annexation, whereby a chaotic Hobbesian world would be redeemed by the ordering principles of democracy. Post-Mexican War travel works written amid further calls for expansion into Mexican territory—among them Asa B. Clark's *Travels in Mexico and California* (1852) and Robert A. Wilson's *Mexico: Its Peasants and Priests* (1856)—continued to reflect patterns of cultural domination that lasted into the twentieth century.

The portrayal of Mexico and Mexicans in the antebellum years thus frequently depended upon racial and religious bigotry, and elements of tendentious rhetoric were common in travelogues, fiction, and historiography devoted to all of Hispanic America. In the Anglo-American novel the merger of domestic romance with the ideology of manifest destiny was underpinned by the novelists' employment of historical frameworks and allusions to the violent and pagan past of Mexico. Before William Prescott's histories of the region were available, Robert Montgomery Bird, for example, had written *Oralloossa* (1832), a play about the killing of a Peruvian Inca prince by Pizarro, and had popularized Cortés's conquest and the decline of the Aztec Empire in novels like *Calavar; Or, the Knight of the Conquest* (1834) and *The Infidel; Or, The Fall of Mexico* (1835). John Stephens's popular travel works, cited above, had benefited from the vogue for works of exoticism such as Timothy Savage's Peruvian travel fantasy *The Amazonian Republic* (1842), Edward Maturin's *Montezuma; The Last of the Aztecs* (1845), Joseph Holt Ingraham's *Montezuma, the Serf* (1845), and Charles Averill's *Aztec Revelations* (1849), fictions of American empire that were built upon barely concealed racist constructions and theories of savagism. A strikingly unusual work combining diverse themes of the western conquest was Lewis Garrand's *Wah-To-Wah, and the Taos Trail; or, Prairies Travel and Scalp Dances, with a Look at Los Rancheros from Muleback and the Rocky Mountain Campfire* (1850), a semi-autobiographical work of mountain life that included an account of the 1847 "Taos Massacre," a brief uprising against the Americans newly in military occupation by Pueblo Indians and Mexicans. In language that might later have been turned against the U.S. theory of manifest destiny by Mexico itself, Garrand characterized the triumph of American power as the codification of progressive history: "the extreme degradation into which [the Mexicans] are fallen seems a fearful retribution upon the destroyers of [the] Aztec Empire."

The romance of ancient Latin American history, however, was most vividly exemplified by William H. Prescott's three-volume *History of the Conquest of Mexico* (1843), one of the most internationally admired histories of its day and the greatest example of the progressive historicism adopted by Garrand, Bird, Stephens, and others. In a masterpiece of Romantic style, Prescott (1796–1859) portrayed the conquest of the Aztecs by Cortés as a prefiguring of the rise to supremacy of the United States. In Prescott's epic account, Aztec barbarism, made especially melodramatic in Prescott's depictions of sacrificial rites, was balanced by a clear portrayal of Spanish greed and plundering—notably in the Poe-like grotesquerie of the city of Tenochtitlán, a virtual charnel house after Cortés's final assault—thus implying an unsettling parallel in the United States' own conquest of North American Indians and Mexicans. But the more powerful implied analogy for most readers in the United States was between the failure and fall of Aztec civilization and that of the contemporary Mexican government. "We cannot regret the fall of an empire, which did so little to promote the . . . real interests of humanity," Prescott wrote.

Its fate may serve as a striking proof, that a government, which does not rest on the sympathies of its subjects, cannot long abide; that human institutions, when not connected to humanity and progress, must fall—if not before the increasing light of civilization, by the hand of violence; by violence from within, if not from without. And who shall lament their fall?

Whatever reflection upon America's own destiny could be read into Prescott's masterwork, the advent of actual war reduced irony to a minimum and brought forth vigorous reassertions of America's millennial promise. Readers relied on Gregg's *Commerce on the Prairies* and Prescott's *History of the Conquest of Mexico* for information about the region; but they took their main view of the war from journalists, soldiers, and fiction writers. Accounts of the military campaign, especially the famous expedition of Alexander Doniphan, were written by a number of participants. F. A. Wislizenus, the German explorer, was on a scientific expedition in the Southwest when he was swept up in the war and made a medical officer with Doniphan, experiences recounted in *Memoir of a Tour to Northern Mexico* (1848). Thomas B. Thorpe (1815-75), better known as the author of "The Big Bear of Arkansas" and other tall tales collected in such volumes as *The Mysteries of the Backwoods* (1846), also described his view of the war in *Our Army on the Rio Grande* (1846) and *Our Army at Monterey* (1847). A significant number of soldiers acted as newspaper correspondents, providing the first significant coverage of an American war and helping to magnify the patriotic outpouring of sentiment that accompanied it. To many, the war seemed a fulfillment of the promises of the American Revolution, which had recently been reawakened in a number of popular histories by Benjamin Lossing, Jared Sparks, George Bancroft, and others. "Yankee Doodle" was the most famous song in the field and at home, and Zachary Taylor replaced Andrew Jackson, who died in 1845, as the nation's favorite soldier-statesman. While Thoreau and Emerson took exception to the war and James Russell Lowell (1819–91) employed the satiric poetry of *The Biglow Papers* (1848) to attack the war as an imperialistic blunder by corrupt politicians, the majority of poets and essayists celebrated American victories and heroism in an orgy of romantic and chivalric images. A compendium of the jingoistic literature of the war was edited early on by William McCarty in *National Songs, Ballads, and Other Patriotic Poetry, Chiefly Relating to the War of 1846* (1846). As a contemporary journalist wrote in his account of Doniphan's campaign, "the American eagle seemed to spread his broad pinions and westward bear the principles of republican government."

The simultaneously invigorating and enervating spirit of manifest destiny is nowhere more clear than in the fiction the Mexican War produced. The stage for such works, however, had been set by fictional portraits of Mexico before the war. Timothy Flint's *Francis Berrian, or the Mexican Patriot* (1826) dramatized Mexico's 1821 revolution in terms of its New England hero's image of the American Revolution—with the irony that by the time of the Mexican War the spirit of the American Revolution would justify war *against* Mexico. Justin Jones's somewhat later portrayal of Mexico's postrevolutionary period, *The Rival Chieftains* (1845), exemplified an increasingly widespread view that the chaos and exoticism of Mexico, "the El Dorado of the New World," made it the perfect scene for romance and novelistic enchantment. The first fiction of New Mexico by an Anglo-American who had actually been there, Albert Pike's *Prose Sketches and Poems* (1834), divides its attention between the beauty and desolate terror of the prairies and sketches of the Mexicans as colorful but at the same time crude and villainous.

Such portraits of Mexicans reached a climax in imaginative writing about the war. For example, the extravagant nationalistic rhetoric that accompanied the portrait of the American Revolution in George Lippard's *Washington and His Generals* (1847) appeared in a slightly revised form in his very popular *Legends of Mexico* (1847). Lippard (1822–54), the author of a variety of gothic tales in other settings, created a commanding paradigm for much of the subsequent fiction about the war by relying on exotic and terrifying scenes, the rescue of endangered maidens or innocent people from dark-skinned ogres, and attacks on the corrupt, even perverse, superstitions of Catholicism. The war, in Lippard's view, was the "Crusade of a civilized People, against a semi-barbarous horde of slaves." As the fulfillment of the nation's destiny initiated by the American Revolution, moreover, the conquest of Mexico would prove the supremacy of Anglo-American blood, spilled and purified in contest with the doomed American Indian, and the legitimacy of democratic principles, forged by revolution and sustained by a Puritan God:

A vigorous People, rugged as the rocks of the wilderness which sheltered them, free as the forest which gave them shade, bold as the red Indian who forced them to purchase every inch of ground, with the blood of human hearts. To this hardy People—this people created from the pilgrims and wanderers of all nations—this People nursed into full vigor, by long and bloody Indian wars and hardened into iron, by the longest and bloodiest war of all, the Revolution, to his People of Northern America, God Almighty has given the destiny of the entire American Continent. . . . As the Aztec people crumbled before the Spaniard, so will the mongrel race, molded of Indian and Spanish blood, melt into, and be ruled by, the Iron Race of the North.

The arc of liberty connecting the Revolution to the Mexican War and symbolizing the march of the United States across the continent is perfectly contained in Lippard's concluding image: "THE unsheathed sword of WASHINGTON resting upon the map of the NEW WORLD."

Lippard's prediction that the Americans would absorb the Mexicans points to a quandary that would confront those who advocated the conquest of "All Mexico" in coming years: would the inevitable amalgamation of the races save the Mexicans or destroy the Anglo-Americans? Even during the debate over annexation of New Mexico and California, John Calhoun and others who opposed President Polk's militaristic designs argued that Mexico was unassimilable. War fiction itself, because it turned so often to the categories of gothic romance in which a Mexican maiden was rescued from villainous brutes or corrupt Catholic priests to become the bride of an American hero, appeared to endorse absorption. The large number of novels and novelettes the war produced played constantly with variations on the theme of rescue and romance. As in the fiction of Indian captivity and the urban gothic novel (itself often violently anti-Catholic), romance in its sexual dimensions—capture, the threat of assault, rescue, and marriage—structured the military exploits recounted in numerous tales, including Arthur Armstrong's *The Mariner of the Mines: Or, the Maid of the Monastery* (1850), William L. Tidball's *The Mexican Bride; Or, the Ranger's Revenge* (c. 1858), George Lippard's *'Bel of Prairie Eden: A Romance of Mexico* (1848), Lorry Luff's *Antonita, The Female Contrabandista* (1848),

Justin Jones's *Inez, the Beautiful: Or, Love on the Rio Grande* (1846) and *The Volunteer: Or, the Maid of Monterey* (1847), Harry Halyard's *The Chieftain of the Churubusco, or, the Spectre of the Cathedral* (1848), Robert Greeley's *Arthur Woodleigh: A Romance of the Battle Field of Mexico* (1847), Charles Averill's *The Mexican Ranchero; Or the Maid of the Chapparal* (1847), and Eliza Ann Billings's *The Female Volunteer* (1851). To cite two typical examples: in Newton Curtis's *The Hunted Chief; Or, the Female Ranchero* (1847), the American hero at the fall of Monterey weds the Mexican woman who has fought throughout disguised as a male ranchero; and in Averill's *The Secret Service Ship* (1848) the marriage of the white hero and the Mexican woman symbolizes the triumph of American strength over Mexican weakness, or "femininity," as well as the resulting union of the two nations ("rapid and brilliant is the conquest of Peace by the glorious, ever victorious Flag of our Union"). Figuring territorial acquisition as sexual conquest and conjugal union, the fiction of the Mexican War thus projected the fulfillment of American destiny in expansion and in the absorption of a West that simultaneously included the geography and the customs and identity of the Mexican people.

The Mexican War continued to attract periodic romantic assessment for several decades, but its great contemporary interest was soon engulfed by the crisis over slavery and sectionalism. A number of soldiers who got their training in Mexico went on to significant careers in America's own internal cataclysm, and the question of African American slavery, which had played a significant role in arguments over the value of Mexican lands, would be resolved as a consequence of the Civil War. By the 1860s, however, the future geographical shape of the continental United States was complete. In the previous decade, a wealth of land and resources, with numerous potential transcontinental routes, had been made available to expansion by force of arms and helped give rise to the very conflicts that appeared to make civil war inevitable. With the American victory in the Mexican War, the questions of manifest destiny, the "Indian problem," and slavery became bound together even more tightly, as did the literatures those questions produced.

The Other Side

The American victory in the war against Mexico dramatically changed the course of American cultural history, making the West a region of even greater economic and political importance while at the same time ensuring that it would remain contested territory. Much of the region's literature, in both oral and written forms, appeared predominantly in Spanish until the twentieth century, when Mexican culture gave way, at least by political definition, to Mexican American culture. Parts of the territories of Texas, New Mexico, Arizona, and California could be defined as "border" regions even before 1848, however, and any account of the literature of the newly conquered territory must include recognition of its historical sources and of the suppression of Mexican cultural voices by Anglo-American domination. The difficulty in assessing the region's native Mexican literature is tied in turn to the ignorance and hostility with which it was treated by Anglo-Americans for the next hundred years. Because there remains a vast amount of as yet unstudied historical, journalistic, autobiographical, and literary material in libraries and archives of California, Texas, the Southwest, and Mexico, it was only at the end of the twentieth century becoming possible to give an adequate account of the literary history of the region. Even so, there were a number of significant *Mexican* works written in or about the greater Southwest before, during, and soon after the antebellum period which may be said to constitute the backgrounds (and in some instances what some scholars might identify as the beginnings or sources) of modern Chicano literature.

Even with the inclusion of very early narratives of the Spanish conquest, the currently documented literary record of the region is very scattered before the nineteenth century. The story may begin with Alvar Núñez Cabeza de Vaca, who was one of the few survivors of a failed Spanish conquistadorial expedition to Florida and endured an excruciating overland trek along the Gulf of Mexico. His *Relación*, composed in 1542, appears to be the first authentic written account of the Southwest and its native tribes as seen by an outsider. The most significant exploration of New Spain, Coronado's expedition up the Colorado River and across the central Great Plains in 1540, was recounted by a number of the participants, but the most important chronicle is Pedro de Nágera de Castañeda's *Relación de la jornada a Cíbola* (c. 1565), which is marked by evocations of the marvelous similar to those appearing in Spanish literature of the same period by Miguel de Cervantes Saavedra and others. The Spanish search for the "golden lands" of the North, in some instances linked to a quest for Aztlán, the Aztec land of origin, worked its way into several imperial texts and histories of the period. Fray Diego Durán's *Historia de las*

Indias de Nueva España (1579-81) and the anonymous *Códice Ramírez* (1853-7) based the myth of an Edenic Aztlán on the legends of native informants, whereas *Crónica Mexicáyotl* (1610), originally written in Nahuatl by Alvarado Tezozomac, and *Crónica miscelánea* (1652), by Fray Antonio Tello, tentatively identified Aztlán with the Pueblos of the Southwest. Later historical works, such as Manuel Orozco y Berra's *Historia antigua y de la conquista de México* (1880) and Alfredo Chavero's volume of the same name published in 1887, argued for yet other geographical locations of Aztlán, and in 1885 William G. Ritch, the secretary of the Territory of New Mexico and president of the New Mexico Bureau of Immigration, published a highly commercial work intended to promote immigration to the region entitled *Aztlán: The History, Resources and Attractions of New Mexico* (also issued under the title *Illustrated New Mexico*). More important than attempts to pinpoint a geographical Aztlán, which remained a matter of historical debate and diverse appropriation on through the twentieth century, are the ways in which Aztlán came to be embraced by some modern Mexican Americans, particularly those identifying with the movement for Chicano nationalism, as their spiritual homeland. A history of the region, in the form of an epic poem dedicated to Phillip III, survives in Gaspar Pérez de Villagrá's *Historia de la Nueva México* (1610), which celebrated Juan de Oñate's crossing of the Rio Grande to colonize New Mexico and appeared fourteen years before Captain John Smith's *General History of Virginia*. Composed in thirty-four cantos, Villagrá's *Historia* traces the history of New Mexico from Mexico's Aztec origins through the period of exploration that led up to Oñate's venture. In its account of the battle between the Spanish and the Acomas, its detailed portrait of the landscape and the working lives of the explorers and vaqueros, and its reflections on the cultural conflict entailed in colonial conquest, Villagrá's epic may be said to have provided the early groundwork for subsequent Mexican American literature.

A few other narratives, by both explorers and priests, appeared during the next two centuries, but the most significant firsthand accounts of the modern period date from the late eighteenth and early nineteenth centuries in the journals of explorers, missionaries, and political leaders, among them Fray Junípero Serra, Gaspar de Portolá, Miguel Costansó, Juan Bautista de Anza, Fray Juan Díaz, and Fray Francisco Gracés. Many such texts had very little circulation until their study by modern scholars; but Fray Geronimo Boscana, at the mission of San Juan Capistrano, recorded traditional Native American legends and creation myths in *Chinigchinich* (1831), which became widely known later when it appeared as an appendix to Alfred Robinson's *Life in California* (1846). Even though New Mexican religious poetry, folk songs, and religious drama such as Corpus Christi plays are documented from the sixteenth century forward, it is only near the period of independence that extensive examples of such literature began to be recorded by contemporaries. The late-eighteenth-century *Los comanches*, a heroic folk drama in verse, recounts the war between the conquistadores and the Comanche chief Cuerno Verde in 1774, though the drama takes one of its central features, the abduction of Christian children by infidels, from earlier Spanish versions of the drama (in which Moors took the place of Comanches) and belongs to a larger genre of such folk works portraying the contest between Christianity and "barbarism" known in both Spain and America as *moros y cristianos*. A play from the early 1840s, *Los tejanos*, depicted the 1841 defeat of the invading Texas Santa Fe expedition by the forces of General Manuel Armijo and offered a form of nationalistic commemoration and political satire that promoted New Mexican territorial integrity even as it adumbrated future threats against it.

The most important literary genre of the region, which would form the basis for much modern Chicano poetic literature, is the corrido, a narrative ballad sung or spoken with musical accompaniment. In addition to documenting the rise of borderland political and economic conflicts, which would remain integral to much Mexican American literature and to Chicano cultural nationalism, the corridos afford the best testimony to the oral, folkloric roots of modern Chicano literature. Descended in part from Spanish ballad forms and widespread in Mexico, the corridos flourished in the Mexican-American border area, especially in Texas, from the 1830s to the 1930s, and continued to be performed and recorded in the twentieth century. In addition to having an important place in Spanish-speaking theater, which was well established in San Antonio, San Francisco, and Los Angeles by the 1860s, corridos were printed along with other folktales, *decimás*, and canciones in Spanish-language newspapers and in bilingual newspapers such as the *New Mexican*, founded in 1849. Although only a few printed fragments from the pre-1848 years have been recovered, the majority of the nineteenth-century corridos were devoted to episodes and legends of Indian warfare, to love affairs, to cattle drives, and, especially, to the extensive civil conflict along the Rio Grande. Even when the cultural abrasion depicted is nonviolent or comic, the corrido in its early forms highlights the uneasy truce of the newly colonized region. "El corrido de Kiansis," for example, portrays the professional rivalry between Mexican vaqueros and Anglo cowboys, with the latter made out to be less than competent hands on the cattle drive.

The most famous of the corridos would appear several decades later, but its construction and its themes illuminate an oral tradition that began much earlier. "El corrido de Gregorio Cortez" concerns the legend of the best known of several rebel figures whose resistance to Anglo-American rule (or, as in the case of Cortez, the Anglos' overt lawlessness and racism) is commemorated by folk ballads. Hunted down and imprisoned along with his wife, Leonor Diaz Cortez, after his 1901 killing of an Anglo sheriff who was attempting to make an illegal arrest, Gregorio Cortez was later pardoned, but not before he had been immortalized as defending his rights "*con su pistola en la mano*" (with a pistol in his hand). Throughout the variants of this corrido, Cortez, though he is represented as a single man pressured into revolt by political injustice, is an individual whose actions express the will of the larger Mexican-American border community, which finds its greater cultural struggle epitomized by his rebellion. In many versions of the Cortez corrido, the hero's violent acts and subsequent legal prosecution are diminished in favor of a focus on his symbolic resistance to the massed authority of the dominant Anglo-American world. The last half of one variant recorded and translated by Américo Paredes reads:

> En el condado de Kiancer
> lo llegaron a alcanzar,
> a poco más de trescientos
> y allí les brincó el corral.
>
> Decía el Cherife Mayor
> como queriendo llorar:
> —Cortez, entrega tus armas
> no te vamos a matar.
>
> Decía Gregorio Cortez
> con su pistola en la mano:
> —Ah, cuánto rinche montado
> para un solo mexicano!
>
> Ya con ésta me despido
> a la sombra de un ciprés

aquí se acaba el corrido
de don Gregorio Cortez.

(And in the county of Kansas
They cornered him after all;
Though they were more than three hundred
He leaped out of their corral.

Then the Major Sheriff said,
As if he was going to cry,
"Cortez, hand over your weapons;
We want to take you alive."

Then said Gregorio Cortez,
With his pistol in his hand,
"Ah, so many mounted Rangers
Against one lone Mexican!"

Now with this I say farewell
In the shade of a cypress tree,
This is the end of the ballad
Of Don Gregorio Cortez.)

"El corrido de Gregorio Cortez," though written about events half a century after the Mexican War, reflects the scattered evidence of comparable motifs in the earlier corridos. Juan Nepomuceno Cortina, who organized a guerrilla band to occupy Brownsville, Texas, to protest Anglo abuse in the 1850s, is the subject of surviving ballad fragments that anticipate the corridos devoted to Cortez. Likewise, Ignacio Zaragoza, the hero of the battle at Puebla (in which Mexico's victory over invading French forces on May 5, 1862, gave birth to the national holiday Cinco de Mayo), became the subject of an 1867 corrido that is technically Mexican in origin but, like other such works infused with nationalistic consciousness, is equally significant for an understanding of the origins of Mexican American culture.

Especially in the border area between Mexico and the United States, where the problem of national identity would remain acute on through the twentieth century, the corridos thus put political sentiment in a popular form and directly reflected the experiences of Mexican men and women, whose lives were shaped by conflicting ideological forces and often marked by violent racism. The period between 1821 and 1848 in particular necessitated wrenching decisions about national loyalty for some Mexicans in the Southwest. For example,

Lorenzo de Zavala wrote a group of important essays about Mexico's independence from Spain, entitled *Ensayos históricos de las revoluciones de México*
(1831); but when he advocated independence for Texas in an anti-Mexican,
pro-American travel narrative entitled *Viaje a los Estados Unidas del Norte
de America* (1834), he lost his Mexican citizenship. Of particular interest as a
counterview of the Mexican War is Ramón Alcaraz's *Apuntes para la historia de la guerra entre México y los Estados-Unidos* (1848), translated in 1850 as
The Other Side, which provides excellent detail about key battles and Mexican
military leaders and is a useful corrective to the chauvinistic American versions of the war. Contemporary histories of the New Mexico region by its
residents include Don Pedro Bautista Pino's *Exposición sucinta y sensilla de
la provincia del Nuevo México* (1812); Antonio Barreiro's *Ojeada sobre Nuevo-
México* (1832), a work that supported a more vigorous imperial trade policy
toward New Mexico and warned Mexico of the territory's vulnerability to U.S.
invasion; and José Agustín de Escudero's *Noticias históricas y estadísticas de la
antigua provincia del Nuevo-México* (1849), a volume that essentially combined
the texts of Pino and Barreiro. From the other side of the cultural divide came
El Gringo; or, New Mexico and Her People (1857) by William W. H. Davis,
U.S. attorney for the Territory of New Mexico from 1853 to 1856, and the letters of Madame Calderón de la Barca, the English wife of a Spanish minister
to colonial Mexico, which were published in 1931 as *Life in Mexico* and offer
an impressive if often Eurocentric portrait of the social world and the role of
women in New Mexico in the years 1839–40.

The most comprehensive contemporary account of the region's history
from the Mexican American point of view would not appear until 1875 in
Mariano Vallejo's five-volume *Recuerdos históricos y personales tocante á la Alta
California*, cited at the outset of this chapter. Military commander of Alta
California from 1836 to 1842, Vallejo surveyed the entire history of Mexican-
Anglo relations in California in his often autobiographical study. Aware that
much of his own cultural heritage, as well as the political and property rights
of many *californios*, had been abrogated by the annexation of California by the
United States, Vallejo nonetheless tempered his criticism with a patriotic view
of the nation of which he had become a prominent citizen. In a forward to his
monumental work that combined familiar American revolutionary rhetoric
with an equally familiar belief in the progress of empires, he wrote (in Spanish)
that he considered himself

an eyewitness to the efforts of self-sacrificing military men and missionaries who, by dint of trials, sleepless nights, privations, and incredible perseverance, succeeded in wrestling from the control of savage Indians this beautiful land, which, redeemed from the bloody grasp of idolatry and raised by its sons to the heights of prosperity, stretches forth its loving arms to the oppressed of monarchical Europe and offers them the shelter of its fertile countryside, a fountain of wealth and prosperity.

That Vallejo wrote in Spanish, however, was but one index of the ambivalence that marked the range of early Mexican American literature. Both the pressure of acculturation and resistance to it were embedded in the bilingualism of much southwestern and California culture, a fact later captured by Jesús María H. Alarid in an 1889 poem entitled "El idioma," in which the author affirmed that English would be the national language of Mexican Americans but that they must never cease to speak and write in Spanish as well. Like the first histories and autobiographical narratives in California and the Southwest, the first Mexican-American novels, Eusebio Chacón's *El hijo de la tempestad* (Son of the Storm) and *Tras la tormenta la calma* (Calmness after the Storm), both published in 1892, were written in Spanish. But neither the language nor the border literature of Mexican America belonged in fact to the United States on the one hand or to Spain's colonial world on the other. Both were Mexican in origin and essence; and although the cultural traditions and literature of the region would, over time, become partially merged with the dominant ideological forms of Anglo America, they would maintain their own voices and historical particularity, rooted in the folk traditions passed down and recorded in such modern collections as Juan B. Rael's *Cuentos españoles de Colorado y Nuevo Mexico* (*Spanish Tales from Colorado and New Mexico*, 1977) and Elaine Miller's *Mexican Folk Narrative from the Los Angeles Area* (1973), as well as in pre-1848 historical and autobiographical narratives. Marked by colonialism but also by a wealth of indigenous traditions, the literature that pointed toward artistic expressions of Chicano and Latino nationalism in the twentieth century remains to be adequately interpreted both in its own terms and as an essential part of early American literary history.

Golden Dreams

By the end of the 1840s the opening of transmontane routes to the West, the U.S. victory in the Mexican War, and the discovery of gold in California released a wave of Euro-American pioneer emigrants that rapidly moved toward the coast and began to settle throughout sizable areas of the Great Plains and the Rocky Mountain West. The myth of the Great American Desert popularized by Pike, Long, Irving, Parkman, Gregg, Farnham, and others was disputed and disproved. As theories that free land in the West would accommodate surplus labor from the East emerged, and as Free Soil politics arose in opposition to the extension of slavery, a national vision of a western agrarian utopia of yeoman farmers served to reanimate the image of America as the "garden of the world." Drawing on conceptions of natural rights expounded by Locke and Jefferson, the agrarianist theory that resulted in the Preemption Act of 1841 and the Homestead Act of 1862 was based on independence, the right to private property, and the discipline of work. The various crusades for a transcontinental railroad by Asa Whitney, Thomas Hart Benton, and Stephen Douglas, among others, represented conflicting ideological interests but shared a vision of the American continent in which the mapping of the western garden would reveal the material value latent in a transcendent myth. The relative ease of acquisition and settlement of rich, abundant land on inland and coastal plains and the lure of mineral wealth in the Rockies and Sierra Nevada sparked a sudden, massive migration (and an often violent displacement of American Indians) that vividly transformed the destiny of the United States within a matter of decades.

Between the Mexican War and the Civil War, the primary Euro-American documents of the far frontier (besides the many scientific reports of the Army Corps of Topographical Engineers and others employed in the reconnaissance of transcontinental rail routes, mineralogical deposits and geographical formations, and Indian encampments) were devoted to promoting settlement in the West. Among the significant travel and emigration guides are Andrew Child's *Overland Route to California* (1852); two publications that warned explicitly against a utopian vision of gold wealth, James Abbey's *California, A Trip Across the Plains* (1850) and J. S. Shepherd's *Journal of Travel Across the Plains to California and Guide to the Future Emigrant* (1851); Charles Dana's *The Garden of the World*, cited above; and Joseph Colton's *Colton's Traveler and Tourist's Guide-Book Through the Western States and Territories* (1856), which was probably the most popular as a celebration of American industry and progress, featuring mileage, maps, and detailed information about the Mississippi Valley and the Great Plains regions. As Colton's guide suggests, the "West" continued to mean virtually all the territory beyond the Mississippi River. Yet the growing literary treatment of the frontier Middle West in personal narratives and frontier fiction was a sign in its own right that settlements would soon crowd out those seeking an unrestricted life in the wilderness or on the prairie.

If the desire for land and later for gold drove most men and women toward the Pacific, other forces as well governed the promise of frontier liberty. Reenacting the original Puritan settlement of America in new terms, for example, the Mormons wanted freedom from religious persecution. A Christian sect that grew to have an enormous following in the twentieth century, the Mormons orginated under the leadership of Joseph Smith, who transcribed and published several sacred works, including *The Book of Mormon* (1830), purportedly the text of a fifth-century prophet who forecast a New Jerusalem and millennial salvation in America. The Mormons were driven ever westward from their original church home in New York State, and after Smith was murdered by a mob in Illinois, they set out for Utah under Brigham Young. Guided by writings on the West by Lansford Hastings and John Frémont, Young established a new colony at Salt Lake in 1847. Both members and visitors wrote a variety of commentaries on the colony. Accounts of the migration are recorded, for example, in *Memoirs of John R. Young, Utah Pioneer of 1847* (1920) and *William Clayton's Journal* (1921), whereas the Mormons' early political and social organization is described in J. Howard Stansbury, *An Expedition to the Valley of the Great Salt Lake of Utah* (1852), James Linforth, *Route from Liverpool to Great Salt Lake Valley* (1855), and Thomas B. H. Stenhouse, *The Rocky Mountain Saints* (1873). In addition to condemnations of the kind that drove them from the East, the Mormons became increasingly the object of satire and exposé in popular fiction. Like the anti-Catholicism of gothic fiction, anti-Mormonism in the novel focused on sexual immorality, in particular the Mormons' advocacy of polygamy. Revelations of what were declared to be the bondage and perversions of Mormon marital life appeared in domestic melodramas such as Metta Victor's *Mormon Wives* (1854), Maria Ward's *Female Life Among the Mormons* (1855), and Ann Eliza Young's *Wife No. 19: or, the Story of a Life in Bondage* (1875), the supposed confessions of a former wife of Brigham Young. Despite these and other attacks on Mormon faith and enterprise, the Mormon migration, which resulted in one of the most stable and economically successful religious communities in American history, embodied in microcosm the revolutionary advent and popular pursuit of the ideal symbolized by the American West.

Nothing more completely summarized the often dreamlike meaning of the West than California during the Gold Rush. The narratives of exploration and the emigrant guides had already proclaimed California the land of America's future; after the Mexican War and the discovery of gold in 1848, the region became, like Ahab's gold doubloon in *Moby-Dick*, which alluded to it, a mirror of each pioneer's dreams. The symbolic significance of California was pinpointed by popular writer Bayard Taylor in the very title of the travel report he filed for Horace Greeley's *New York Tribune: Eldorado; or, Adventures in the Path of Empire* (1850). Completing and capping America's drive toward empire, California, according to Taylor, proved that the essence of America was hard work, risk, and a democratic leveling that made labor respectable and prosperity across the classes acceptable.

Various journals and emigrant guides to the gold country appeared immediately, including Henry Simpson's *Three Weeks in the Gold Mines* (1848), William Kelley's *A Stroll through the Diggings of California* (1852), the future California Supreme Court justice Lorenzo Sawyer's *Way Sketches* (1850), and Alonzo Delano's fine geological study, *Life on the Plains and Among the Diggings* (1854). The Australian William Shaw warned of the demoralizing effects of "gold mania" in *Golden Dreams and Waking Realities* (1851), and the Scottish writer John D. Borthwick argued in *Three Years in California* (1857) that the "Golden Legend," "one of the most wondrous episodes in the history of mankind," would momentously transfigure world trade. Life in the mines themselves—with its wild mix of races, rough frontier justice, and kaleidoscope of fulfilled and shattered dreams—was quickly recorded as history by J. Quinn Thornton in *Oregon and California in 1848* (1849) and in sketches such as Leonard Kip's *California Sketches With Recollections of the Gold Mines* (1850). Most famous of all were Louise Amelia Knapp Smith Clappe's *Dame Shirley Letters*, which first appeared in the San Francisco *Pioneer Magazine* in 1854–5. Based on her own experiences in the mining country in 1851–2 and written under the name Dame Shirley, these letters ostensibly to her sister in Boston recorded in magnificent detail the danger, profanity, and gamble of mining life, conveying at the same time a perfect sense of what Alexis de Tocqueville had diagnosed as the dreamy restlessness of Americans, who seemed never content but always in search of new wealth or greater freedom and adventure.

Most of the fiction devoted to the Gold Rush was cheap melodrama like George Payson's *Golden Dreams and Leaden Realities* (1853) and *The New*

Age of Gold (1856); gothic romance like the anonymous *Amelia Sherwood; or, Bloody Scenes at the California Gold Mines* (1849); or travel fantasy like Fanny Foley's *Romance of the Ocean: A Narrative of the Voyage of the Wildfire to California* (1850). The only fiction to raise more complicated issues were the legendary 1854 treatment of the bandit Joaquin Murieta by the Cherokee writer Yellow Bird (John Rollin Ridge) and Charles Averill's *Kit Carson: The Prince of the Gold Hunters* and its sequel *Life in California, or, The Treasure Seeker's Expedition* (both 1849), rambunctious adventure stories that presaged Frank Norris's *McTeague* in probing the "boundless power of unbridled lust for gold."

In the best writing about California in the 1850s, however, gold was not a rigid symbol but a metaphor evocative of the apparent triumph of American destiny. In the events transpiring within just three years, the Reverend Walter Colton wrote in *The Land of Gold; or, Three Years in California* (1850), the region "has sprung at once from the shackles of colonial servitude to all the advantages and dignities of a sovereign state." Although Colton noted that the miners were still in need of women, whose "smiles garland the domestic hearth," he considered the acquisition of California and the discovery of gold an omen of future greatness and issued an evangelical appeal to emigrants to settle and purify the region as a prelude to universal conquest:

Our globe was invested with no claims of utility till it had emerged from chaos; then verdure clothed its hills and vales; then flowing streams made vocal the forest aisles; then rolled the anthem of the morning star. . . . The tide of Anglo-Saxon blood stops not here; it is to circulate on other shores, continents, and isles; its progress is blent with the steady triumphs of commerce, art, civilization, and religion. It will yet flow the globe round, and beat in every nation's pulse.

The moral redemption to be accomplished by California needed to begin in California itself, claimed Eliza Farnham, wife of the travel writer Thomas Jefferson Farnham and author of a volume on midwestern emigration entitled *Life in the Prairie Land* (1846). Her *California, In-doors and Out* (1856) agreed with Colton and with a number of frontier novelists in arguing that women and the transforming powers of homemaking would be the key to California's success, notably because the domestic ideal was an emblem of democratic powers at work: "the loyalty that other nations pay to kings and queens, to old institutions, and to the superiority of caste, is paid by [men in America] to women." Without wives and mothers in a world of violent greed and vigilante justice, said Farnham, adopting a metaphor from mining geology, the "beautiful proportions of the moral nature will be gradually broken down, as the surface of the stone is hollowed, and its original form in part destroyed by the unceasing friction."

Easily the most dramatic prophecy to grow from the acquisition of California and the military and scientific conquest of the Rocky Mountain West appeared in a work by explorer, writer, and later governor of the Colorado Territory William Gilpin (1813–94). In a series of addresses collected as *The Central Gold Region. The Grain, Pastoral and Gold Regions of North America* (1860), he argued that the heart of this region, from the Great Plains to California, lay in the hemispheric band, postulated by Alexander von Humboldt, known as the isothermal zodiac. Falling in the path that had previously produced the empires of China, India, Greece, Rome, Spain, and Britain, the regions of the American West were thus set to usher in the great empire of North America. By means of an emigration "resembling the undulation of the sea, which accompanies the great tide-wave," a pastoral, Anglo-American empire, operating according to the "universal instincts of peace" and having at its command enough gold to accomplish the "*industrial* conquest of the world," would soon arise. With "moral grandeur" distinct from that of Europe, it would represent the fruition of the American Revolution; its "*untransacted destiny*" would be to "unite the world in one social family—to dissolve the spell of tyranny and exalt charity—to absolve the curse that weighs down humanity, and to shed blessings around the world." The pioneer heroes would lead the way in this millennial project, and a transcontinental railroad would be the material sign of its fulfillment. Gilpin's essentially Whitmanian prophecy appeared in a variety of forms on the eve of the Civil War, not least in the arguments of proslavery southerners, who saw the question of empire from a different angle of vision and asserted that the benevolent employment of slave labor could make possible the cultivation of the entire western hemisphere and open limitless trade across the Pacific.

The two views of empire shared an assumption that America's destiny in the 1850s had reached a climactic point and that the true passage to Asia would at last be achieved. Momentarily setting aside the explosive civil war that he saw on the horizon, in 1850 then Senator William Seward contemplated what the Treaty of Guadalupe Hidalgo and settlement of the Pacific coast appeared to promise:

> If, then, the American people shall remain an undivided nation, the ripening civiliza-
> tion of the West, after a separation growing wider and wider for four thousand years,
> will in its circuit of the world, meet again, and mingle with the declining civilization
> of the East on our own free soil, and a new and more perfect civilization will arise
> to bless the earth, under the sway of our own cherished and beneficent democratic
> institutions.

Both in geographical terms and with respect to the conflict over slave labor and sectional power, a crisis was inevitable. The full development of the West, and with it the further decimation of American Indian cultures, would follow the Civil War, but America's modern shape and meaning, recorded in a variety of forms and prophetic detail, were already powerfully clear in the antebellum era's literature of exploration and empire.

To Muse on Nations Passed Away

The Frontier and American Indians

In 1879, Hinmaton Yalakit (Thunder Rolling in the Heights), a Nez Percé leader known to whites as Chief Joseph, delivered an oration in Washington, D.C. His words summed up an escalating history of betrayals by settlers and government officials:

> The earth is the mother of all people, and all people should have equal rights upon it. You may as well expect the rivers to run backward as that any man who was born a free man should be contented when penned up and denied liberty to go where he pleases. If you tie a horse to a stake, do you expect that he will grow fat? If you pen an Indian up on a small spot of earth, and compel him to stay there, he will not be contented, nor will he grow and prosper. I have asked some of the great white chiefs where they get their authority to say to the Indian that he shall stay in one place, while he sees the white men going where they please. They cannot tell me. . . . Whenever the white man treats an Indian as they treat each other, then we will have no more wars. . . . Then the Great Spirit Chief who rules above will smile upon this land, and send rain to wash out the bloody spots made by brothers' hands across the face of the earth. For this time the Indian race are waiting and praying.

American Indians would wait in vain. Chief Joseph's oration, one of many such protests that form a powerful genre of resistance literature, looked both backward and forward from the historical midpoint in the long process of Indian Removal and the destruction of tribal integrity that was a consequence of the Euro-American conquest of the West. His words in the nation's capital are a simple reminder that American literature of the frontier was always a literature of political and cultural conflict, one in which language itself was a weapon of subjugation and an agent of transformation.

The acceleration of the U.S. westward expansion following the American Revolution put sudden, overwhelming pressure on resident Native American tribes, especially those east of the Mississippi River. The origins of the warfare waged against most tribes during the nineteenth century lay in the colonial period, but the several decades before and after America's own struggle for independence were crucial to the long-term imperial thrust. During the first half of the nineteenth century, the French and Indian Wars were central to American development and the progress of settlement across the continent. France's enormous cession of Indian land to Britain, the Indian's loss of allies, and the lessening of colonial reliance on Britain for protection created the conditions for the American Revolution and expansion east of the Mississippi. The Louisiana Purchase in 1803 gave the United States presumptive control over Indian territory west of the Mississippi and made possible the creation of a formal policy of Indian Removal. Prompted by a national ideology whose expressed intentions ranged from benevolent paternalism to virtual genocide, treaties negotiated between Indian tribes and the United States or state governments were often violated by American officials themselves and more often by the frontiersmen who wanted new land.

The War of 1812 marked important defeats for American Indians in both the North and the Southeast and elevated to national fame General William Henry Harrison and General Andrew Jackson. Both were vociferous on the subject of removing Indians from territories coveted by whites. Harrison asked: "Is one of the fairest portions of the globe to remain in a state of nature, the haunt of a few wretched savages, when it seems destined by the Creator to give support to a large population and to be the seat of civilization?" Although they sometimes took their ideas of Indian life from the Romantic philosophy and literary archetypes promulgated by those followers of Rousseau who valued the "state of nature" over the promised advance of Euro-American "civilization," most Euro-Americans accepted the verdict rendered by the essayist and novelist Hugh Henry Brackenridge in 1793: "I consider [that] men who are unacquainted with the savages, like young women who have read romances, have as improper an idea of the Indian character in the one case, as the female mind has of real life in the other." The "virtue" of primitive life, Brackenridge maintained, was an illusion of Enlightenment thought; true knowledge of

Indian life proved that tribes standing in the path of white settlement would have to be assimilated, removed, or vanquished. Settlers and governmental officials agreed.

Advanced with differing degrees of urgency by Thomas Jefferson, James Monroe, and John Quincy Adams as the best solution to warfare over land, the government's policy of Indian Removal was solemn doctrine for Jackson, who became known among many Indians as Sharp Knife. Although it was preceded by a good deal of public and congressional debate (which often had more to do with the future use of the lands than with tribal rights), the practice of Removal, begun in the 1820s, technically "allowed"—but in point of fact forced—Indians to exchange their tribal lands for territory west of the Mississippi. The policy became official with the passage of the Removal Bill in 1830 and with Jackson's refusal to abide by two Supreme Court decisions, *Cherokee Nation v. Georgia* (1831) and *Worcester v. Georgia* (1832), which held that the laws of the state of Georgia were subordinate to federal jurisdiction over the Cherokees. Although Georgia could therefore not permit the seizure of Cherokee lands by white settlers, the Cherokees were defined by the court as "domestic dependent nations"—in effect, a foreign country and people within the United States—and placed legally in a position of paternalistic dependence upon the federal government for protection and redress. Jackson simply ignored the continued illegal actions of the state of Georgia, and by 1838 most members of the "Five Civilized Tribes" (the Cherokee, Creek, Seminole, Chickasaw, and Choctaw) had been forced to follow what they came to call the Trail of Tears into newly created Indian Territory west of the Mississippi.

However indefensible Jackson's policy and his flouting of the Supreme Court, it is unlikely that federal interference could have halted the Euro-American drive on the frontier and the consequent challenge to Indian rights in territory farther and farther west. Jackson was not alone in believing that the expansion of white civilization was foreordained and that Removal was therefore not only expedient but also a humane alternative to war. Whatever the good intentions of some of its advocates, however, Removal was a process whose practical effects amounted to extermination. The burden of Jackson's views, summed up in 1830 in his Second Annual Message, demonstrated this clearly enough:

To follow to the tomb the last of his [the Indian's] race and to tread on the graves of extinct nations excite melancholy reflections. But true philanthropy reconciles the mind to these vicissitudes as it does to the extinction of one generation to make room for another. . . . Philanthropy could not wish to see this continent restored to the condition in which it was found by our forefathers. What good man would prefer a country covered with forests and ranged by a few thousand savages to our extensive Republic, studded with cities, towns, and prosperous farms, embellished with all the improvements which art can devise or industry execute, occupied by more than 12,000,000 happy people, and filled with the blessings of liberty, civilization, and religion?

In the context of Jackson's era, which boasted few defenders of an egalitarian society without regard to what were assumed to be inherent racial or national characteristics, his rationale for Removal was not in the least radical. Nevertheless, the ultimate result of the policy, degradation and extinction, was not difficult to forecast. Speckled Snake, a Cherokee, predicted as much in his answer to Jackson's advocacy of Removal through a policy of benevolent paternalism:

Brothers! We have heard the talk of our great father; it is very kind. He says he loves his red children. *Brothers*! When the white man first came to these shores, the Muscogees gave him land, and kindled him a fire to make him comfortable. . . . But when the white man warmed himself before the Indian's fire and filled himself with the Indian's hominy, he became very large; he stopped not for the mountain tops, and his feet covered the plains and the valleys. His hands grasped the eastern and the western sea. Then he became our great father. He loved his red children; but said, "You must move a little farther, lest I should, by accident, tread on you." With one foot he pushed the red man over the Oconee, and with the other he trampled down the graves of his fathers. . . . I have heard a great many talks from our great father, and they all began and ended the same.

Through Removal the population of American Indians east of the Mississippi was reduced from the 1820s through the 1840s to a quarter of its original size. In the case of the Cherokees alone, about four thousand out of twenty thousand died from disease and starvation in the journey from Georgia to Oklahoma. The Sauks and Foxes, the Winnebagos, and the Ojibwa (Chippewa), along with the southeastern tribes, were among those forced to cede or sell land and move west, where they were thrust into conflict with resident tribes of Sioux, Blackfeet, Osages, Pawnees, Comanches, Arapahos, and others. The policy of Removal, because it sought to provide a homeland for dispossessed tribes, was considered by most to be in many respects *more benevolent* than forcing Indians to adopt a culture not their own. But such programs as the government's appropriation of $10,000 a year starting in 1819 for a Civilization Fund to educate and Christianize Indians, although mildly successful with some tribes, were a meager form of benevolence. As Tocqueville wrote in *Democracy in America* of the forced migration of Creeks, Cherokees, and Choctaws, "it is impossible to destroy men with more respect [for] the laws of humanity."

Yet Tocqueville too considered Native Americans to be resistant to "natural laws" of progress. In this he shared the views of Lewis Cass, governor of the Michigan Territory from 1813 to 1831 and secretary of war under Andrew Jackson. Along with Jackson, Cass was a primary architect of the policy of Removal, arguing in several influential essays in the *North American Review* in the late 1820s that the Indian, unlike the Euro-American, was indolent and "stationary," content to live in the same circular routines as the bear, the deer, and the buffalo: "He never looks around him with a spirit of emulation, to compare his situation with that of others, and to resolve upon improving it." Or as the more expressive metaphor of Francis Parkman (1823–93) later put it: "[T]he Indian is hewn out of rock. You can rarely change the form without the destruction of the substance. . . . He will not learn the arts of civilization, and he and his forest must perish together." Parkman's comments appear in his *The Conspiracy of Pontiac* (1851), which played a large role in fixing the idea of Indian "doom" as part of American's prevailing mythology for the rest of the century. His careful identification of Indians with the natural world—both destined for defeat and cultivation by a greater race—is representative of white conceptions of the Indian's quasi-human form, as is his equally careful paternalistic imagery: "We look with deep interest on the fate of this irreclaimable son of the wilderness, the child who will not be weaned from the breast of his rugged mother." Widespread cultural perceptions of the American Indian as a "child" of nature—both innocent and given to uncontrolled violence— reenforced the policy of Jackson and others who developed a paternalistic structure of care and discipline to promote Removal. The natural metaphors employed by Cass and Parkman would proliferate in the nineteenth-century depictions of American Indians. In both political and psychological terms they situated Euro-American conquest within an epic pattern that was claimed to be at once providential and natural, unfolding according to observable laws of national purpose.

As the new nation was mapped and settled by white pioneers, Native American tribes occupied smaller and more remote areas of the map, in many cases ever more distant from their ancestral lands, while at the same time they became increasingly popular as subjects of American cultural expression and academic research. The absorption of the figure of the Indian into America's mythic consciousness, a process begun with the narratives of captivity and Indian warfare in the colonial period, was accelerated in the nineteenth century. Indian chiefs or heroes could become celebrities once they were no longer threatening as warriors, and whole tribes could be portrayed as virtuous and tragic to a public that had already been assured of final white triumph and saw battle and captivity as part of the ordained mission of America in the New World. A spirit of nationalism, prevailing attitudes toward "primitive" or "savage" life, and land hunger combined to create the conditions for a literature that largely supported Indian Removal even if it scorned the often violent or dishonest methods by which it was accomplished. During the period from the government's first official policy of Removal through the completion of pioneering routes west across the plains and mountains to the Pacific coast (roughly from the mid-1820s through the 1850s) novelists like James Fenimore Cooper, ethnographers like Henry Rowe Schoolcraft, historians like Thomas McKenney, and poets like Henry Wadsworth Longfellow dramatized American Indians as a people who belonged to a passing phase of human development, destined to die out if they remained unable to accept acculturation into the new nation. Not always sinister but nonetheless tragic, Removal gave direction to the representation of American Indians in the cultural documents of Euro-Americans and, at times, to the self-representation by Indians themselves.

Not surprisingly, the lives and voices of American Indians were often distorted in the texts that tried to portray them. Relatively few documents written by, or recorded from, Indians in the pre-Civil War period survive, and those that do are suspect either because they reflect less their native traditions than the expectations of the white audience to whom they were presented or because of problems in translation. Even so, there are a number of Indian texts written in English, as well as a far larger number of traditional stories and legends recorded and translated by researchers like Schoolcraft and George Catlin, which to some degree counter the denigrating or misguided views of Indian life depicted in popular Euro-American fiction and poetry. Native American cultural expression, largely nonliterate until the twentieth century, is difficult to conceptualize according to the chronological divisions and interpretive traditions of Euro-American literary history. Moreover, the isolation of Indian culture into an American "antebellum" period or even under the heading of either "American Indian" or "Native American," which falsely universalizes the traditions of hundreds of diverse tribes, imposes artificial definitions that are at times as inadequate and restricting as the Anglo-American penchant for speaking metonymically of "the Indian." Nonetheless, traditional native culture not only remained powerful during the exterminating wars of the nineteenth century but also began to be systematically recorded in written Euro-American forms for the first time. Because the history of American Indian literature in the antebellum period was inevitably a history of cultural appropriation and erasure—but one in which Native American culture did survive, under overwhelming and violent pressures—the language, ideology, and analytic methods of the dominant white world often ironically provided the primary means by which Indian cultural expression was preserved.

Living Monuments of a Noble Race

In the literature of western expansion, even those documents that did not focus on American Indians often took for granted that the "Indian problem" was in the process of being solved. Because Indian tribes seemed destined to recede or vanish in the face of advances by white pioneers, however, the Indian often became for white writers a nostalgically or ironically charged symbol, capable of representing a variety of ideas: the loss of innocence that progress entails; a mythic age that would give historical scope to an America eager to assert its nationalism; or a primitivistic stage of social organization preferable to an increasingly urban, industrial world. Most of all, perhaps, the Indian could be figured as a noble hero, tragic in defeat but in pride and stoicism also a mask—at times a mirror—for white anxiety over the destruction of Native American tribal life.

A representative measure of prevailing cultural and political attitudes toward Indians at midcentury can again be found in Parkman's *The Conspiracy of Pontiac*, which differs little in outlook from the work of other historians and ethnologists but stands out for its lyrical view of the continent's swift transfiguration. It is also a good example in popular literature, not so much of the cultural "removal" of Indians from the American landscape, but of their containment within a carefully circumscribed area of thought. Just a few years earlier in *The California and Oregon Trail* (1849) Parkman had presciently depicted the escalating slaughter of buffalo as though their death were coincident with that of the Indians who relied on hunting them, both destined to vanish in what Parkman represented as a natural process. In the *Conspiracy of Pontiac*, a work comparable to *Moby-Dick* in its epic sweep at a climactic moment of mid-nineteenth-century history, Parkman locates the American Indian's vanquishing and death in the past by making the French and Indian Wars and Pontiac's uprising the last obstacle to white supremacy on the continent. As Melville's *Pequod* sinks into the maelstrom after its captain's monomaniacal pursuit of Moby Dick, a hammer wielded by the Indian Tashtego pins a screaming sky hawk against the mainmast. Parkman did not share Melville's tragic vision of America's western expansion, but his epic account of Pontiac likewise symbolized the meaning of that expansion by portraying the "American forest and the American Indian at the period when both received their final doom." Like Cooper and other novelists who set their accounts of Indian warfare in the past, Parkman displaced anxiety over contemporary violence and Removal into another era, rendering Native Americans fatalistically "lost"—already part of a mythic past—and thereby generating a powerful historical depth for America's ideological identity. A portrait of the defeated Pontiac, musing upon Lake Erie in 1766, reveals the scope of Parkman's own vision:

> Little could he have dreamed . . . that within the space of a single human life, that lonely lake would be studded with the sails of commerce; that cities and villages would rise upon the ruins of the forest; and that the poor momentoes of his lost race—the wampum beads, the rusty tomahawk, the arrowhead of stone, turned up by the ploughshare—would become the wonder of school-boys, and the prized relics of the antiquary's cabinet.

Along with national artworks like Horatio Greenough's sculpture *Rescue Group*, erected at the Capitol in 1853, and mundane artifacts of cultural and economic policy like the Indian-head penny, first minted in 1859, Parkman's 1851 rendering of Pontiac indicated that one phase of American history, that encompassing the first decades of Removal, was reaching a close. In a journal entry of 1859, Thoreau, long a philosophical student of Native American relics and names, could declare that the arrowhead was a kind of "stone fruit" or a seed, slow to germinate, that would "bear crops of philosophers and poets." In fact, however, the poetic appropriation of Indians as a primary element in American mythology had begun long before.

Because few writers had direct knowledge of Native American life, most relied on romantic clichés and frontier tales of savage violence. As Washington Irving remarked in an 1848 essay, "Traits of Indian Character," Indians were likely to have been doubly mistreated: "The colonist often treated them like beasts of the forest; and the author has endeavoured to justify him [the colonist] in his outrages." Hardly immune to romanticism himself, Irving found that the "proud independence, which formed the main pillar of savage virtue, has been shaken down, and the whole moral fabric lies in ruins." Turned into a "ruin" in both aesthetic and moral terms, American Indians were just as significant a problem for the intellectual as they were for the government official. For both, the disappearance of the present tribes could be understood as part of the same geohistorical process that was sweeping forward the Euro-American race. The ideology of Removal was required to perform a double function. On the one hand, it had to provide a philosophy to justify purging the continent of "alien" and potentially deadly people. On the other hand, it had to create a political and cultural medium in which conquest could be naturalized or set within a panoramic elaboration of predestined history, as in Cornelius Matthews's novel *Behemoth: A Legend of the Mound-Builders* (1839), which treats the remains of the prehistoric forerunners of contemporary American Indians as the North American equivalent of Greek antiquities. "A decaying bone, an old helmet, a mouldering fragment of wall," Matthews wrote, can make us feel our "kindred with generations buried long ago."

Irving, for one, was not sanguine about the survival of American Indians in actuality or in their dignified remembrance in national mythology:

If, perchance, some dubious memorial of them should survive, it may be in the romantic dreams of the poet, to people in imagination his glades and groves, like the fauns and satyrs and sylvan deities of antiquity. But should he venture upon the dark story of their wrongs and wretchedness; should he tell how they were invaded, corrupted, and despoiled, driven from their native abodes and the sepulchres of their fathers, hunted like wild beasts about the earth, and sent down with violence and butchery to the grave, posterity will either turn with horror or incredulity from the tale, or blush with indignation at the inhumanity of their forefathers.

The "dark story" would get told only with difficulty, and even the most generous accounts struggled against ingrained notions of savagism and the tendency to romanticize Native American life in compensation for its destruction. With some irony, the Indians' own words and stories, whether preserved in oral tradition or by sympathetic travelers, would become literary artifacts, not unlike the stone and clay relics that pioneer farmers (and natural philosophers like Thoreau) would find for generations. An anthropological or archeological attitude toward Indians thus preceded actual fieldwork; Indians were memorialized in the very moment they were doomed, celebrated as part of America's innocent, mythic past even as they were pushed ever westward and declared to be savages beyond the bounds of civilized life.

In the Euro-American literature devoted to American Indians, as in that devoted to slavery, official speeches and documents, ethnographic materials, and historical commentary are equal in importance and often in literary quality to the work of novelists, dramatists, and poets. Moreover, the questions of African American slavery and Indian Removal were not unrelated but together belonged to the central dilemma of race in its relation to the promise of the American Revolution. The Declaration of Independence spoke with alarm of the "merciless Indian savages" who threatened colonial life, and Washington, Jefferson, Adams, and others of the early national generation were often less than sympathetic to the Indians' plight as long as they were perceived to be military enemies. Yet black slaves and American Indians, however they might both be ranked below whites in the hierarchy of "nature" (as would Mexicans by the 1830s), hardly constituted a single issue. In fact, as Tocqueville noted in *Democracy in America*, their situations could be seen as nearly opposite: "the Negro has reached the ultimate limits of slavery, whereas the Indian lives on the extreme edge of freedom" and enjoys a kind of "barbarous independence." Tocqueville's portrait of the American Indian was sympathetic—if nonetheless informed by an ineradicable belief in savagism—but his theory of the Indian's "freedom" bears notice because it defines the double attitude American culture would hold more and more rigidly as the century passed and Indian tribes perished. In this prevailing theory, Indians were noble, courageous, and independent; but they were also improvident, childlike, superstitious, vengeful, and thus a threat to stable and complex social order.

Both official policy and popular literature promulgated this double attitude, as did some Native Americans who converted to Christianity and accepted white social and economic culture. The result was an image of the American

Indian often placed in polar opposition to the advancing Euro-American society: primitivism versus civilization, demonic revenge versus Christian charity, or nomadic hunting life versus property rights and agricultural development. The defining characteristics of "savage" life advanced by politicians, historians, and imaginative authors alike included Indians' propensity to fight by guerrilla methods and to indulge in scalping and other brutalities; their lack of Christian forgiveness and idealization of vengeance; their weak family structure and immature sense of organized society; and their stoic willingness to endure intense pain and hardship. That the same savage traits were also assigned to white pioneers who chose a wild frontier life over the confinement of society only underlines the fact that the idea of the Indian and the idea of the frontier were often inseparable in both geographical and psychological terms. As Thoreau said he might devour a woodchuck raw in order to incorporate its "wildness," so Indians and their ways might be sought out by the frontiersman, the renegade from society, or writers determined to place their work at the borders of a developing frontier tradition. Yet Indians, like their land and its riches, would likewise be devoured in the process—either literally exterminated or else assimilated into the nation's culture, subtly changing it perhaps but submitting at last to its dominating myths. In any event, official policy would remain divided between the advocates of virtual annihilation and those like Jedediah Morse, who in his *Report to the Secretary of War . . . on Indian Affairs* (1822) predicted both the necessity and the enormous difficulty of the "godlike work" of education and acculturation.

Some portraits were legitimately sympathetic to the Indians' plight; others simply took advantage of the popular rage for melodrama and sentiment on stage and in prose fiction. On occasion a virtual catalogue of major ideas appeared in a single work, as in James S. French's novel about General William Henry Harrison's campaign against the Shawnee chief Tecumseh, *Elkswatawa; or, the Prophet of the West* (1836). Both the novel and its subject are instructive examples of the mythologizing process at work, and *Elkswatawa* is best seen in the context of other treatments of its events and ideas that demonstrate how fiction and drama overlapped with historiography and Indian narrative to create a multidimensional artifact of composed American Indian life.

In the face of relentless advances of white settlers, Tecumseh had set out in 1811 to organize the tribes of the entire Mississippi Valley in an alliance. Along with his brother Elkswatawa, known as the Prophet, Tecumseh espoused a form of Indian nationalism that rejected all corrupting influences of Euro-American life. Defeated by Harrison at the battle of Tippecanoe, an event that helped precipitate the War of 1812, Tecumseh's forces fell into disarray and his powerful leadership was dissipated. Yet over the next several decades, as the conclusion of the war and the advent of Indian Removal opened the Mississippi Valley to unimpeded white pioneer expansion, Tecumseh was readily incorporated into a national myth, as though his defeat necessitated ritual internalization. For example, whereas William R. Wallace's *The Battle of Tippecanoe* (1835) made Tecumseh's enemy, General Harrison, the hero in an ornate patriotic epic, George H. Colton's heroic poem *Tecumseh; Or the West Thirty Years Since* (1842) depicted the Shawnee chief as a savage hero, destined to fall to a greater force. Colton memorialized that fall by providing Tecumseh with a pseudoglorious "War Song" to mark his passing:

> I smell the carnage of the battle!
> Terrible is the strife,
> Where gushes the tide of life!
> But 'tis joy, as we sink,
> Of the red stream to drink,
> That warms from a foeman our hatchet and knife!

Even poems with opposing heroes, that is to say, could accomplish much the same cultural work. In a more critical vein, Benjamin Drake's *Life of Tecumseh* (1841) portrayed Tecumseh as brave and humane, even a military genius (Drake quotes James Hall, who called the Shawnee chief a "Napoleon of the West"), whereas the white advance was seen to be the result of "insatiable cupidity and a wanton disregard of justice." The less sympathetic portrait in Benjamin B. Thatcher's *Indian Biograph* (1832), though it made Tecumseh a great statesman and patriot, recognized a fatality in the fact that he used his great genius in fighting "only for wild lands and wild liberty." What were claimed to be Tecumseh's own words, quoted in a variety of texts, became ironic evidence of Euro-American destiny—for example, this 1811 speech, advocating the unity of all Indians and invoking aid from the British, which was recorded in a popular captivity narrative, John Dunn Hunter's *Memoirs of a Captivity Among the Indians of North America* (1824):

Brothers.—Who are the white people that we should fear them? They cannot run fast, and are good marks to shoot at: they are only men; our fathers have killed many of them: we are not squaws, and we will stain the earth red with their blood.

Brothers.—The Great Spirit is angry with our enemies; he speaks in thunder, and the earth swallows up villages, and drinks up the Mississippi. The great waters will cover their lowlands; their corn cannot grow; and the Great Spirit will sweep those who escape to the hills from the earth with his terrible breath.

It is in this context that both Tecumseh's famous oration and a representative novel like French's ought to be read. Speeches by both Tecumseh and General Harrison are quoted in *Elkswatawa*, and Tecumseh appears as a brave, almost magnificent figure; but these elements are subordinated to the archetypal story of the rescue of a white heroine from captivity. Because it converges with the battle of Tippecanoe, the rescue becomes emblematic of the justification for warfare often urged by politicians and military leaders: that frontier settlers had to be saved from marauding Indians. The white Indian hater, evocatively named Earth, returns to a peaceful life in civilized society at the end of *Elkswatawa*, suggesting that the killing of savage Indians is only a temporary and practical phase of American progress, which must itself momentarily employ savage methods in order to triumph. Tecumseh's humanity and courage, and the idealism of his brother, the Prophet Elkswatawa, whose vision of a pristine, communal native existence is tragically betrayed, are thus traits to admire but ones that, significantly, now belong to a past subject to the emerging generic laws of the frontier novel. Tecumseh, one could say, is deliberately staged as both a historical and political icon within these texts, a figure whose sacrificial role translates imperial warfare into naturalized destiny.

The popular expectations of Romantic historical fiction shaped most novelistic treatments of American Indians, and in some cases their rationale became an explicit part of the author's concerns. James Fenimore Cooper, William Gilmore Simms, and Nathaniel Hawthorne are only the most famous of the many authors who sought to develop a theory of the Romance suitable to an American setting. Like Hawthorne's preface to *The Scarlet Letter*, such theories exploited the possibilities of American exceptionalism but at the same time worked to discover the historical depth and cultural resonance that critics, both foreign and domestic, claimed the nation lacked. In the case of American Indians, the Romance thus joined forces with ethnography, and for imaginative writers such as Irving and Thoreau, and historians such as McKenney and Schoolcraft, the Indian's demise became perfectly representative of America's potential antiquity even as it authorized a progressive futurity.

Although most writing by whites about American Indians in the period from 1820 through 1865 at least implicitly reflected such a dual vision, it is especially prominent in the major historical and ethnographical work that preserved in written form a large body of Native American history and legends while attempting to give a coherent, if inevitably distorted, account of it in Euro-American terms. The histories produced in the antebellum period, because they were usually governed by nationalistic assumptions about the superiority of the new American government and its people, constitute a significant statement of the "Indian problem." Although most historians took for granted the Indian's eventual displacement, several accounts that were not prominently ethnological in character sought to provide reliable and sympathetic information about Native American life before it disappeared. Among these are Henry Trumbull's *History of the Indian Wars* (1811; revised, 1841), John G. Heckewelder's *History, Manners, and Customs of the Indian Nations* (1818), Benjamin B. Thatcher's *Indian Biography* (1832), Harvey Newcomb's *The North American Indians* (1835), John Frost's *Indian Wars of the United States* (1840), and Samuel Goodrich's *Lives of Celebrated American Indians* (1843). One of the best-known works, Samuel Drake's *Biography and History of the Indians of North America* (1832), although not as comprehensive or informed as the later works of McKenney, Schoolcraft, and Catlin, is especially important as a compendium of history, biography, captivity narratives, and Native American oratory. In addition to Drake's own critique of the methods of white progress, his reliance on primary (but translated) Indian documents, such as Speckled Snake's reply to Jackson, noted above, makes his a study of strongly counter-pointed voices.

This was not always true of more prominent work. The period's leading national history, George Bancroft's *A History of the United States* (1834–75), depicted Native American culture as politically dignified but socially primitive—a combination of simplicity, immorality, and irrationality. In his section on "The Red Men East of the Mississippi," for example, Bancroft noted that "the American savage has tongue and palate and lips and throat; the power to utter flowing sounds, the power to hiss"; but before contact with Europeans, none of the eastern tribes "had discriminated the sounds which [they] articulated" and formed an alphabet, "and the only mode of writing was by rude imitations and symbols." The savage's "system of morals" was but a "license to gratify his animal instincts," and even if the red men carried the federal form of government to a perfection rivaling the ancient Hellenic councils, they were still "deficient in the power of imagination and abstraction" and "inferior in reason and in ethics."

Bancroft's chapter is a good index of the ways in which historical and ethnological writing about Indians overlapped. Both assumed that writing was the primary technology that distinguished whites from Indians; by the same token, writing, along with the collecting of legends and artifacts, was seen to be the primary means by which Indians would be preserved, since expectations for the survival of tribal life were slim. The force of this assumption was codified when Albert Gallatin founded the Bureau of American Ethnology in 1842, centralizing the enormous labor to catalogue Indian languages and customs that took place over the nineteenth century, an effort according to prevailing standards of inquiry that constituted one of the first large-scale scientific projects in the United States. The foremost American ethnologist of the nineteenth century, Lewis Henry Morgan (1818–81), created over his career a paradigmatic anthropological picture of American Indians as sublime but simple, the noble victims of white rapaciousness yet destined to wither under the powerful advance of a superior culture. Morgan's most influential work appeared in the 1870s, and by then he spoke straightforwardly of the preservation of Indian life within the structures of anthropological museum work. In an essay entitled "Montezuma's Dinner," which appeared in 1876, he remarked: "The question is still before us as a nation, whether we will undertake the work of furnishing to the world a scientific exposition of Indian society, or leave it as it now appears, crude, unmeaning, unintelligible, a chaos of contradictions and puerile absurdities." If persons willing to undertake such work could be found, Morgan insisted, "it will be necessary for them to do as Herodotus did in Asia and Africa, to visit the native tribes at their villages and encampments, and study their institutions as living organisms, their condition, and their plan of life."

Morgan's own research began many years earlier, however, and his *Ancient Society* (1877), which put forward a theory of the social evolution of all world races from a common origin, grew out of studies among Native Americans, in particular the Iroquois. His later work was less prone to the condemnations of "savage" traits that are scattered throughout his first important study, *League of the Ho-de-no-sau-nee, or Iroquois* (1851). The *League* appeared in the same year as Parkman's *Conspiracy of Pontiac* and the first volume of Schoolcraft's monumental *Historical and Statistical Information,* and the three works all represented in their different ways the common belief that the Indians' reign was finished, suitable now only for historical and ethnological evaluation. Based on his famous "Letters on the Iroquois" in the *American Review* in 1847, Morgan's *League* offers a detailed account of tribal government, numerous renderings of tales and mythic beliefs, and descriptions of family life and customs. As a people without sophisticated literacy or industrial arts, however, the Iroquois are depicted by Morgan as trapped in the hunter state, referred to as "the zero of human society." The Iroquois are united with the phenomena of the natural world, but they pay the price by falling "under the giant embrace of civilization, victims of the successful warfare of intelligent social life upon the rugged obstacles of nature." Morgan's arguments on behalf of Indian land rights and his detailed, ostensibly objective record of Iroquois culture thus remain in conflict with his view that the Iroquois are themselves an aspect of "rugged nature" and his consequent belief in the superiority of the Euro-American community.

Equally important in establishing American Indians as a subject of study was the painter and writer George Catlin (1796–1872). Some of his work, like the notorious accounts of a painful Mandan initiation ceremony, recorded in most detail in *O-kee-pa: A Religious Ceremony and Other Customs of the Mandans* (1867), was attacked by Schoolcraft; but Catlin's description of the Mandan ceremony was defended by Morgan and corroborated by later researchers. If Catlin's work is less professedly scientific than Morgan's, his descriptive observations, if not his romantic racial speculations, are comparatively reliable. He grew up in frontier Pennsylvania and, like Morgan, was trained for a legal career, but he abandoned law for portrait painting and seized upon American Indians as his life's work. In 1832 Catlin began an eight-year journey among the western and southern Indians, visiting some forty-eight different tribes and producing over five hundred portraits, landscapes, and paintings of artifacts. Setting out by steamboat up the Missouri, Catlin wrote to his publisher that he was intent on the Indians' rescue—the rescue "not of their lives or their race (for they are 'doomed' and must perish)" but rather "of their looks and their modes," so that "phoenix-like, they may rise from a 'stain on a painter's palette,' and live again upon canvass, and stand forth for centuries yet to come, the living monuments of a noble race." The record of the Indian's image, then, the resurrection from his dying body of a mythic presence in the monumental form of hundreds of canvases, was all Catlin could hope to achieve. Artistic and literary representation would take the place of tribal survival (as Cooper had already begun to prove in his Leatherstocking Tales) and would fix an artistically objectified figure of the American Indian at a moment of tragic heroism stranded outside the progressive flow of historical time.

Recorded in *Letters and Notes on the Manners, Customs, and Condition of the North American Indians* (1841), Catlin's trip ranks among the most significant Euro-American imperial explorations of the century. It gave him the means to set down in pictures and words "the living manners, customs, and character of an interesting race of people who are rapidly passing away from the face of the earth—lending a hand to a dying nation, who have no historians or biographers of their own to portray with fidelity their native looks and history." Catlin also organized a popular show of his paintings and artifacts and staged dances and ritual performances by actual Indians in the United States, England, and France in the 1840s. From 1852 to 1857 he undertook another long exploring trip through Central and South America and the Far West, which he recorded in several volumes, including *Last Rambles Amongst the Indians of the Rocky Mountains and the Andes* (1867). These travels reinforced his impression that increasingly Indians could be seen on the frontiers only "as a basket of *dead game*—harassed, chased, bleeding, and dead." Catlin abhorred the general misuse of the term "savage" and responded to the tribes he visited in respectful terms. Yet he also perpetuated the naive hypothesis that Native Americans untouched by white life—those beyond the frontier—remained nobly pure, whereas contact with white traders and pioneers inevitably degraded the native tribes. For Catlin, a perfect exponent of the paradox of ethnography, civilization was certain "to obliterate the grace and beauty of Nature." His extensive painted catalogue of Indian customs, utensils, clothing, houses, and faces was intended to preserve from extinction a race who, like the buffalo, had "taken up their *last abode*."

Despite their devotion to Indian study, neither Catlin nor Morgan worked from within the governmental structure that was responsible for administering American law on the frontier. Thomas McKenney, author with James Hall of the three-volume *History of the Indian Tribes of North American* (1836–44), labored diligently within the government to preserve a record of Native American life even as he may be said to have overseen its vanquishing. As superintendent of Indian trade, an office in the War Department, McKenney (1785–1859) administered the system of government trading posts, and as head of the Bureau of Indian Affairs, created in 1824, he became a strong advocate of philanthropic reform among Indian tribes. On several occasions McKenney helped to negotiate treaties in the field with Indians of the North and the Southeast. Although he was thrown out of office by Jackson in 1830, McKenney fundamentally believed, along with the president, that Removal was the only way to save the Indians—*and* to make their lands available for cultivation.

McKenney came to office largely ignorant of actual Indian life, and his early volume *Sketches of a Tour to the Lake* (1827), which covers the trip with Lewis Cass to negotiate with the Ojibwa, is sometimes mistaken in its facts. Later works such as *On the Wrongs and Rights of the Indians* (1846) and his *Memoirs* (1846) continue to lament Indian vengefulness and improvidence, and McKenney always endorsed conversion to white values of agriculture, education, and Christianity. His major work, the *History* written with Hall, contains reproductions of numerous portraits of Indian chiefs and leaders by Charles Bird King and James Otto that McKenney had assembled in an "Indian Gallery" of the War Department. The reproductions accompany biographical and historical chapters on many tribes and about a hundred and fifty individuals, among them Red Jacket, Kiontwogky (Cornplanter), Sequoyah, Osceola, Black Hawk, and Major Ridge. Most of the biographical text has been attributed to McKenney, but a separate essay signed by Hall outlined a recognizable theory of savagism. Nomadic, improvident, and lacking a "code of empires" that could be integrated into international law, the Indian tribes of America are in essence depicted as part of the kingdom of animals. "Lost in the most degrading superstition," Hall remarks, "they look upon Nature with a vacant eye, never inquiring into the causes, or the consequences of the great revolutions of Nature, or into the structure or operations of their own minds." McKenney's view was less pessimistic. Like Catlin, he had a genuine humanitarian interest in Indian reform—certainly preferable, he thought, to genocide—but his great work also turned into a virtual museum of antiquities in his own lifetime. His Indian Gallery became part of the Smithsonian in 1858 (most of the portraits were destroyed in an 1865 fire). It effectively marked the absorption or elimination of many Native American tribes in the eastern

United States, and it is strikingly emblematic of their cultural containment by Euro-American writers and politicians in the antebellum period.

Easily the most important Euro-American work of ethnographic preservation of Native American culture was done by Henry Rowe Schoolcraft (1793–1864). A geologist and Indian agent from 1822 to 1841 in the Great Lakes region, Schoolcraft married an Indian, lived with various tribes and studied their languages (especially the Ojibwa, Ottawa, and Lakota), and attempted both to catalogue every fact of Native American civilization he uncovered and at the same time to justify its displacement by a superior culture. He accompanied McKenney and Cass on a treaty expedition in 1820 and recorded the event in *Narrative Journal of Travels Through the Northwestern Regions of the United States* (1821). His explorations of the valley and sources of the Mississippi are detailed in *Travels in the Central Portions of the Mississippi Valley* (1825) and *Narrative of an Expedition through the Upper Mississippi* (1834). These works, along with the earlier *A View of the Lead Mines of Missouri* (1819) and a poem about the Mississippi River entitled *The Rise of the West* (1830), demonstrate Schoolcraft's ability to combine precise geological and geographical observation with a theory of U.S. expansion. Like other trappers, miners, and explorers, Schoolcraft saw the land with double vision: on the one hand, he valued aesthetically its pristine beauty; on the other, he was aware of its speculative value in real estate and mineral rights. Because he saw Indians the same way, Schoolcraft's work of recording Native American customs and history, which occupied the last half of his life, fails to make clear sense of a great wealth of data.

Before his six-volume *Historical and Statistical Information Respecting the History, Condition, and Prospects of the Indian Tribes of the United States* (1851–7), Schoolcraft had already written several ethnological treatments of Indians and their literature, all of which were reprinted numerous times under various titles during the next several decades. *Algic Researches* (1839) collected a group of Ojibwa and Ottawa legends and myths. Reprinted in expanded form in 1856 as *The Myth of Hiawatha*, the volume capitalized on the fact that Longfellow had relied heavily on Schoolcraft's tale of Manibozho, an Ojibwa trickster figure, for his famous poem *The Song of Hiawatha*. (Whittier, Lowell, and other writers would also be inspired by Schoolcraft's materials.) He used the legend of Manibozho and the rest of the volume's tales to corroborate his theory that the apparent ambiguities and monstrosities in the tales are a result of Indian "barbarism." *Onéota* (1844–5), a collection of primary materials and essays by various hands, and *Notes on the Iroquois* (1846), a report to the federal government on the prospects for converting the tribe to market agriculture, reached a similar conclusion. The Indian's supposedly barbaric state, they argue, makes white reform difficult, even for the agent, like Schoolcraft, who attempts to be as faithful as possible to the language and forms of Native American culture.

Schoolcraft, by then superintendent of Indian affairs, was commissioned by the secretary of war in 1847 to collect statistics and cultural material illustrating the present condition and future prospects of all Native American tribes. He gathered information from a variety of sources, including his own previous writings, and within several years began to publish his massive *Historical and Statistical Information*. As in earlier works, he approached his material with a combination of sympathy and perplexity, if not contempt. His point of view is without question that of the superior who acknowledges certain strong and admirable personal traits in Indians but finds them culturally weak, socially uncouth, and morally degenerate. His purpose, he remarks, is to furnish a basis, in both political and philosophical terms, for the government's Indian policy. Indians for Schoolcraft are "fallen," in a state of decline; they worship nature, not God; and they hunt instead of raising grain and developing industrial arts (on these factual points alone, Schoolcraft, like many other Euro-American observers, was often simply wrong). Schoolcraft was committed to the theory that the Indian's degradation was a result of neglecting "higher and sublime principles." At times he seems almost impulsively unable to interpret properly the fascinating abundance of material he collects, and his volumes are often a chaos of evidence. And yet Schoolcraft's governing myth continually serves to organize potentially intractable native material. For example, his account of the importance of the Oneida Stone as a symbol of that tribe's collective nationality intersects with his minerological interest in the formation, which then becomes indicative of the primacy of "scientific" over "primitive" thought. Strategically extending his mischaracterization of the Oneida as a hunting society, Schoolcraft writes that no observer witnessing the vista of farms and villages visible from the top of the stone can "view this rich scene of industrial opulence, without calling to mind that once proud and indomitable race of hunters and warriors, whose name the country bears." That tribe, however, was "destined to fall before the footsteps of civilization," and today its people are dead, scattered, or subjugated to the "social liberality" of "the school, the church, the farm, and the workshop." The scientifically based ideal of market production—central to the collective "tribal" life of Euro-American progress—is thus derived from the totemic stone in such a way that the now-vanquished tribe becomes a symbolic father race to the new Americans.

The volumes of Schoolcraft's *Historical and Statistical Information* vary in their contents and organization, but each typically contains historical accounts of various tribes, etymological and mythological studies of their languages, histories of migrations and warfare, and sections on geography, mineralogy, antiquities, medicine, totems, demonology, and graphic arts, all held together by Schoolcraft's theories of savage decline. They are illustrated by the brilliant plates of Seth Eastman, a military officer who, while stationed at Fort Snelling, Minnesota, studied and sketched Ojibwa and Sioux scenes that he hoped to assemble in an Indian Gallery. When Catlin turned down Schoolcraft's request for illustrations (because the government had refused to purchase his paintings), Eastman prepared hundreds of plates, which appeared in *Historical and Statistical Information* as well as in two 1853 volumes: *The Romance of Indian Life* and *The American Aboriginal Portfolio*, coauthored with his wife, Mary Eastman. The very concept of an "aboriginal portfolio" suggests the contradictory imposition of the artifice of representation upon the artifacts of native culture and Native Americans themselves.

The Eastmans' volumes demonstrated with visual clarity that the two decades following the initiation of Removal in 1830 coincided with the escalating white appropriation of the Indian's world as the territory of romance. Their earlier volume, *Dahcotah; or, Life and Legends of the Sioux* (1849), was a rambling compilation of anecdotes and ethnographic materials, most valuable for its brief sketches centering on the lives of frontier women. But its preface by Caroline Kirkland succinctly incorporates the mythologized imperial portrait of the American Indian generated by a frontier ideology. "The study of Indian character is the study of the unregenerate human heart," and only determined benevolence can rescue the savage from his enslaving traits of envy and revenge. By the same token, the Indians virtually "live" poetry, and we should "write it out for them." Their great poetic value lies in their "aboriginality," in their role as "our" lost past which can serve as the basis for a nationalistic literature: "nothing is wanting but a Homer to build this Iliad material into 'lofty rhyme,' or a Scott to weave it into border romance." The models were thus still foreign for Kirkland and Eastman, as they were for

Cooper, Morgan, and Schoolcraft, but the material was purely "American," not least because it was by then so fully enveloped in the shroud of fantastic legend. The picture frame, like the book of Indian life, became a domain of distorting ethnographic appropriation at just the moment American novelists like Hawthorne, Cooper, and Melville were most concerned to define the fictive territory of American Romance.

Schoolcraft's masterwork, appearing at the midpoint of the period later known as the American Renaissance, participates in the triumph of a mythology of American mission and savage decline that animates some of the most important imaginative works of the antebellum years. That is not to say, however, that *Historical and Statistical Information* is itself pure fabrication. If it fails to meet modern anthropological standards and systematically imposes an alien ideology on the materials it surveys, it nonetheless remains a powerful study, both as an expression of Schoolcraft's own representative mind and as a collection of primary Native American material, including pre-Columbian antiquities, detailed linguistic studies, portraits and illustrations of contemporary artifacts, speeches and biographies of famous chiefs, and delineations of Indian dream theory. All of this is juxtaposed to countervailing documents such as cranial measurement statistics, President Monroe's 1825 speech on Removal, and bloody captivity narratives. There are also apocryphal reports of atrocities in warfare, such as the passage quoted from Jonathan Carver's 1788 volume *Travels through the Interior Parts of North America* (later echoed in a famous scene in Cooper's *The Last of the Mohicans*), which described the 1757 massacre of British troops and civilians at Fort William Henry: "Many of these savages drank the blood of their victims, as it flowed warm from the fatal wound." By containing a mixture of contrary impulses originating in observed American Indian culture and in the often demonizing mythology of Euro-American cultural production, Schoolcraft's *Historical and Statistical Information* is a comprehensive expression of antebellum frontier ideology. The encyclopedic character of the work—its incorporation of myth, technical lore, scientific speculation, and political judgment—along with its habit of symbolic self-constitution parallels other contemporary epic expressions of the American imperial imagination such as Thoreau's journals, Whitman's poetry, and Melville's fiction.

From the standpoint of literature, however, Schoolcraft's work is most valuable for recording numerous Native American tales, songs, orations, and legends in paraphrase or in translation. Imagining the wilderness to be a storehouse of symbolic language corresponding to primitive consciousness, Schoolcraft, like many of his contemporaries, saw the Native American mind as inherently "poetic" and spiritual, yet he paradoxically refused to admit that Indian traditions or oral expressions could constitute a proper literature. In particular, Schoolcraft found pictographic material to be "the literature of the Indian" written in the "language of idolatry," evidence of an elaborate craft but one that showed the Indian to be unchanged since pre-Columbian times. Besides recording events of warfare, religion, love, prophecy, cosmology, hunting, and the like, pictography could also become an ironic emblem of its own limitations. Thus, when Schoolcraft reproduces a complicated Ojibwa pictographic petition to President Taylor in 1849 asking for retrocession of lost land, its ethnological value is dwarfed by its practical futility. Similarly, the legends often point apocalyptically to the ultimate results of white conquest, as in the case of Manibozho, the trickster-warrior said to be living in the ice of the Arctic Ocean: "We fear the white race will some day discover his retreat and drive him off. Then the end of the world is at hand, for as soon as he puts his foot on the earth again, it will take fire, and every living creature will perish in the flames."

Like some other Native American stories of the period, this legend appears to displace onto whites the annihilation suffered by Indians; but in any case it is a more accurate rendition of Native American thought than Longfellow's appropriation of the legend in *Hiawatha*. Schoolcraft wrote that his aim in the massive research he conducted was "to furnish a true basis for the governmental policy to be pursued with [the Indians] as tribes and nations, and for the pursuit of the momentous object of their reclamation and salvation as men." What he did not recognize (or chose not to articulate) was that the twin projects of removal and salvation, although they were often announced in the same language, were built on a contradiction as fundamental as that between progress and genocide.

Under the Stars of Adversity

Schoolcraft's achievement in fieldwork and analysis is a telling combination of fine perception and cultural misunderstanding. As a result, there is the risk that his tales and artifacts will be ignored altogether or will appear as unrevealing as the arrowhead of which Thoreau wrote in his journal, "it is no disgusting mummy, but a clean stone, the best symbol or letter that could have been transmitted to me . . . no single inscription on a particular rock, but a footprint— rather a mindprint—left everywhere, and altogether illegible." Whatever the ethnocentric limitations of Schoolcraft's work or that of other nineteenth-century white writers, however, the period's imperial ethnography remains a valuable resource on Native Americans. Modern readers, for example, have made important use of Schoolcraft's collected legends, the pictographic poetry and political orations, and the vast number of verses and songs, such as these Ojibwa war songs recorded in 1824:

> Todotobi penaise
> Ka dow wiawiaun.
>
> I wish to have the body of the fiercest bird,
> As swift—as cruel—as strong.
>
> Ne wawaibena, neowai
> Kagait ne minwaindum
> Nebunaikumig tshebaibewishenaun.
>
> I cast away my body to the chance of battle.
> Full happy am I to lie on the field—
> On the field over the enemy's line.

More than anything else, perhaps, Schoolcraft's project commandingly represents the Euro-American perspective on the great diversity of Indian cultural expression. Little appreciated even in some current interpretations of Native American life is his early recognition that the dimensions of Native American "literature" would have to include not just songs, chants, and oral legends but also pictography on animal skins or walls, totem poles, ornate pottery or weaving, inscriptions on bark, pipes, or other ceremonial objects, beaded belts or bands, and other forms of expression in signs and artifacts central to Native American traditions.

The records made by Schoolcraft and others in the antebellum period highlight the ironic fact that American Indian texts (i.e., written documents) were seldom produced or transcribed until the 1830s, coincident with the acceleration of Removal. Moreover, the primary collected examples of the Indian's voices—their war rhetoric and their protests against violated promises and treaties—were typically framed by an alien ideology by the time they reached the American public. Virtually all examples of recorded Native American literature prior to the twentieth century were a combination of transcription and translation, with the attendant potential for misrepresentation, intentional or not, that those processes imply. Much of the collected written literature, even that from decades or centuries earlier, was compiled under the auspices of the Bureau of American Ethnography and published in their bulletins beginning in the 1880s, the point of final military defeat for most western tribes. Especially in the case of tales, songs, and poems, Native American literature is traditional and communal. With the exception of specific autobiographical works written in English by Indians, no single author can or in many cases should be identified, and the date of a work's origin is difficult to ascertain. In many instances, too, the work was originally performed in song, dance, chant, or ritual drama, and however precise the descriptions by Schoolcraft, Catlin, or others, these components can seldom be reconstructed with complete authenticity.

From the pre-Civil War period, the preserved written literature of American Indians is generally of three kinds: myths, tales, and songs transcribed by ethnologists; war or treaty orations recorded by witnesses; and autobiographical works, essays, and some prose fiction by Indians or their amanuenses. Although ethnological transcription of Indian literature has taken place primarily since the beginning of the twentieth century, scholars and writers in the early nineteenth century often recognized the vital significance of the oral tradition of Native Americans. Writing in the *North American Review* in 1815, for example, Walter Channing called upon that tradition as one means of establishing a national American literature. Sounding a common theme, Channing remarked that the United States as yet had no national character and doubted, therefore, that it could be said to have a national literature. Even though circumstances in colonial and postrevolutionary America had been "peculiarly opposed to literary originality," however, Channing argued that the oral traditions of America's "aborigines" could be said to constitute the nation's proper native literature. Channing joined other commentators—missionaries, ethnologists, and novelists like Cooper—in pointing to the unique sounds and metaphoric figures of Native American language:

The language of the Indian . . . was made to express his emotions during his observance of nature, and these emotions were taught him at a school, in which the master was nature, and a most unsophisticated heart the scholar. Hence it is as bold as his own unshackled conceptions, and as rapid as his own step. It is now as rich as the soil on which he was nurtured, and ornamented with every blossom that blows in his path. It is now elevated and soaring, for his image is the eagle, and now precipitous and hoarse as the cataract among whose mists he is descanting. In the oral literature of the Indian, even when rendered in a language enfeebled by excessive cultivation, every one has found genuine originality.

Channing's assessment, despite its fanciful and stilted language, points to those features of American Indian literature that modern scholars and poets have continued to recognize as central to its traditional forms. Although it is very difficult to generalize about a literature produced by hundreds of diverse tribes speaking as many languages and dialects, there is a pervasive emphasis in Indian literature on a consonance between expressed form and natural or physiological process. Native American literature is grounded in the rhythms of nature and the body; it often employs repetition and stylized ceremonial forms to create on organic compact with the surrounding visual and aural world. Frequently, commonplace events or daily actions are infused with mystic or spiritual elements, and a dreamlife or sense of other dimensions of the universe pervades the basic forms of linguistic or sign expression. Harmonious wholeness with the universe is the subject of much ceremonial material, whose chants and songs function to restore unnatural divisions between self, spirit, community, and the natural world. For example, a widely translated Navajo night chant designed to heal the rift of spiritual being fuses the separated self with a world at once natural and cosmic. As a small portion of the chant indicates, the calling forth of the divinity of rain links the spiritual journey of regeneration to the earth's cycles of growth and production:

> With the rainbow landing high on the ends of your wings, come to us soaring.
> With the near darkness made of the dark cloud, of the he-rain, of the dark mist,
> and of the she-rain, come to us.
> With the darkness on earth, come to us.
> With these I wish the foam floating on the flowing water over the roots of the
> great corn.
> I have made your sacrifice.
> I have prepared a smoke for you. . . .
> Happily I recover.
> Happily my interior becomes cool.

Happily my limbs regain their power. . . .
Happily abundant passing showers I desire.
Happily an abundance of vegetation I desire.
Happily an abundance of pollen I desire. . . .
Happily may fair white corn, to the ends of the earth, come with you.
Happily may fair yellow corn, to the ends of the earth, come with you.
Happily may fair blue corn, to the ends of the earth, come with you. . . .

Native American oral literature is thus inherently tribal and communal, inspired by and focused on links across generations and geographically diverse communities rather than on aesthetic distinction or individual self-expression. Ceremonial expression—composed of song, chant, story, and dance—serves to integrate private emotion into a cosmic network of experience that unites men and women with the processes of the earth; and this multi-dimensional language itself becomes a conduit of shared tribal knowledge. Mysticism is thus not the province of special study or of a select priestly order but is instead an essential component of the holistic consciousness all share in the experience of ancestral culture.

In most cases the traditional legends and songs cannot be said with certainty to belong to a particular period, and it is therefore difficult or counter-productive to interpret American Indian literature according to the chrono-logical divisions of Euro-American literary history. Many important tales and songs concern the creation of the earth or of a particular tribe, often when a hero leads his or her people forth from a cave, lake, or underground world. As in other literary traditions, flood myths, stories of regeneration after natural catastrophe, and accounts of the creation or spiritual dimensions of the world's phenomena predominate. Native American sacred myths often emphasize a complete integrity of body and spirit and an intersection of human belief and action with the natural world of mineral, plants, animals, weather, and the astronomical heavens. For example, the beginning of a Pawnee creation myth personifies divine beings above as stars but humanizes the creation of the earth as a story of courtship and consummation:

Over all is Tirawa, the One Above, changeless and supreme. From Tirawa come all things: Tirawa made the heavens and the stars.

The Pathway of Departed Spirits [the Milky Way] parts the heavens. In the begin-ning, east of the path was Man: west of the path was Woman. In the east was creation planned: in the west was creation fulfilled. All that the stars did in the heavens foretold what would befall upon the earth, for as yet was the earth not made.

In the west dwelt the White Star Woman, the Evening Star, who must be sought and overcome that creation might be achieved. From the east went forth the Great Star, the Morning Star, to find and overcome the Evening Star, that creation might be achieved. . . .

A Cherokee creation myth combines poetic vision of elemental creative powers lodged in godlike animals with an apprehension of the primordial processes of geological and biological formation:

The earth is a great island floating in a sea of water, and suspended at each of the four cardinal points by a cord hanging down from the sky vault, which is of solid rock. When the world grows old and worn out, the people will die and the cords will break and let the earth sink down into the ocean, and all will be water again. . . . At first the earth was flat and very soft and wet. The animals were anxious to get down, and sent out . . . the Great Buzzard, the father of all the buzzards we see now. He flew all over the earth, low down near the ground, and it was still soft. When he reached Cherokee country, he was very tired, and his wings began to flap and strike the ground, and wherever they struck the earth there was a valley, and where they turned up again there was a mountain. . . . Men came after the animals and plants. At first there were only a brother and a sister until he struck her with a fish and told her to multiply, and so it was. In seven days a child was born to her, and thereafter every seven days another, and they increased very fast until there was danger that the world could not keep them. Then it was made that a woman should have only one child a year, and it has been so ever since. . . .

Native American creation theory is less a part of systematic religious worship in the Euro-American sense than it is the basis for an integrated moral philosophy and epistemology that includes all human interaction with nature. In counterpoint to traditional beliefs whose figures are firmly grounded in the physical world, a substantial portion of Native American thought is highly abstract. The account given by the California Luiseno tribe of the origin of the world begins with a remarkable combination of subtle abstraction and metaphoric juxtaposition of ideas about sexual division and the engendering of the world:

The first [things] were *Kyuvish*, "vacant," and *Atahvish*, "empty," male and female, brother and sister. Successively, these called themselves and became *Omai*, "not alive," and *Yamai*, "not in existence"; *Whaikut Piwkut*, "white pale," the Milky Way, and *Harurai Chatutai*, "boring lowering"; *Tukomit*, "night," with the implication of "sky," and *Tamayowut*, "earth." She lay with her feet to the north; he sat by her right side; and she spoke: "I am stretched, I am extended. I shake, I resound. "I am diminished, I am earthquake. I revolve, I roll. I disappear." Then he answered: "I am night, I am inverted (the arch of the heavens). I cover, I rise, I ascend. I devour, I drain (as death). I seize, I send away (the souls of men). I cut, I sever (life)."

These attributes were not yet; but they would be. The four double existences were not successive generations: they were transitions, manifestations of continuing beings.

Then as the brother took hold of her and questioned, she named each part of her body, until they were united. He assisted the births with the sacred *pavuit* stick, and the following came forth singly or in pairs, ceremonial objects, religious acts, and avenging animals:

Hair (symbolic of the spirit).
Rush basket and throwing stick.
Paint of rust from springs and paint of pond scum.
Water and mud.
Rose and blackberry, which sting for Chungichnish.
Tussock grass and sedge, with which the sacred pits for girls were lined.
Salt grass.
Bleeding and first periods.
These were human; and so were the next born, the mountains and rocks and
    things of wood now on earth. . . .

Despite the unique description of the first things created by the mystic incestuous union—a relatively common element in Native American natural theology—the Luiseno story is conceptually closer to modern scientific theory than are most accounts of the origin of the universe in mythic Western or Indian traditions.

As many creation myths suggest, animal figures, usually treated with the respect due those possessed of divine or magic powers, are central to Native American oral tradition. Numerous tales concern trickster figures who can change into other persons or into inanimate objects, but most often into animal forms. Like folktales from many traditions, the trickster tale usually points out a good or bad moral model for the community, and in some cases challenges or satirizes institutional powers: the tribal leadership, the wisdom of ancestors, the magic of religion or medicine, or dealings with enemy tribes or Euro-Americans. Often the trickster is at the center of erotic or crude stories and jokes, but he may also take part in legends of heroism or romance central to the tribe's self-conception. Manibozho (Schoolcraft's and Longfellow's Hiawatha) is the hero of numerous Ojibwa and Menomini trickster tales. Especially prevalent are tales of Coyote, a cunning and deceitful but also often foolish figure, who is sometimes represented as responsible for the advent of much of the world's evil. Yet he is likewise a figure of comic or ironic power, evanescent and fluid, embodying a primal force that bears responsibility for the conflicts between hardship and triumph that constitute the destiny of tribal peoples. In a Caddo myth set before the origin of death, for example, the tribe decides that because the world is getting too crowded, people should die for a period before returning to earth; Coyote, however, wants people to die forever. The medicine men build a grass house where the dead are to come to be restored to life, but when the first one comes, in the form of a spirit that inhabits a whirlwind circling the grass house, Coyote closes the door and prevents the whirlwind from entering. Grief is thus introduced into the world, the legend says, and ever since, the spirits of the dead have wandered the earth in whirlwinds until they find the road to the Spirit Land.

Both myths and trickster tales have been transcribed in verse form as well, suggesting the vocal lyricism of Native American oral tradition. Although the use of dance, chanting, and drums and other instruments changes the nature of transcribed songs and poems, many works on such topics as love, illness, death, hunting, war, thanksgiving, birth, fertility, and dreams have been set down to resemble traditional English lyrics. A number of tales or verses, such as this Osage song of the maize, incorporate into the divine cycle of planting and cultivation the spirits of the dead, whose voices here bring the corn crop to maturity:

> Amid the earth, renewed in verdure,
> Amid the rising smoke, my grandfather's footprints
> I see, as from place to place I wander,
> The rising smoke I see as I wander. . . .
>
> Amid all forms visible, the little hills in rows
> I see, as I move from place to place.
>
> Amid all forms visible, the spreading blades
> I see, as I move from place to place. . . .

Some transcribed texts depict visionary quests, often undertaken in connection with puberty or death rites, while others, drawing on the widespread belief in the existence of animal souls and even in the spirits of inanimate objects, concern ceremonies or taboos related to food or the handling of certain objects. A portion of an elaborate Mescalero Apache song cycle devoted to the rites of adolescence for young girls links the beginning of womanhood to the creative power latent in the arrival of dawn:

> The sunbeams stream forward, dawn boys, with shimmering shoes of yellow.
> On top of the sunbeams that stream toward us they are dancing.
> At the east the rainbow moves forward, dawn maidens, with shimmering shoes
> and shirts of yellow, dance over us.
> Beautifully over us it is dawning . . .
> Above us among the mountains, with shoes of yellow I go around the fruits and
> the herbs that shimmer.
> Above us among the mountains, the shimmering fruits with shoes and shirts of
> yellow are bent toward him.
> On the beautiful mountains above it is daylight.

That the imagistic symbolism of dreams, or the spirit world, is highly respected is evident in the significance accorded encounters with animal totems or ancestors, prophetic indications of success in coming hunts, travels, and wars, and transhistoric visions of tribal regeneration of the kind recorded in John G. Neihardt's classic text, *Black Elk Speaks* (1932). Dream songs are a particularly important aspect of American Indian tradition in that they typically have a powerful mystic significance for each person, directing the individual to a closer spiritual communion with the natural world. The Iroquois in particular created a sophisticated dream theory, which held that the deepest expression of the soul could be communicated in dreams, in what would later be understood to be the symbolic language of the unconscious. The poetic materials in which Schoolcraft saw superstition and idolatry were in fact a source of complex beauty and long, carefully articulated traditions and philosophies. Ritual song, dense metaphoric patterns, and a spiritual animation of the natural world therefore frequently intersect in the Native American text. In the Navajo song of the Black Bear, for example, the attributes of divine power ascribed to the bear also represent an extension of his intimate relationship to the tribe. The kinetic figures of the song are drawn at once from the human and from the inanimate world; repetition and catalogue (in some respects not

unlike that of Whitman's poetry) create a ceremonial voice and motion for the
surrogate tribal singer who takes on the bear's role in performance:

> My moccasins are black obsidian,
> My leggings are black obsidian,
> My shirt is black obsidian.
> I am girded with a black arrowsnake.
> Black snakes go up from my head.
> With zigzag lightning darting from the ends of my feet I step,
> With zigzag lightning streaming out from my knees I step,
> With zigzag lightning streaming from the tip of my tongue I speak.
> Now a disk of pollen rests on the crown of my head.
> Gray arrowsnakes and rattlesnakes eat it.
> Black obsidian and zigzag lighting stream out from me in four ways.
> Where they strike the earth, bad things, bad talk does not like it.
> It causes the missiles to spread out.
> Long Life, something frightful I am.
> Now I am.
>
> There is danger where I move my feet.
> I am whirlwind.
> There is danger when I move my feet.
> I am a gray bear.
> When I walk, where I step, lightning flies from me.
> Where I walk, one to be feared I am.
> Where I walk, Long Life.
> One to be feared I am.
> There is danger where I walk.

Some of the most important and most frequently recorded American Indian
literature appears in the form of war songs or oratory connected with battle
and with treaties or their violation. That such material is among the most often
transcribed attests both to the prevailing Euro-American portrait of Indians
as noble, doomed warriors and to the underlying need, within the ideology
of imperial advance, to depict Indian tribes as inherently belligerent. Because
the translated records are almost always open to question, Indian oration of
necessity belongs to a world defined in part by dramatic invention. In fact, the
treaties themselves, beginning in the colonial period, were considered by some
historians of culture to be the earliest American drama. Benjamin Franklin,
among others, thought them important enough to print for a general reading
public. Unfolding somewhat in the form of chronicle plays rich in symbolic

and performative oratory, the treaty records often dramatized ritual exchanges of words and gifts between Indians and whites. The roles of agents and interpreters were critical to the ceremony, the place was often chosen for its symbolic significance (marking a frontier, a sacred meeting place, or the confluence of paths or territories), and dances or chants sometimes formed a necessary part of the compact. The history of treaties, however, was one of disappointment and betrayal for American Indians, and the transcribed literary record of orations and songs takes its principal power from the language of tragedy and protest. The Winnebago chief Red Bird sang the following death song in 1827 upon surrendering to the U.S. troops after a bitter series of raids prompted by white violations of Winnebago property:

I am ready.
I do not want to be put in chains.
Let me be free.
I have given away my life—
(*Stooping, he picked up a pinch*
of dust and blew it away.)
—it is gone like that!
I would not take it back.
It is gone.

Another brief lyric that speaks all the more powerfully for its condensed, imagistic form was recorded by the Cheyenne George Bent, a witness to the 1864 massacre of hundreds of Arapaho and Cheyenne, including women and children, at Sand Creek, Colorado:

At the beginning of the attack Black Kettle, with his wife and White Antelope, took their position before Black Kettle's lodge and remained there after all others had left the camp. At last Black Kettle, seeing that it was useless to stay longer, started to run, calling out to White Antelope to follow him, but White Antelope refused and stood there ready to die, with arms folded, singing his death song:

Nothing lives long,
Except the earth and the mountains,

until he was shot down by the soldiers.

A much more extensive record of oratory connected with contention over tribal land, or more specifically with treaties and their violation, survives from the antebellum period, and the conceptions expressed often stand in stark contrast with prevailing Euro-American views of the progress of civilization on the frontier. At the heart of many such speeches by Indians is a radically different understanding of the interaction between the human and natural worlds, one more closely tied to seasons, migratory patterns, and the open spaces of the prairies than to property rights and physical or legal strictures. The Comanche chief Ten Bears asked the white peace commissioners who joined the prestigious group of Indian leaders assembled at the Medicine Lodge council in 1867, "[W]hy do you ask us to leave the rivers, and the sun, and the wind, and live in houses? Do not ask us to give up the buffalo for the sheep." Remarking that he was born on the prairie, "where the wind blew free, and there was nothing to break the light of the sun . . . where there were no enclosures, and where everything drew a free breath," Ten Bears said he wanted to die there, and "not within walls."

In the decades following the Civil War the American government systematically imposed an alien notion of property rights on plains Indians by deliberately slaughtering buffalo in order to destroy the migratory patterns of western tribes and force them onto reservations. This strategic decimation of Indian and animal life was implicit at the outset of Removal, however, as Parkman recognized in the analogy, noted earlier, that he drew in *The California and Oregon Trail* between the killing of buffalo and the demise of American Indians. That is to say, not just war but killing itself became part of a "natural" process. Some four decades earlier the Pawnee chief Petalesharo anticipated such a result in the rapidity of white settlement. Attending a conference with President Monroe in 1822, Petalesharo (Man Chief) spoke with dignity of an Indian view of natural resources that stood in opposition to the market and labor values of the whites:

Let me enjoy my country, and pursue the buffalo and the beaver, and the other wild animals of our country, and I will trade their skins with your people. I have grown up and lived thus long without work—I am in hopes you will suffer me to die without it. We have plenty of buffalo, beaver, deer and other wild animals—we have also an abundance of horses—we have everything we want—we have plenty of land, if you will keep your people off it. . . . Let us exhaust our present resources before you make us toil and interrupt our happiness. . . . Before our intercourse with the whites (who have caused such a destruction in our game), we could lie down and sleep, and when we awoke we would find the buffalo feeding around our camp—but now we are killing them for their skins, and feeding the wolves with their flesh, to make our children cry over their bones. . . . I know that the robes, leggings, mockasins, bear claws, etc. [presented as gifts] are of little value to you, but we wish you to have them deposited and preserved in some conspicuous part of your lodge, so that when we are gone and the sod turned over our bones, if our children should visit this place, as we do now, they may see and recognize with pleasure the deposits of their fathers, and reflect on the times that are past.

The intimate relationship with the animal world observed by most Native Americans thus grew from practical events of daily life that were not to be separated from the ceremonial significance of tribal memory. Little Crow, a Santee Sioux, echoed Parkman's analogy in a figurative address to a Minnesota war council in 1862 that was prophetic:

We are only little herds of buffalo left scattered; the great herds that once covered the prairies are no more. See!—the white men are like locusts when they fly so thick that the whole sky is a snowstorm. You may kill one—two—ten; yes, as many as the leaves in the forest yonder, and their brothers will not miss them. Kill one—two— ten, and ten times as many will come to kill you. Count your fingers all day long and white men with guns in their hands will come faster than you can count.

Although he converted to Catholicism and cooperated with whites fully enough to have the city of Seattle named after him in 1854, Seathl (Dwamish) responded to the honor after the organization of the Washington Territory in a forceful, unsettling oration:

There was a time when our people covered the land as the waves of a wind-ruffled sea cover its shell-paved floor, but that time long since passed away with the greatness of tribes that are now but a mournful memory. I will not dwell on, nor mourn over, our untimely decay, nor reproach my paleface brothers with hastening it as we too may have been somewhat to blame. . . . It matters little where we pass the remnant of our days. They will not be many. The Indian's night promises to be dark. Not a single star of hope hovers above his horizon. Sad-voiced winds moan in the distance. . . . Ane [yet] when the last Red Man shall have perished, and the memory of my tribe shall have become a myth among the White Men, these shores will swarm with the invisible dead of my tribe, and when your children's children think themselves alone in the field, the store, the shop, along the highway, or in the silence of the pathless woods, they will not be alone. In all the earth there is no place dedicated to solitude. At night when the streets of your cities and villages are silent and you think them deserted, they will throng with the returning hosts that once filled them and still love this beautiful land. The White Man will never be alone.

Because Seathl's moving oration, it is now known, was embellished by a journalist far beyond its original scope, it also offers an object lesson in the problem of textual authenticity. In the twentieth century, however, a letter reportedly sent from Seathl to President Franklin Pierce in 1855 was also discovered. It reiterates some of the same themes of the oration and sums up the contrasting conceptions of life that inevitably pitted Euro-American settlers against the native inhabitants, all the more remarkably in that it also obliquely links its ecological attack on white development to a common antebellum critique of Jacksonian mobility and disinterest in ancestral authority:

> The earth is not [the white man's] brother, but his enemy, and when he has conquered it, he moves on. He leaves his father's graves, and his children's birthright is forgotten. . . . There is no quiet place in the white man's cities. No place to hear the leaves of spring or the rustle of insect's wings. . . . The Indian prefers the soft sound of the wind darting over the face of the pond, the smell of the wind itself cleansed by a mid-day rain, or scented with a piñon pine. The air is precious to the red man. For all things share the same breath—the beasts, the trees, the man. . . . What is man without the beasts? If all the beasts were gone, men would die from great loneliness of spirit, for whatever happens to the beast also happens to man. All things are connected. Whatever befalls the earth befalls the sons of the earth.

The most famous and frequently reprinted orations, which revealed much about both the speakers and the Euro-Americans who made use of the orations, belonged to the most notorious warriors, such as Tecumseh and Black Hawk. Their lives and symbolic fame, like that of the earlier imposing figures of King Philip and Pontiac, were the subject of white writers in a variety of genres and became entangled in white frontier mythology and its burgeoning literature of conquest. In all cases—whether in Drake's record of Tecumseh's challenge to Harrison, the treaty orations collected by Schoolcraft and others, or Black Hawk's edited and translated autobiography—the appropriation of the Indian's words by the languages of ethnology and literary production inevitably raises problems of accuracy. Of special importance during the age of Euro-American conquest is the appearance of the first major documents composed in English by Native Americans, in which the problem of translation gives way to a more comprehensive question about the assimilation of one culture to another. Inevitably, written English was for Indians both a means of wider communication and a sign of cultural fragmentation and loss.

The first such written histories appeared in the antebellum period alongside the first significant histories of the Indian nations by whites. William Warren completed his *History of the Ojibways* in 1853 (although it went unpublished until 1885), but it followed by several decades *Sketches of Ancient History of the Six Nations* (1827) by David Cusick (Tuscarora),which begins with historical-mythological tales of creation, migration, and warfare, and follows the history of the Iroquois through the establishment of the League. Among the most important works of literature written in English by American Indians in the antebellum period were autobiographical conversion narratives, which were themselves a form of history writing firmly set in the Protestant tradition of spiritual autobiography. Although some of the narratives, such as *A Memoir of Catherine Brown, A Christian Indian of the Cherokee Nation* (1825), were prob-ably transcribed into English by missionaries, a few important autobiographies composed in English were published during the decades of Removal. They typ-ically display little of the keenness of vision or richness of figurative language evident in the transcribed orations of Seathl or Tecumseh. Indeed, they must be measured against the far stronger assertions of resistance to the Christian mission evident in some orations. A good instance of such Indian counterargu-ment appears in the reply of the Iroquois chief Sagoyewatha (He Who Causes Them To Be Awake), known to whites as Red Jacket, to a representative of the Boston Missionary Society in 1805. Sagoyewatha ironically subverted some of the missionary's central tenets while focusing on a contrast between the written and oral tradition that Cooper and other white writers would appropriate in distinguishing between the language of civilization and the "book of nature":

You say that you are sent to instruct us how to worship the Great Spirit agreeably to his mind; and if we do not take hold of the religion which you white people teach, we shall be unhappy hereafter. You say that you are right and we are lost. . . . We understand that your religion is written in a book. If it was intended for us as well as for you, why has not the Great Spirit given it to us; and not only to us, but why did he not give to our forefathers the knowledge of the book, with the means of under-standing it rightly? . . . How shall we know when to believe, being so often deceived by the white people?

Sagoyewatha's oration destroyed the logic of Euro-American missionary work, which lay at the heart of arguments about manifest destiny and the regenera-tion of America's savages through conquest. It also cast an important light on the historical accuracy and ideological motivations of conversion documents ascribed to or written by American Indians. By internalizing the national myth of Christian mission, the autobiographical conversion narratives expressed clearly the power of political containment, which could operate as effectively in language as in arms.

The first American Indian to write extensively in English was the Pequot William Apess (1798–1839). His autobiography, *A Son of the Forest. The Experience of William Apes, a Native of the Forest* (1829), is a conversion narrative that plays on his transformation from what is represented as native, natural ignorance to the educated light of Christian grace. He notes at the outset that he is descended from King Philip but, shrewdly playing on the rhetorical value of this genealogy, undermines his distinctive character by noting that we are all— white and Indian alike—"descended from *Adam*." Converted to Methodism at age fifteen, Apess was raised among whites (he was one quarter white) after a brutal childhood among separated parents and violent, alcoholic grandparents. Despite lapses of faith and service in the army in the War of 1812, he eventually became a missionary, a living "monument of [God's] unfailing goodness." *A Son of the Forest* is less interesting as autobiography than as a text that mirrors Christianity's uneasy complicity in the process of conquest. Apess's appendix to the volume attacks the notion of savagism and follows a common evangelical argument that Indians are descendants of ancient Israelites; but it also reproduces a doggerel "Indian Hymn" that makes the Indian into a crude minstrel figure:

> God lub poo Indian in da wood
> So me lub God, and dat be good.

Nevertheless, Apess's subsequent writings were increasingly articulate on behalf of Native American rights. *Experience of Five Christian Indians of the Pequot Tribes* (1833) was more critical of white aggression and treaty violations; and *Indian Nullification of the Unconstitutional Laws of Massachusetts Relative to the Marshpee Tribe* (1833) contained a strong attack on the state's illegal acts against tribal property and a brief for tribal self-government. Apess's critique of Euro-American conquest reached a peak in his *Eulogy on King Philip* (1836), a fiery pamphlet that depicts his ancestor Philip to be a hero as glorious as those of the American Revolution—a "noble" figure, made by the "God of Nature," but no savage. The *Eulogy* ridicules Puritan piety and the "hideous blasphemy" of their wars. Increase Mather's famous account of the war, says Apess, relies on prayers that are but "the foundation of all the slavery and degradation in the American Colonies, towards colored people." The pamphlet borrows from the tradition of the jeremiad in advocating Euro-American reform *and* Christian conversion among the Indians, but its most memorable passages belong to the rhetoric of tragic lamentation. Would the Euro-Americans, Apess rhetorically asks, like to see *their* wives and children "slain and laid in heaps, and their bodies devoured by the vultures and wild beasts of prey? and their bones bleaching in the sun and air, till they moulder away, or were covered by the falling leaves of the forest?" Like Euro-American writers such as Parkman and Cooper, whose works were often set in the colonial period but acted out anxieties coincident with the destruction of Indian tribes, Apess cast back to the seventeenth century for genocidal scenes prophetic of tragedies that were occurring as he wrote.

Less starkly eloquent but at once more complex and more popular than Apess's autobiography was George Copway's *The Life, History, and Travels of Ka-ge-ga-gah-bowh* (1847), which immediately went through six editions and was issued in revised forms for a number of years. Copway (1818–69), a Canadian Ojibwa who became a Methodist missionary before moving to the United States in 1846, benefited from the vogue of ethnological work in the 1840s. His *Life* included romanticized yet detailed accounts of Ojibwa tribal life along with the dominant story of his own conversion; its combination of native exoticism and alien subjugation by the ideology of mission was thus perfectly suited to public reading tastes. Copway's second important work, *Traditional History and Characteristic Sketches of the Ojibway Nation* (1850), was more critical of Euro-American practices but focused primarily on geography, tribal history, ethnographic material, and the transmission of Ojibwa oral legends. The same year, he wrote *The Ojibway Conquest*, a narrative poem about the Ojibwa defeat of the Sioux in the Great Lakes region, and dedicated it to Thomas McKenney. Copway lectured extensively in America and Europe, briefly edited a journal entitled *Copway's American Indian*, and wrote futilely in favor of a separate Indian state east of the Missouri River. He enjoyed the admiration of Irving, Cooper, Longfellow, and Parkman, perhaps the surest sign that his message was largely consistent with their own in its adherence to the archetypes of savagism combined with a mild liberal critique of the rapacity of civilized progress. Throughout most of his work American Indian life is viewed nostalgically, doomed in direct ratio to Copway's own proselytizing for Christianity and the ideals of white culture.

Two other Ojibwa missionaries wrote autobiographical accounts of their tribal lives and personal conversions: Peter Jacobs, *Journal of the Reverend Peter Jacobs* (1857); and Peter Jones, *History of the Ojibway Indians* (1861), which departs from type in condemning the white man as an agent of Satan and includes a good deal of ethnographic material in the vein of Schoolcraft. However, neither surpasses Copway in celebrating education, cultivation, and refinement—in particular the *written* English language, which Copway believed would allow him to live beyond his mortal life. Written English is thus allied to Christian salvation, both aspects of the civilizing process that were said to distinguish the "reclaimed" savage from his or her illiterate and heathen people. Renouncing the savage life of hunting and warfare, says Copway, "I now take the goose quil[l] for my *bow*, and its point for my *arrow*." Despite the often absorbing record of Ojibwa culture contained in the *Life*, and despite its impassioned attacks on alcoholism, land greed, and Removal, it is Copway's faith in the "arts of civilized life," which he thought would overcome the Indian's benighted ignorance and lead to "intelligence and virtue," that dominates the volume and established its great popularity with his white audience. Although his autobiography is more interesting and historically valuable than that of Apess, Copway over the course of his career was more thoroughly assimilated by the very society that defined for him the paradoxical taint of "noble savagery" he might conceal but could never completely escape.

Two of the most important Native American writers of the early nineteenth century were Cherokee, Elias Boudinot and John Rollin Ridge, whose importance stemmed in part from the unique features of Cherokee culture. The Cherokees stood alone among Native Americans in what was judged to be the sophistication of their agricultural and educational systems according to Euro-American models by the 1820s. With Sequoyah's invention in 1821 of an eighty-six-character syllabary, referred to as his "talking leaves," the Cherokees developed a European form of literacy and initiated a bilingual newspaper, the *Cherokee Phoenix*, edited by Boudinot from 1827 to 1832. Interested less in Cherokee improvement and self-government than in the cession of their lands, however, the state of Georgia abolished Cherokee national government. As noted above, an 1832 Supreme Court decision upholding Cherokee rights was ignored by the state and ridiculed by President Jackson, with the result that in 1835 the Cherokees were forced to sign the Treaty of Echota, authorizing their removal to western lands. Precisely because of their advances in industry and

learning, it was argued by both whites and some influential Cherokee leaders
that the tribe would be better off with apparent political independence in a new
sovereign territory. John Ridge (the father of John Rollin Ridge) thus argued
for resettlement as a form of cultural preservation, but his view of "civilization" was infused with a classic doubleness. In an 1826 letter to Albert Gallatin,
Ridge outlined the Cherokee Nation's political, economic, and cultural structure, but he concluded with an ambivalent assertion of Cherokee destiny:

Mutability is stamped on everything that walks on the Earth. Even now we are forced
by natural causes to a Channel that will mingle the blood of our race with the white.
In the lapse of half a Century if Cherokee blood is not destroyed it will run its
courses in the veins of fair complexions who will read that their Ancestors under the
Stars of adversity, and curses of their enemies became a civilized Nation.

In 1839 John Ridge, his father (Major Ridge), and Elias Boudinot were executed by other Cherokees in accordance with an 1829 Cherokee law that made
the cession of tribal land a capital offense.

Educated at a Moravian mission school and then in Connecticut, Boudinot
(1804–39) took the name of his benefactor, the revolutionary statesman and
president of the American Bible Society Elias Boudinot. The elder Boudinot
was the author of the widely cited *Stars in the West* (1816), which argued that
Native Americans were descended from ancient Hebrews and would thus,
when converted, augur a new millennium. (The theory, dating from both the
Spanish conquests in Mexico and colonial New England writing, appeared in a
variety of forms in legitimate histories of the Indian tribes, works of religious
inspiration such as *The Book of Mormon*, and in popularizations of the idea such
as Ethan Smith's 1823 volume *Views of the Hebrews*.) The Cherokee Boudinot
gave up complete assimilation after a furor over his interracial marriage, but
he argued ardently as a teacher, a missionary, and a writer and translator for
the acculturation of his tribe. The weekly *Cherokee Phoenix* was a compendium of news, cultural notices, laws, and advertisements for material goods—a
catalogue, Boudinot thought, of the civilizing process at work. He supported
Removal because he had faith in territorial integrity and believed that the fate
of the Cherokee Nation in Georgia would be "servitude and degradation." In
numerous public letters and pamphlets such as "An Address to the Whites"
(1826) and "Letters and Other Papers Relating to Cherokee Affairs" (1837)
and in a fictional tract entitled *Poor Sarah; or, The Indian Woman* (1833), he

outlined his fear that the Cherokee Nation, if it failed to accept the proposed treaty, would become the "relics of a brave and noble race." His execution only highlighted the ironic pressures of his role as both an apologist for Removal and a staunch advocate of Indian rights and national sovereignty.

John Rollin Ridge (1827–67), known also by his chosen name of Yellow Bird, was only twelve years old when he witnessed the killing of his father and grandfather in Oklahoma. After a brief eastern education in Massachusetts and a marriage in Arkansas, he followed the Gold Rush to California, where he became a journalist and poet. His *Poems*, published posthumously in 1868, are largely light verse combined with nationalistic celebrations of American progress and the grandeur of the West. Much of the poetry, in fact, appears to justify Euro-American supremacy in the hemisphere. Yet his journalistic writings on the Indian's condition, later collected in *A Trumpet of One's Own* (1981), have a more independent cast, indicating his advocacy of a separate Cherokee state as part of the Union, criticizing the gold miners' brutality toward "Digger" Indians, and calling for continued belief in Indian spiritual practices instead of the adoption of a sterile and impractical Christianity.

Yellow Bird's most important work, however, was the double-edged novel *The Life and Adventures of Joaquin Murieta* (1854), which posed as the true story of a legendary California bandit and may have been based on the exploits of one or more contemporary figures. Half Mexican and half Indian, Murieta as drawn by Yellow Bird incarnates the urge for vengeance brought about by anti-Mexican prejudice in the gold fields. In addition to being a popular mythic model for future western outlaws in American literature, the figure of Murieta may be understood to be Yellow Bird's own indirect statement about the justification for revenge against whites felt by American Indians, whether in California, Georgia, or Oklahoma. Although his father and grandfather were killed by other Cherokees, it seems likely that Ridge saw their deaths in the same light as the legend's story of the rape of Murieta's mistress, the murder of his brother, and the theft of his land. The fictional bandit, that is, unleashes the vengeance that neither the Mexicans nor the Cherokees could act out on any scale comparable to the violent force exercised in their conquest.

The contradictions of assimilation evident in the educated Boudinot and the acculturated Cherokees is even harsher in the case of Black Hawk (1767–1838), chief of the Sauks, who led a bitter Illinois frontier war in 1832 rather than submit to the resettlement required by a treaty of 1804. Black Hawk's 1833

Autobiography, also published as the *Life of Ma-Ka-Tai-Me-She-Kia-Kiak*, records this more radical struggle. Its voice of resistance would not prevail, but the autobiographical act, fully expressing the paradox of white conquest and Indian assimilation, gave greater permanence to the oratorical powers Black Hawk had used in 1832 to set the stage for warfare with the whites and to prophesy the course of nineteenth-century American empire:

> The Great Spirit created this country for the use and benefit of his red children, and placed them in full possession of it, and we were happy and contented. Why did he send the palefaces across the great ocean to take it from us? . . . Little did our fathers then think they were taking to their bosoms, and warming them to life, a lot of torpid, half-frozen and starving vipers, which in a few winters would fix their deadly fangs upon the very bosoms that had nursed and cared for them when they needed help.
>
> From the day when the palefaces landed upon our shores, they have been robbing us of our inheritance, and slowly, but surely, driving us back, back, back towards the setting sun, burning our villages, destroying our growing crops, ravishing our wives and daughters. . . . They are now running their plows through our graveyards, turning up the bones and ashes of our sacred dead, whose spirits are calling to us from the land of dreams for vengeance on the despoilers.

The same sentiments are recorded in the *Autobiography*, though with somewhat different effect. As in the case of the oration, the composition of Black Hawk's story by a white translator (Antoine LeClaire) and a white editor (J. B. Patterson) reflects the American Indian's submission to an alien language, but the autobiography places the Indian's language in a more elaborate and controlled system of cultural expression. Black Hawk's text borrows elements from the conversion narrative but can more profitably be compared to the *Confessions* of the slave rebel Nat Turner, which were recorded and printed in similar circumstances at about the same time. The voices of both Black Hawk and Nat Turner were thus allowed to speak—even to protest the destruction or enslavement of their people and to justify their countering acts of violence—but at the same time their transcribed words were contained within structures of confession and capitulation, and further screened by the commercial process of publication and sale. Whereas Nat Turner was executed, however, Black Hawk became a popular public figure, a distinction that symbolizes the fact that the African American rebel remained a specter of terror whereas the Indian rebel by then could more easily be absorbed into the narrative of Romantic nationalism.

Captured and jailed in 1833, Black Hawk was taken east to meet the man his story designates our "great Father" and the "great brave"—President Jackson—and to tour several cities. He came away understandably impressed with the technological power and sheer size of white civilization, ready to voice the subjugation recorded at the end of his text: "The tomahawk is buried forever! We will forget what has past—and may the watchword between the Americans and the Sacs and Foxes, ever be—'*Friendship!*'" Whether or not this ending is an honest expression of Black Hawk's sentiments (it accords with his public statements), the autobiography is factually reliable and, if ornate, clear evidence of his general distrust of white society. The account of his early life, including warfare against the Ojibwa and Osage and service with the British in the War of 1812, describes the increasing deceit and incursions by white frontiersmen into tribal territory. The war resulting from the seeming betrayal of Black Hawk's rival Keokuk is reduced to the question of land, stated simply by Black Hawk:

My reason teaches me that land *cannot be sold.* The Great Spirit gave it to his children to live upon, and cultivate, as far as is necessary for their subsistence; and so long as they occupy and cultivate it, they have the right to the soil—but if they voluntarily leave it, then any other people have a right to settle upon it. Nothing can be sold, but such things as can be carried away. . . . I told [Governor Cole and James Hall] that the white people had already entered our village, *burnt our lodges, destroyed our fences, ploughed up our corn, and beat our people*: that they had brought *whiskey* into our country, *made our people drunk*, and taken from them their *horses, guns*, and *traps*; and that I had borne all this injury, without suffering any of my braves to raise a hand against the whites. . . . I had appealed in vain, time after time, to our agent, who regularly represented our situation to the great chief at St. Louis, whose duty it was to call upon our Great Father to have justice done to us; but instead of this, we are told *that the white people want our country, and we must leave it to them.*

Black Hawk's defeat left him spiritually dignified but a broken man, nursing the illusion that the Mississippi River would successfully protect his tribe from further advances of Euro-American settlement. His eastern tour, anticipating later appropriations of native figures for commercial enterprise, made him a momentary celebrity. He was interviewed by McKenney for his *History of the Indian Tribes of North America*, and his activities were portrayed in gossip columns of the day and later in a number of histories of Indian affairs, as well as in individual volumes like Benjamin Drake's sympathetic *The Life and*

Adventures of Black Hawk (1838) and Elbert Smith's epic poem, *Ma-Ka-Tai-Me-She-Kia-Kiak; or, Black Hawk and Scenes in the West* (1848). Smith's further subtitle, *A National Poem*, suggests the dual purpose that Black Hawk, like other heroic Indian figures, served: at once a noble warrior defying the superior might of white technology and still virtually an extension of the richly described western landscape waiting to be subordinated:

> The red man of the wood, like morning dew,
> Has disappeared, except a harmless few.

If Black Hawk thought the land could never be sold, his adversaries thought it could never resist the superior force of cultivation and market improvement. Although he retained less control of his own story than other Native American autobiographers such as Apess and Copway, Black Hawk produced a life story in many ways more alive to the contradictions of military and governmental paternalism and more aware of the costs of compromise with Euro-American values.

La Belle Sauvage

Although the Euro-American fiction devoted to the frontier and the figure of the Indian is superior in both quality and scope, poetry and drama often combined the vanquishing of Indians with a rhetoric of nationalism. Longfellow's *The Song of Hiawatha* (1855) was only the most famous of these productions. In the period between the American Revolution and the War of 1812, a number of poets and dramatists, adopting the same archetypes of sentimental romance and tragic defeat found in the novel, had begun to fix in stylized forms the elegiac images of the Indian that would come to prominence during the era of Removal. Three decades before Longfellow's poem appeared, Lydia Sigourney's epic poem *Traits of the Aborigines of America* (1822) had already provided a sweeping history of American Indians, complete with a plethora of biblical and classical allusions.

Less grandiose and more typical in its range of concerns was William Cullen Bryant's poetry. "The Indian Girl's Lament" is a romantic song for a slain lover, for example, and in "An Indian Story" a brave rescues his captive maiden. Bryant's popular poem "The Prairie" is an excellent example of the Euro-American naturalization of conquest, moving from a tone of melancholy doom to one celebratory of the triumph of civilization. The laws of nature ensure that one society always succeeds another, just as the American Indians once conquered the Mound Builders:

> The red-man came—
> The roaming hunter-tribes, warlike and fierce,
> And the mound-builders vanished from the earth. . . .
> The strongholds of the plain were forced, and heaped
> With corpses. The brown vultures of the wood
> Flocked to those vast uncovered sepulchres . . .
> Thus change the forms of being. Thus arise
> Races of living things, glorious in strength,
> And perish, as the quickening breath of God
> Fills them, or is withdrawn. The red-man, too,
> Has left the blooming wilds he ranged so long. . . .

The process of conquest and expansion is thus demonstrated to be part of an unfolding national drama, directed by God's intercession, in whose most recent scenes the Indian has "left," first the eastern woodlands and now the midwestern prairies.

Reflecting the same fascination with commanding leaders and biography contained in the histories of American Indian tribes and warfare (as well as in nineteenth-century American historiography in general), popular poems on Indians were often devoted to single heroic figures. The brave Indian was often depicted as a magnificent outcropping of the natural landscape that resisted settlement but could not prevent it; in him were summed up the noble traits ascribed to Indians resolutely facing the superior force of white soldiers and pioneers. At times, however, the Indian's lament had a philosophical acuteness that was not entirely the result of the myth of American mission. James W. Eastburn's *Yamoyden, A Tale of the Wars of King Philip* (1820), for example, furnished epigraphs for a number of novels. Its conventional romantic adventure, set against the backdrop of King Philip's War, rendered a melancholy lesson for the powerful:

> Tis good to muse on nations passed away,
> For ever, from the land we call our own;

Nations, as proud and mighty in their day,
Who deemed that everlasting was their throne.

Longfellow's *The Song of Hiawatha* capitalized on the twin vogues for
heroic representation of defeated Indians and for ethnographic detail of the
kind available in Schoolcraft. The poem's unusual meter derived from the
Finnish epic *Kalevala*, and the story borrowed from the Native American legends in Schoolcraft, Catlin, and Heckewelder. Like Daniel Bryan's 1813 epic
about Daniel Boone, *The Mountain Muse*, Longfellow's *Hiawatha* acts out
in cultural form the conquest of native life with the native's own complicity. By combining European and Native American mythologies and yoking
Native American mysticism to the principles of Christianity, Longfellow cre-
ates a god-hero whose exploits belong to legend but whose purpose is to sanc-
tify the rise of a Western, Christian, agricultural empire in the United States.
The sensual, earthy elements of the legendary materials are made genteel for
Longfellow's audience; and Hiawatha appears not as the devious trickster
figure of the Manibozho legend but as a classical hero who bestows order
upon his nation and prepares the way for the Euro-American arrival. After
Hiawatha commands his people to heed the Christians' "words of wisdom"
("For the Master of Life has sent them / From the land of light and morning!"),
the poem's conclusion links the hero's departure and death to an image of the
evening West:

> And the evening sun descending
> Set the clouds on fire with redness,
> Burned the broad sky, like a prairie,
> Left upon the level water
> One long track and trail of splendor,
> Down whose stream, as down a river,
> Westward, westward Hiawatha
> Sailed into the fiery sunset,
> Sailed into the purple vapors,
> Sailed into the dusk of evening.

Hiawatha's message ameliorates white conquest, and in his death and disappearance he, like the Indians of America, is symbolically absorbed by the
West—the Christian eternity, the temporary home of removed Indians, and
the ultimate goal of Euro-American manifest destiny.

The artifice of Hiawatha's character was acceptable to an audience conditioned by fiction and drama—and even by the ethnological writing that burgeoned by the middle of the century—to imagine Indians as romantic, domesticated stage figures. The drama in particular heightened this distorted expectation. From one point of view, as noted above, the historical record of legal interchange and treaties between whites and Indians constituted a version of American drama, a series of chronicle plays structured by symbolic action and oratory. But the Indian plays that gained a popular audience by the 1820s and evolved over the course of the century into the circus-like melodrama epitomized by Buffalo Bill Cody's famous "Wild West Exhibition" were fantasy representations of Indian life and Euro-American benevolence. Stage versions of Cooper's *The Last of the Mohicans* and Bird's *Nick of the Woods* were particularly well received, no doubt because the distinction between stage melodrama and dramatic narrative was already a rather fine one in the books themselves. Perhaps the earliest dramatization of Indian relations, Robert Rogers's *Ponteach* (1766) was unique in its critical treatment of the white colonists' betrayal and cheating of Pontiac. Following the lead of Indian biographies, later battle plays such as Richard Emmons's *Tecumseh; or, The Battle of the Thames* (1836) and Alexander Macomb's *Pontiac; or The Siege of Detroit* (1838) glorified white victory over strong, noble enemies. In those stage works, as in the proliferation of warrior songs and legends, Indian nobility in action and in speech was deliberately detached from the real world of armed conflict and dispossession and frozen in the timeless world of performance. Long after the events that prompted it, the famous speech of Logan justifying his revenge for the destruction of his family, included in Jefferson's *Notes on the State of Virginia*, became a rhetorical set piece in nineteenth-century primers and was made the concluding oration of Joseph Doddridge's *Logan: The Last of the Race of Shikellemus, Chief of the Cayuga Nation* (1823). Even more markedly than the reprinting of Indian oratory in histories, ethnological collections, or autobiographical narratives like that of Black Hawk, the drama at once highlighted the stoic dignity of American Indians and imprisoned their voices in a form of ceremonial utterance almost entirely at odds with their own native cultures.

The most popular and now notorious among dramatizations of Native-American life were those devoted to the story of Pocahontas. As its title suggests, James Nelson Barker's operatic *The Indian Princess; or La Belle Sauvage* (1808) anticipated much literary treatment of American natives in portraying the famous daughter of Powhatan as an exotic but ideologically astute heroine and in providing its hero, Captain John Smith, an opportunity to praise the new American nation:

> Oh, enviable country! thus disjoined
> From old licentious Europe! may'st thou rise,
> Free from those bonds which fraud and superstition
> In barbarous ages have enchain'd *her* with;—
> Bidding the antique world with wonder view
> A great, yet virtuous empire in the west!

Other plays casting Pocahontas as the archetypal melodramatic heroine include Robert Dale Owen's *Pocahontas* (1838), Charlotte Barnes Conner's *Forest Princess* (1848), and George Washington Custis's *Pocahontas; or, the Settlers of Virginia* (1827), the last distinguished for its placing of Pocahontas's rescue of Smith at the end of the action, thus heightening the redemptive import of her marriage to John Rolfe and Powhatan's final benediction: "Let their union be a pledge of the future union between England and Virginia . . . looking thro' a long vista of futurity, to the time when these wild regions shall become the ancient and honour'd part of a great and glorious American Empire."

Despite the unavoidable fact of Pocahontas's marriage to Rolfe, the Indian plays were pervaded by problems of courtship and marriage but seldom suggested the possibility of mixed marriage or miscegenation. Rather, they displaced problems of government and military paternalism, often enforced by policies of starvation and violence, to the stage drama of domesticity. When physical union between races was represented by Custis and others, anticipating the apparently more acceptable union of white soldiers and Mexican women portrayed in numerous novels after the Mexican War, it took on a ritual, symbolic character. The representation of Pocahontas's life and marriage thus became a sacrament of absorption authorizing the empire being brought to fruition at the time Custis and his contemporaries were writing. It violated the prohibition of racial mixing established in *The Last of the Mohicans*; but it did so in a far more distant past and in the name of generating out of an erotic union between Indian nature and English property an imperial vision of America that would restrict the dangerous potential for contamination in frontier life.

The most popular of all Indian plays, John Augustus Stone's *Metamora; or The Last of the Wampanoags* (1829), was written for the famous actor Edwin Forrest, who portrayed Metamora (King Philip) as an honorable and unrepentant hero who dies with a curse of the white race on his lips. Because the Indian drama relied so heavily on simplistic characterizations of warfare, treaty, and Indian life, it was best known even in the decades of its greatest popularity more for its rhetorical fireworks than for its power to reveal the significance of the Indian's demise. Stone's play was parodied in John Brougham's *Metamora; or, The Last of the Polywogs* (1847), whose later companion piece *Po-Ca-Hon-Tas; or, The Gentle Savage* (1855) anachronistically mixed in lampoons of various ethnic groups and contemporary political events in order to ridicule the artificiality of the literary use of Native American language, the stage gimmicks of the Pocahontas plays, and the public rage for Longfellow's *Hiawatha*. Such satire brought to the surface tendencies that were implicit in most of the drama devoted to the Indian question: a willingness to distort historical circumstance in the interest of national mythology and a psychological need to envision the destruction of native culture in melodramatic forms that would make conquest appear glorious and cathartically burn off in faked tragedy any doubts the audience might entertain about the wisdom and justice of western expansion.

The drama often played on two themes that were intimately related: the idea of the noble Indian hero and the ordeal of white captivity. Likewise, these themes are often dominant in the fiction devoted to American Indians, which in large part reflected the prevalent characteristics of the era's domestic fiction. The cultural power of the novel as a form therefore lay to a great extent in its use of the sentiment generated by familial violence and captivity, an emotive argument to which standard histories and biographies also resorted. However sympathetic the fictional portrait of Indian life or of such Indian heroes as Pontiac, King Philip, and Black Hawk, the novel's stock use of melodramatic plots, its tendency to celebrate the epic conquest of a "virgin land," its fascination with the exotic, and its easy sentimentalizing of dead or dying Indians made it inherently incapable of treating Native American culture with accuracy or objectivity.

One direct source of these distortions was the long-standing popularity of captivity narratives, whether actual or fictional, which had in essence been the colonies' first imaginative literature and which remained through the nineteenth century a widely read and influential genre. The colonial captivity narrative, such as Mary Rowlandson's, made its heroines or heroes representative of a larger community whose resolve was being tested by the satanic forces in the wilderness. Outside God's community all was primitive, demonic. White aggression was converted into victimization, and the rescue or return of the captive often appeared as a sign of grace. The captive's gravest risk was not death but rather the temptation to identify with the alien way of life and become a savage. As a literature organized along psychogeographical boundaries that justified Euro-American advance while also revealing deep anxieties about it, the captivity narratives were often sensational, even incredible, at the same time that they posed as factual accounts of life beyond the frontier. By the end of the eighteenth century, the captivity narrative had begun to merge with sentimental fiction, so that a popular work like Ann E. Bleecker's *History of Maria Kettle* (1793) resembled less a historically valid captivity narrative than it did a gothic melodrama.

The rise of the novel and the accelerating process of western expansion and Indian Removal were coincident in America, and episodes of captivity played an important part in novels treating frontier life as a symbolic moment in the drama of American historical development. Because they were based on dubious evidence or conformed to the dictates of popular fiction and national ideology, many of the dozens of captivity narratives printed and reprinted throughout the antebellum period are spurious or, at the least, factually unreliable. Set in a liminal realm of the national imagination, at a moment of critical political redefinition, the post-Revolution captivity narrative mixed explorations of anxiety about the revolt against paternal order and authority with evocations of the loss of moral structure and social coherence possible on the frontier. The relatively widespread use of captivity narratives in the work of historians and ethnologists of the day tended not to contradict the elements of the gothic present in the fiction but instead to corroborate them within an apparently scientific context. The historian John Frost, author of a number of works on warfare with American Indians and frontier life, recorded a series of sketches of pioneer women under attack or in captivity in *Heroic Women of the West* (1854). Schoolcraft employed the narratives in his massive *Historical and Statistical Information*, and Drake included them in his *Biography and History of the Indians of North America* (1832) and also issued scholarly collections of them. In such volumes as *Indian Captivities* (1839) and *Tragedies in the Wilderness*

(1841), he claimed historical accuracy but implicitly developed a theory of savagism consistent with his focus on "barbarous rites and ceremonies."

Especially as it was transfused into fiction, captivity thus justified white violence as a means of rescuing the besieged frontier community and, by linking violence to the notion of a vulnerable family, reworked the popular stereotypes of seduction fiction. Actual tragedies in the wilderness merged with hypothetical or fantastic violence and suffering. For example, the *Narrative of the Captivity and Sufferings of Mrs. Mary Smith* (1818) not only plagiarized previous narratives but served an explicit ideological purpose by reveling in the supposed cannibalistic torture and sexual abuse of young virgins during the Creek Wars of 1813–14, with the heroine eventually rescued by a brave soldier of Andrew Jackson's troop. Similarly, the *Narrative of the Capture and Providential Escape of Misses Frances and Almira Hall* (1832), although based on actual captivities, was transmuted into straightforward propaganda against Black Hawk by its focus on the Indian's butchering of white settlers. In the *Narrative of the Massacre, by the Savages, of the Wife and Children of Thomas Baldwin* (1836), two children are burned at the stake, thus setting the stage for the hero's transformation into an archetypal hermit and Indian hater. One of the most striking narratives, corresponding to a later phase of warfare against western tribes, is Royal B. Stratton's *The Captivity of the Oatman Girls* (1857), which recounted the stories of several family members held by Apaches and Mohaves in New Mexico in order to predict the coming achievement of manifest destiny:

But this unpierced heathenism that thus stretches its wing of night upon these swarming mountains and vales, is not long to have dominion so wild, nor possess victims so numerous. Its territory is already begirt with the light of a higher life; and now the footfall of the pioneering, brave Anglo-Saxon is heard upon the heel of the savage, and breaks the silence upon his winding trail.

Although the majority of captivity narratives and captivity fictions relied on a theory of savagism to authorize the destruction of American Indians, a few narratives, such as John Dunn Hunter's *Manners and Customs of Several Indian Tribes Located West of the Mississippi* (1823) and *Memoirs of a Captivity Among the Indians of North America* (1824), which recorded his captivity since childhood among the Kansas and Osage, were decidedly more sympathetic and accurate in their accounts of Native American culture. One of the most remarkable of such narratives concerned the life of John Tanner (1780?–1847), who was captured at age nine and lived for about thirty years among the Ojibwa. After marrying within the tribe and raising a family, he found it impossible to return to white society. Set down by Edwin James in *A Narrative of the Captivity and Adventures of John Tanner* (1830), his story offers a detailed account of Native American life, including hunts, marriage, warfare, and ritual ceremony. The narrative is thus an important ethnological source, and it records a variety of songs and reproduces a number of pictographs with transliteration, translation, and commentary. Even as he lamented the Euro-American destruction of Native American culture, however, Tanner (at least by James's account) accepted that destruction as the certain result of Euro-American military and material strength. Moreover, that technological superiority was not unrelated to what Tanner designated as the limits of native cultural development. The oratory and music of American Indians are vehement and repetitive rather than refined, Tanner argues, and their lack of a useful documentary language symbolically marks their relation to the conquerors: "without literature to give perpetuity to the creation of genius, or to bear to succeeding times the record of remarkable events, the [Native] Americans have no store house of ancient learning to open to the curiosity of the European race." Not only the wealth of oral and material culture that had survived through centuries of transmission but the evidence of Tanner's own text partially contradicted this assertion of inferiority. Yet his recognition of the power of European culture, combined with his personal preference for life among the Ojibwa, left him stranded between two worlds, his text a sign of the frontier that divided them.

Perhaps only the life of Mary Jemison bears comparison to that of John Tanner for the cultural paradoxes it contains. In her case, the issue of gender further increased the difficulty she faced in a life split between two worlds. In captivity narratives based on actual events, as in the novels built around episodes of bondage, women are often central figures. This fact is most clearly reflected in the great popularity of such novels as Cooper's *The Last of the Mohicans* and in Bancroft's dramatic rendering of Jane McCrea's captivity in his *History* (1834), which capitalized on one of the best-known American paintings of the era, John Vanderlyn's *Death of Jane McCrea* (1804), a work depicting the imminent slaughter of McCrea by two Indians, with implicit suggestions that the violence is a form of sexual violation. Although women thus occupied a symbolic role of vulnerability in the bulk of the narratives and fiction, a stunning exception is James E. Seaver's *A Narrative of the Life of Mary Jemison* (1824), which was an immediate best-seller and went through a number of editions during the nineteenth century. Mary Jemison's captivity, after the killing of her family in the French and Indian Wars, led her to live the rest of her life among Indians. She married first a Delaware, then a Seneca, and finally lived alone with half-blood children who could not easily return to white society. Her story thus went beyond melodrama. Its realistic account of life "as an Indian" gave witness to the decline and subjugation of two tribes during her lifetime, and her own "savage" acculturation can be seen as a kind of atonement for the policy of Removal. Most important, however, the narrative tells in detail the story of a woman's daily life on the frontier, her management of house and land, and makes her in effect the female equivalent of Daniel Boone, not only surviving but prospering in the wilderness.

Measured against other captivity narratives, Mary Jemison's story was quite atypical in the strength and independence accorded her. However, if the heroine of the frontier was often drawn with expressive characteristics corresponding to the sentimental pattern of domestic romance, she could nevertheless be shown to have achieved a kind of freedom and individual identity more available on the frontier than in eastern society. Several women writers found particular success in the genre of frontier fiction by rendering the transition from scenes of violence and captivity to a life of agrarian settlement and domestic labor. Catharine Sedgwick's *Live and Let Live* (1837), Marian Susanna Cummins's *Mabel Vaughan* (1857), Caroline Soule's *Little Alice; or, The Pet of the Settlement* (1863), and Metta Victor's dime novels *Alice Wilde, the Raftsman's Daughter* (1860) and *The Backwoods Bride* (1860) use novelistic accounts of family life to portray an agricultural West in which the domesticated community tended to break down, if not erase, class distinctions and promote an idealized vision of labor on the land, one that was at times more in accord with Native American social practice, including its reliance on matrilineal rule. At the same time, some important fiction by women anticipated later populist writing in challenging the idyll of the agricultural West. Elizabeth Fries Ellet's historical work *Pioneer Women of the West* (1852) and Eliza Hopkins's novel *Ella Lincoln; or, Western Prairie Life* (1857) presented reliable versions of the woman pioneer's experience, the latter undermining the sentimentality of marriage by portraying clearly the "homely faces and undraped outlines" of women on the prairie. Similarly, Alice Cary, the author of *Clovernook* (1852–3), two volumes depicting the transformation of frontier Ohio from a pastoral to an industrial economy, and the less valuable *Married, Not Mated* (1856), concentrated on the somber and melancholy side of family life: "Poverty is the pioneer about whose glowing forges and crashing forests burns and rings half the poetry that has filled the world."

As noted in the previous chapter, pioneer journals, most of them published years later, and emigrant guides provide some of the most exceptional writing by frontier women. A British emigrant, Rebecca Burlend, recorded her family's journey to an Illinois farm in *A True Picture of Emigration* (1848), but the most important observer of midwestern frontier life was Michigan author Caroline Kirkland (mother of the realist writer Joseph Kirkland), whose several volumes on emigrant life are a full account of its hardships and rewards. Kirkland (1801–64) was inspired by Tocqueville, and her work often matches his precision and insight, whether discussing the philosophical question of liberty on the frontier or weather and natural resources. *A New Home—Who'll Follow?* (1839) and *Forest Life* (1842) were specifically composed as guides to the new territory, but Kirkland's strength lay particularly in her presentation, through fine details of domesticity, of the harsh but sometimes liberating life discovered by frontier women. In *Western Clearings* (1845) she looked back on the land fever of the mid-1830s and the resultant growth of social classes and diversity in labor, thus adding a political-economic dimension to her personal portrait of the garden world of the West.

Because the roles of women were in part determined by assumptions common to the domestic novel and the captivity narrative, the frontier romance often added to the captivity narrative's basic plot of capture and rescue elements of repetition, temptation, seduction, white villainy, and national purpose. Captivity became a stock device in the novels of Cooper, Simms, Timothy Flint, Catharine Sedgwick, and others, for whom the providential rite of passage was the essence of expansionist spirit. A number of the most successful captivity novels set their action in the seventeenth century, thus establishing historical depth for America's national ideology. Like Parkman's *Conspiracy of Pontiac* and the better-known novels of Cooper and Simms, they too displaced the violence of contemporary warfare and Indian Removal into a previous era and so legitimized the inevitability of the vanquishing of the Indians. Lydia Maria Child's *Hobomok* (1824) concerns a noble tribal chief who marries an apparently widowed Puritan woman but gives her up along with their

half-blood son when the former husband unexpectedly returns. White sava-
gism is thus averted, and the half-blood child, who goes off to England for
his education, is a symbol of what the Native American should become: an
Anglicized, obedient child. Catharine Sedgwick's *Hope Leslie* (1827), Eliza
Cushing's *Saratoga* (1824), Joseph Hart's *Miriam Coffin* (1834), John T. Irving's
The Hawk Chief (1837), Anna Snelling's *Kabaosa* (1842), and Eastburn's poem
Yamoyden all similarly employed captivity as a means to represent the final
absorption of American Indian life by the Euro-American world and to release
anxiety generated by the energy of national conquest. Featuring elements central to most literatures of empire, they utilized stock dramatic devices as a
means of testing the nation's capacity to decimate native cultures in the name
of expanding the Jacksonian area of freedom.

Anchoring this strategy in the age of the American Revolution, Josiah
Priest's *Stories of the Revolution* (1836) and *A History of the Early Adventures
of Washington Among the Indians of the West* (1841) borrowed from structural
devices of the Indian drama in mixing captivity narratives with glorification
of America's founding heroes. If he was not a brutal devourer of women and
children, the Indian hero could in this way sometimes be elevated and partially
cleansed by his alliance with white national figures or, as in *Hobomok*, by his
contact with white family life. Yet even in those cases where life among Indians
is depicted as in some ways preferable to white colonial life (e.g., *Hope Leslie,
Yamoyden,* or John H. Robinson's *Kosato; The Blackfoot Renegade* [1850]),
the ultimate purpose of the test is to explain the demise of the Indian tribes.
Edward S. Ellis's *Seth Jones; or, The Captive of the Frontier* (1860), one of the
first dime novels, reduces the action of countless examples of the genre to a
simple formula: "When the Anglo-Saxon's body is pitted against that of the
North American Indian, it sometimes yields; but when his mind takes the place
of contestant, it *never* loses."

The Euro-American body might fail or become contaminated by savagery,
but the mind would prevail—this message permeates American frontier literature. Underlying the portrayal of women and families at risk from savagery is
a pervasive fear of miscegenation, which is latent in the Pocahontas stories and
elsewhere but has its full articulation in *The Last of the Mohicans*. These texts are
typically less vile than the antimiscegenation literature directed against blacks
and abolitionists in the period, but they are nonetheless revealing of the relationship between popular melodrama and racial fears. In John Neal's witchcraft

novel, *Rachel Dyer* (1828), the half blood is a gothic hero representing a psychic and social struggle between Puritan "light" and demonic "darkness." The mixed-blood hero of Ann Stephens's *Malaeska; the Indian Wife of the White Hunter* (1839), an Indian hater unaware of his own heritage, is prevented from contaminating a white woman in marriage by the last-minute discovery that his mother is an Indian; the mother and son, victims of unnatural amalgamation, then commit suicide. By contrast, the Indian hero of John S. Robb's *Kaam; or Daylight, The Arapahoe Half Breed* (1847) becomes a white hater and assumes the name of "Night." Poe's Dirk Peters, in *The Narrative of Arthur Gordon Pym* (1838), is a deformed Hobbesian creature who probably inspired the similar depiction of a "monkey-like" monster in John Esten Cooke's *Lord Fairfax* (1868), which employs specific parallels to *The Tempest* in order to suggest that the half blood's brutality can be tamed by the beauty of a white woman.

Like the theme of captivity, the theme of mixed blood became a mechanical device, a means of generating the horror of transgressed or collapsed boundaries in the body comparable to boundaries violated and crossed by actual Indian warfare and Removal. The numerous popular novels turned out by hack writers like Osgood Bradbury and Emerson Bennett, and later by the dime novelists, used the two themes in tandem. In Bradbury's *Larooka: The Belle of the Penobscots* (1846), the mixed-blood heroine's exotic sensuality almost leads to incest with her brother; in *Lucelle; or, The Young Iroquois* (1845), the heroine's virtue supports Bradbury's manifesto in favor of intermarriage as a way to "purify" the Native American "stock"; whereas in *Pontiac; or, The Last Battle of the Ottawa Chief* (1848), the French and Indians must twice rescue Pontiac's half-blood daughter from the British so that she can finally marry a French soldier and become—as the "Italian beauty"—the toast of Paris society. Bennett, far from praising miscegenation, saw it as savage evidence of degradation. The captured heroine of *The Forest Rose; A Tale of the Frontier* (1850) is barely prevented from becoming a fierce woman warrior, the final loss of her social role: "By a righteous law of nature, man loves what he can foster and protect; woman, what can cherish and protect her." In *The Prairie Flower; or, Adventures in the Far West* (1849) Bennett's characters are saved from both natives and dangerous mountain men along the Oregon Trail by Kit Carson, and in *Kate Clarendon; or, Necromancy in the Wilderness* (1848), the angelic heroine must be rescued from a rejected suitor, who has joined the other serpents and "swarthy savages" crawling about in the Ohio woods.

As it converged with the standard gothic romance, then, the captivity story, on stage and in fiction, superimposed an ideology of racial superiority upon the stereotypes of popular culture, the two working together to ward off the threat of contamination. Woman's symbolic role as besieged maiden in the gothic novel assumed nationalistic purpose in the captivity novel, where she appeared as the sacred embodiment of racial purity and the vessel of future generations destined to sweep across the opened western territories. Over that destiny, however, loomed the shadow of other races. The apocalyptic threat of miscegenation, anticipating the hysteria of later periods of American and European racial conflict, was voiced in James Kirke Paulding's *Konnigsmarke* (1823) by a black slave figured by Paulding as a witch: "the time shall surely come, when the pile of oppression ye [whites] have reared to the clouds shall fall, and crush your heads. Black men and red men, all colours, shall combine against your pale, white race; and the children of the masters shall become the bondsmen of the posterity of the slave." Paulding's passage was prophetic of later protest against racist ideology by non-Western peoples; but even in the decade before the official policy of Indian Removal was adopted, it revealed volatile fears hidden within the literature devoted to the passing of the noble American savage and the heroic redemption of innocent white captives.

Leatherstocking Nemesis

The portrayal of American Indians in both history and literature, as well as the special power of the captivity narrative and its fictional derivatives in post-revolutionary "family romance," can be fully understood only as developments parallel to the rise of the American frontier hero, the subject of much of the most significant and influential American writing of the period. Indeed, the Euro-American hero and the Native American hero in white literature were in many respects mirror images of one another. The hero of the captivity narrative, as the genre assumed a more novelistic form in the early nineteenth century, was as likely to be a rough frontiersman as a soldier or community leader. Often he was a husband, father, or son driven to vengeful madness by the slaughter or abduction of his family, a paradigm repeated on through twentieth-century popular culture. Whatever shape he took, however, his portrayal was likely to be influenced by the central myth of Daniel Boone

(1734–1820), the famous eighteenth-century land agent, pioneer, and patriarch of Kentucky. First immortalized in an appendix to John Filson's *The Discovery, Settlement, and Present State of Kentucky* (1784), Boone became the inspiration for numerous frontier heroes and the subject of many versions of his own exploits. Filson's Boone is celebrated as the founder of a new republic, a man destined by Providence and by the laws of nature to journey through a dark wilderness and lead his people into a promised land of rich, pristine territory. A true Enlightenment hero, Boone is tempted by the forces of primitivism but remains a harbinger of progress, in particular the agricultural regeneration of the wilderness. Daniel Bryan's epic poem *The Mountain Muse* (1813) portrays Boone as the incarnation of a national aristocratic force that will subjugate the chaos figured both in the sublime but wild landscape and in the undisciplined ferocity of the American Indian.

Boone appeared as a character in a number of histories, plays, poems, and novels, but none as popular or influential as Timothy Flint's *Biographical Memoir of Daniel Boone* (1833), also published as *Life and Adventures of Colonel Daniel Boone*. Flint relied on newspapers, interviews, and folktales in constructing a hero great enough to embody the mythology of a whole nation. This Boone is, among other things, a representative "westerner"—the new type of rough, independent, stoic American man that only frontier life can produce. His necessary identification with the Indian, as part of his immersion in the wilderness, is more emphatic in Flint's version, and his role as a hunter is made prominent (as a young boy, Flint writes, Boone "waged a war of extermination" against animals, in anticipation of his role as an Indian fighter). Flint notes that Boone was surely one model for Cooper's Leatherstocking. But it is clear that the influence went both ways, for Flint's Boone, like Natty Bumppo, is a crack hunter, a tracker with perfect "instinct," and a natural but unlettered Christian: the "woods were his books and his temple." The stories of Boone's own captivity and that of his daughter, like the notorious courtship scene in which the deer Boone is tracking leads him to his future wife, Rebecca, tend toward the fantastic in Flint's account. Like the novelistic version of captivity narratives, the domestic drama highlights the ideological function of the primary myth of Boone's leadership, which is evidence that a new "garden of earth" "had been won from the domination of the savage tribes, and opened as an asylum for the oppressed, the enterprising, and the free of every land." Boone, of course, is driven farther west by the arrival of the very civilization he has made possible. His stoic isolation, like that of Leatherstocking, serves in part to keep him from the corruptions of society, but it may also be seen as an expression of his sacrificial character. As his exploits became more and more mythic, Boone's singularity could also be made to bear the burden of anxiety over violations of the wilderness and decimation of its native inhabitants.

Something of this contradictory vision about its heroes is surely present as well in the public's enthusiastic response to the legends of the idiosyncratic frontier figure recorded in *Narrative of the Life of David Crockett* (1834). A Tennessee state legislator and U.S. congressman, Crockett (1786–1836) was best known as the tall-tale hero of the folklore created to advance his minor political career. Exaggerated stories of his bear hunting and Indian killing, nar-rated and parodied in backwoods slang, made stories about him, including his own dubious *Life*, very popular. He broke with fellow Tennessean Andrew Jackson over land rights and the president's policy of Indian Removal; his career ended, he went to Texas and became immortalized as a slain hero in the battle of the Alamo. As the model for the Indian-killer Earth in *Elkswatawa*, burlesqued by Paulding as the character Nimrod Wildfire in his play *The Lion of the West* (1830), and the subject of numerous frontier rags-to-riches stories and editorials, Crockett nearly became a living caricature of the frontiersman myth, a comic Boone whose braggadocio heightened the illusion of mascu-line virility even as it exposed its tall-tale character. Along with Sam Houston, whose autobiography told the story of his life among the Cherokees and as the father of Texas, Crockett (at least in his own myth) inhabited two overlapping worlds: a powerful world of social and political order, sustained in its drive west by another world of isolated, rugged, outlaw heroes prone to daredevil risk and comic outburst.

As the examples of Boone and especially Crockett made clear, the pro-liferation of violence and the propensity for tall tales on the frontier often transcended attitudes toward Indian savagery. For example, Indiana minis-ter Bayard Rush Hall's *The New Purchase; or, Seven and a Half Years in the Far West* (1843), written under the pen name of Robert Carlton, is one of the most bizarre works about frontier life. The novel combines strong pleas on behalf of violated Indian rights with wild burlesques of hunting, boating, preaching, and "savage" life. Hall's style is an anarchic mix of pathos, bom-bast, and farce, less successfully realized in a sequel entitled *Something for Everybody* (1846). Also curious in the frontier genre, and notable for both its careful observation and its sense of justice across racial and cultural lines, is the work of the German emigrant Karl Postle (1793–1864). Postle traveled widely in the western United States and Mexico and, writing under the pseudonym of Charles Sealsfield, became an important advocate for Native Americans. His novel *Tokeah; or, The White Rose* (1829) was the first in a series of internationally popular books on frontier life and American pioneers, among them *The Cabin Book; or, Sketches of Life in Texas* (1844), *Life in the New World* (1844), and *Frontier Life* (1856).

More typical of the western fiction that began to appear in cheap periodicals in the 1850s and flowered in the dime novel of the post-Civil War years were melodramas such as E. C. Judson's ("Ned Buntline") *Norwood; or, Life on the Prairie* (1850) and David Belisle's *The American Family Robinson . . . Lost in the Great Desert of the West* (1854), a captivity and survival tale that concludes with settlement in California, where "in giant strides science and art triumph over the rough barriers, and open avenues for the advancement of moral reform." In the dime novel and its predecessors, the author often examined characters who, whether out of a sense of justice, a desire for outlaw life, or sheer perversion, not only fled to the frontier but became "white Indians" and often turned their violence back against other white frontiersmen. Charles Webber's *Old Hicks the Guide* (1848), John Richardson's *Wacousta; or, The Prophecy* (1851), Emerson Bennett's *The Renegade* (1848), and H. R. Howard's *The Life and Adventures of John A. Murrell, the Great Western Land Pirate* (1847) contain notable antebellum examples of such renegades. Implicit in the dime novels, as in the Indian drama, was a fantasy enactment of the process of Removal. Judson, for example, would go on to write a series of Buffalo Bill dime novels, later staged as part of Cody's traveling show. Common to virtually all fiction set on the frontier was a sense of the inevitable vanquishing of the Indians and the gradual establishment of social and economic order in an outlaw environment. The lesson of the novel was that both the untamed Indian and the white renegade would be replaced by pastoral and, later, industrial life.

This, too, was the lesson of the fictional character who was to become the most famous of frontier heroes trapped between two worlds. Even the mythological versions of Boone's life were no match for the frontiersman Leatherstocking, created by James Fenimore Cooper (1789–1851) in five novels that depict the hero's life from early years to his death on the far western plains: *The Deerslayer* (1841), *The Last of the Mohicans* (1826), *The Pathfinder*

(1840), *The Pioneers* (1823), and *The Prairie* (1827). Because the novel dealing with Leatherstocking's youth in the 1740s, *The Deerslayer*, was written
last, it represents in part Cooper's self-conscious return to an earlier, socially
less complex phase of American history. Revolving around several episodes of
captivity (as do all the novels except *The Pioneers*), *The Deerslayer* depicts the
formation of Leatherstocking's frontier character against the background of
a now faded, mythic Indian world that has been conquered and reordered by
"paleface" names and customs. Born Natty Bumppo, the hero regresses from
white life, acquiring the names Deerslayer and Hawkeye for his prowess in
killing first an animal, then a man. Like Boone, he is an isolated, stoic figure,
in this novel rejecting the love of Judith Hutter for the comradeship of his
lifelong Delaware companion Chingachgook. But from Judith he receives his
mythic gun, "Killdeer," which symbolizes the male fertility channeled away
from family into ascetic wilderness life and which (at the time Cooper is writing in 1841, after over a decade of Removal) may also be taken to represent
the increased propensity for violence and Indian-hating Cooper's young hero
displays.

In all the novels Leatherstocking is a man torn between two worlds. He
shares the "gifts" of the Indian, fine instincts and often incredible skills in woodcraft, but he has "white" sympathies, relying on a "natural" sense of justice and
implicitly Christian forgiveness, while continually condemning the purported
Indian ideal of violent revenge and the practice of scalping (although he argues
that both belong to the American Indian's particular "gifts"). Leatherstocking
had become a national hero by the time Cooper, after a pause of thirteen years,
returned to him in *The Pathfinder* and *The Deerslayer*. In the former, it is Natty
who falls in love but must, fortunately for his myth, be rejected by the white
heroine. Set amid 1759 battles between the British and the Iroquois near Lake
Ontario, *The Pathfinder*, along with the earlier *The Last of the Mohicans*, depicts
Leatherstocking as a mature scout and warrior. By placing his exploits in the
context of the French and Indian Wars, Cooper called attention to the war's
instrumental role in forming the United States and thus preparing the way
for Euro-American conquest of Indian tribes and territories. Cooper's saga
encompasses that expansion, at once deploring the tragic alienation of the frontier hero Leatherstocking and mourning the "destined" demise of Indians, yet
carefully detailing the social and economic necessity of the land's transfiguration into property and capital.

In the first of the novels, *The Pioneers*, the forces of law, property, and social order (represented by Judge Temple, modeled in part on Cooper's father) are in conflict with Leatherstocking's belief in his natural right to the land and its bounty. A figure of romantic dispossession, Leatherstocking is driven out of the community at the book's conclusion, and the marriage of Temple's young heirs underscores Cooper's belief in the value of lawfully transmitted property. By the time of *The Prairie*, set on the western plains in 1804, just after the Lousiana Purchase, the old man Natty Bumppo is virtually the last of a race of individualistic frontiersmen (even though Cooper was in fact writing at the height of the "mountain man" era). Entangled in a new series of captivities and skirmishes by a dissolute group of squatters, Leatherstocking once again proves his physical prowess and his preference for Indian life over white society before succumbing to a death that seems already coincident with the closing of the initial phase of America's postrevolutionary expansion: "The trapper had remained nearly motionless for an hour. His eyes alone had occasionally opened and shut. When opened, his gaze seemed fastened on the clouds which hung around the western horizon, reflecting the bright colors, and giving form and loveliness to the glorious tints of an American sunset. The hour—the calm beauty of the season—the occasion, all conspired to fill the spectators with solemn awe." Conquest has here become a carefully composed landscape portrait, with the dying scout a memorial witness to the necessary human cost of the nation's future.

The period between *The Prairie's* setting and its composition in 1827 allowed Cooper to see clearly the destiny of the western territories and their inhabitants. Like Lewis and Clark, Leatherstocking, the tragic forerunner of white settlement, had traversed the continent; the mountains and plains were being settled; and Monroe had formulated the policy of Removal, which would accelerate under Jackson. Thus, Cooper in 1826 could speak with symbolic accuracy of the "last" of the Mohicans. In the novel of that name, the young Delaware chief Uncas is the last of his distinguished line; but his father, Chingachgook, who outlives him only to die in a forest fire (by virtual suicide) in *The Pioneers*, might also be considered the "last" of the Mohicans. Even though Hawkeye and Chingachgook triumph over the enemy Indians and rescue the white heroines from captivity, it is "white blood" that prevails in the novel. In Cooper's deepest meditation on the question of miscegenation (which he projected to be the ultimate result of any actual assimilation), the

Euro-American Cora, marked by the black blood of her West Indian slave mother, and Uncas, the Indian who loves her, are sacrificed, while her sister Alice, a submissive woman who has no place on the frontier, is saved for marriage to the soldier Duncan Heyward. Cooper draws the "evil" Magua with something of the enchanting power of Milton's Satan, but though Magua is clearly wronged by whites and justly seeks revenge, he is also destroyed.

The action of *The Last of the Mohicans*, divided into two captivity sequences, pivots around the historical 1757 massacre of the British by French-allied Hurons at Fort William Henry. Cooper's significant enactment of the massacre resembles many of his battle scenes in its stylized caricature of combat, but it is especially important insofar as it turns the image of an Indian attack upon a woman and child, already a widespread literary and political cliché, into the spark initiating a ferocious loss of control:

The savage spurned the worthless rags [of offered clothing], and perceiving that the shawl had already become a prize to another, his bantering but sullen smile changing to a gleam of ferocity, he dashed the head of the infant against a rock, and cast its quivering remains to her very feet. For an instant, the mother stood like a statue of despair, looking wildly down at the unseemly object, which had so lately nestled in her bosom and smiled in her face; and then she raised her eyes and her countenance toward heaven, as if calling on God to curse the perpetrator of the foul deed. She was spared the sin of such a prayer; for, maddened at his disappointment, and excited at the sight of blood, the Huron mercifully drove his tomahawk into her own brain. The mother sank under the blow, and fell, grasping at her child, in death, with the same engrossing love that had caused her to cherish it when living.

At that dangerous moment Magua placed his hands to his mouth, and raised the fatal and appalling whoop. . . . Death was everywhere, and in his most terrible and disgusting aspects. Resistance only served to inflame the murderers, who inflicted their furious blows long after their victims were beyond the power of their resentment. The flow of blood might be likened to the outbreaking of a torrent; and as the natives became heated and maddened by the sight, many among them even kneeled to the earth, and drank freely, exultingly, hellishly, of the crimson tide.

The violence of the Hurons, who are allied with the French and led by the vengeful Magua, dominates the book, and Hawkeye's exploits are all in answer to it. Although French and British incursions have destroyed the existing "harmony of warfare" among Indian nations, turning them unnaturally against one another and corrupting or humiliating their leaders (as in the case of Magua, debased by white alcohol and whipped in public by the father of Cora and

Alice), Cooper's novel inevitably links the doom of the "noble" Indians to the savage violence of the "bad" Indians. Projecting into a past war the exterminating violence that his own generation both feared and set in motion, Cooper authorized the destiny envisioned at the book's end by Tamenund, the ancient chief of the Delaware: "The palefaces are masters of the earth, and the time of the Red Man has not yet come again."

The Last of the Mohicans may lack the freshness of adventure and clear delineation of Hawkeye's character found in The Deerslayer, the broad mythic scope of The Prairie, and the complex interaction of individual freedom with laws and social obligations seen in The Pioneers, but it is nevertheless Cooper's most complete examination of the Indian question as it was defined by the ideology of Removal. Hawkeye's fanatic insistence throughout the book that he is a "man without a cross" (i.e., a man with pure white, uncrossed blood) suggests the double bind that made him for Cooper such a powerful hero: he must reject white society because of its constraints, corruption, and hypocrisy, but his innate, if unlettered Christian sensibility and loathing of what he defines as the cruelty of true Indian customs leave him monastically isolated, a patriarch without a dynasty. When Parkman reviewed Cooper's collected novels in 1852, he recognized Leatherstocking as an "epitome of American history" in the era of exploration and settlement, a "hybrid off-spring of civilization and barbarism," but saw him too in essence as a renegade, emblematic of the savage life by then passing away.

In Cooper's conception, however, Natty Bumppo is also the tragic, sacrificial figure who both forecasts and atones for Euro-American conquest as, indeed, does the body of Cooper's work itself. His other Indian novels are less successful than the Leatherstocking Tales. In Wyandotté (1843), set during the American Revolution, the title character rises from his degraded role as a servant to kill his white master. The Oak Openings (1848) makes its western hero a more refined, less violent bee hunter who survives the Indian wars in Michigan to become a farmer and politician, and portrays the high potential for Christian conversion among the Indians. Indians have a minor role in Cooper's Littlepage novels. In The Redskins (1846), for example, real Indians drive off the "Injins," an anti-rent mob who adopt Indian disguises as a sign of rebellion and defiance of the law. Only in the earlier The Wept of Wish-ton-Wish (1829) does Cooper achieve the complex force of the Leatherstocking series. Set against successive generations of a Puritan community, the novel employs

King Philip's War, the themes of witchcraft and regicide, episodes of captivity, and the threat of miscegenation to chart the rise of New England as a securely held Euro-American territory. With any of these novels Cooper might have secured a place for himself as an important white writer about American Indians. Yet it is his panoramic Leatherstocking Tales, which unite the era's central myth of frontier individualism with a grand dramatization of the military defeat and cultural dispossession of Native Americans, that elevated Cooper above his contemporaries and made him widely read by Europeans, for whom the American frontier was the height of the exotic, and by succeeding generations of Americans, who were eager to discover, as in a mirror, the mythical heroic traits, bloody and disturbing as they may be, of their own national character.

The years from the 1820s through the 1840s, during which the necessity for Indian Removal fully entered public consciousness, saw the most significant production of fiction that made its noble native heroes the "last" of their tribes or families or simply the last to resist absorption or dispersal to western lands and eventually to reservations. Among novels of the period that display the search for a theory of conquest, Nicholas Hentz's *Tadeuskind, the King of the Lenape* (1825) anticipated Cooper's characterization of Uncas by comparing its real, historical chief to the "Torso of Hercules," in effect relegating him to antiquity. Likewise, Charles F. Hoffman's revolutionary novel *Greyslaer: A Romance of the Mohawk* (1840) made Chief Joseph Brant one of nature's doomed "children," and Daniel P. Thompson's later *The Doomed Chief* (1860) celebrated King Philip in the title role but concluded with the graceful suicide of the Native American heroine and a familiar message: "all was lost, forever lost, to the red man." James B. Ransom's *Osceola: a Tale of the Seminole Wars* (1838) depicted an idyllic tribal state contaminated by white contact and threw into relief the emblematic melancholy wasting of Osceola, whose "majestic form soon dwindled to a mere shadow." Like the various portraits of Tecumseh's and Black Hawk's doom, Robert Strange's *Eoneguski; or, The Cherokee Chief* (1839) justified Removal by making its Indian hero a subordinate soldier in Andrew Jackson's 1812 army who fails to fulfill his dying father's command of revenge and in the end chooses a pacific agricultural life in North Carolina.

Employing a strategy of retrospection that he would repeat in his best-known novels of the South, William Gilmore Simms, (1806–70) depicted the emergence of a gentry and a frontier middle-class structure in South Carolina after the extermination of Yemassee Indians in *The Yemassee* (1835). Based on warfare that took place in 1715, the novel confidently asserted the doctrine of Removal, which by then was fully incorporated in the public mind through the southern states' forcible eviction of the Five Civilized Tribes: "Conquest and sway are the great leading principles of [civilization's] existence, and the savage must join in her train, or she rides over him relentlessly in her onward progress." Like Tamenund in *The Last of the Mohicans*, the Yemassee chief Sanutee foresees the death of his tribe. Corrupted by alcohol and white customs, his son Occonestoga is eventually expelled from the tribe and killed by his mother to prevent a ceremonial humiliation. Like Cooper, Simms in his preface depicted the Romance as a combination of novelistic and epic features, and the Indian as a fit subject for "the natural romance of our country." He thought assimilation impossible and had no qualms about inventing Native American mythology in order to create for Indians an antiquity comparable in his eyes to that of Greeks or Saxons, presumably to assert the historical depth of America and at the same time to answer white compunctions about the natives' demise. His essays on Boone, "The First Hunter of Kentucky" (1845), and on "Literature and Art Among the American Aborigines" (a review of Schoolcraft's works published in 1845) supported his contention that the "North American Indian was as noble a specimen of crude humanity as we can find"—that is, a specimen like one of those featured in McKenney's Indian Gallery, belonging now to the past but nonetheless deserving of archeological study: "We are apt to think him no more than a surly savage, capable of showing nothing better than his teeth. . . . We are unwilling to read his past as we are unable to control his future;—refuse to recognize his sensibilities, and reject with scorn the evidence of any more genial attributes." Within a matter of two decades after the official proclamation of Removal, the novel had adapted itself almost seamlessly to an ethnological attitude toward the Native American. The preservation of Uncas and similar native heroes as though in stone monuments was mirrored by the elevation into myth of their closely matched but finally superior white antagonists.

Boone, Crockett, Jackson, and Cooper's Leatherstocking became heroes at the moment the "West" became a definitive aspect of American thought and life. The violent displacement and subjugation of Native Americans were thus an integral part of the process by which both white and Indian archetypal heroes would become permanent elements of American cultural thought. Two authors who had an equally large share in establishing the West as a subject for literature and, in fact, as the distinguishing feature of America's nationalistic culture were Timothy Flint (1780–1840) and James Hall (1793–1868).

Flint, a Massachusetts missionary, first wrote an account of his travels in the Mississippi Valley, *Recollections of the Last Ten Years* (1826), before turning to history and fiction. His *History and Geography of the Mississippi Valley* (1827) is one of the best studies of the region; and *Indian Wars of the West* (1833) contains the central materials of the Boone legend he expanded into the *Memoir* that same year. *Indian Wars* not only gives a partisan rendering of exploration and settlement but also argues for the historical depth and importance of the New World indicated by recent archeological finds. Establishing the American West as a legitimate ground for ideology and for fiction was one of Flint's special goals, reflected, for example, in *George Mason, the Young Backwoodsman* (1829), a novel about the children of a New England minister who moves his family to the Mississippi Valley. "I feel as much interest in the march of these barefooted boys along the deep forest," Flint wrote, "as I do in reading about the adventures and ridiculous distresses of fine dressed lords and ladies." This theme runs through most of Flint's fiction, despite its very diverse settings. In *Francis Berrian, or the Mexican Patriot* (1826), a New Englander brings the spirit of the American Revolution to the 1822 rebellion in Mexico. *The Life and Adventures of Arthur Clenning* (1828) concerns South Seas castaways who live as "Adam and Eve," adopt a native girl (named "Rescue") and teach her English and Christianity, then return to the Illinois frontier and marry her to a Pottawatomie chief before giving up their landed estate in England for frontier life in America. Both Poe's *Narrative of Arthur Gordon Pym* and Melville's *Typee* seem indebted to Flint's *Arthur Clenning*, particularly to the extent that they equate South Seas natives with Native Americans as similarly alien groups. Flint's best-known novel, *The Shoshonee Valley* (1830), is a complex story of a white man and his Chinese wife living in the ethnically diverse Oregon Territory among mountain men, Native Americans of various tribes, Spaniards, Russians, and Asians. A tragic love story, with episodes of captivity, rescue, and warfare, is here balanced by Flint's attempts at anthropological realism, whereby the civilization of the Shoshone appears as a Rousseauistic state that slowly succumbs to the fatal effects of money, alcohol, and debauchery.

James Hall is best remembered now as the source of Melville's chapter in *The Confidence-Man* (1857) entitled "The Metaphysics of Indian-Hating," an ironic meditation on the "Indian problem" derived from Hall's story of Colonel John Moredock in *Sketches of History, Life, and Manners in the West* (1834). After his family was massacred, Moredock became a classic Indian hater—a "Leatherstocking Nemesis," in Melville's words, dedicated to "a calm, clois-tered scheme of strategical, implacable, and lonesome vengeance." Decent and generous in polite society, but driven by violent longings for revenge on the frontier, the figure of Moredock epitomized the cycle of vengeance that expan-sion brought to the surface of individual and national character. Grim violence permeates Hall's sketches and stories, and revenge preoccupies everyone in his frontier world. In his only novel, *The Harpe's Head, A Legend of Kentucky* (1833), a love story holds together a similar (and in this case authentic) tale of two brothers who unaccountably became mad killers. If the theory of sava-gism articulated in his contribution to McKenney's *History of the Indian Tribes of North America* was based on a perceived antagonism between native sav-agery and superior white culture, *The Harpe's Head* portrayed an indulgence in violence, especially among national leaders and chiefs, to be universal. From Nimrod to Black Hawk, Hall writes, "the magnates of the earth have ever taken great delight in killing animals, and cutting the throats of their fellow men."

Besides working as a lawyer and a judge, Hall edited the *Illinois Gazette* (1820–2) and the *Illinois Intelligencer* (1829–32) and was founding editor of the *Illinois Monthly Magazine* (later called the *Western Monthly Magazine*), the first literary periodical in the West. His stories and sketches appeared in a number of volumes with different titles and arrangements, beginning with *Letters from the West* (1828), which sought to establish the West as a legitimate literary sub-ject and attacked European observers who had ridiculed American manners. His work offered credible descriptions of frontier life and developing cities such as Pittsburgh, Wheeling, and Cincinnati. Yet his dominant theme was the one Melville picked out for scrutiny: the sources and practice of Indian-hating in American history and myth. In "The Pioneer," from *Tales of the Border* (1835), the hero's desire for revenge against Indians—his "insatiable thirst for the blood of the savage"—is only overcome when he nearly murders his own captive sister, now living with an Indian husband and children. "The Indian-Hater," collected in *Legends of the West* (1832), portrays a man whom the mere sight of an Indian in a store can drive into frenzy: "His eyes rolled wildly, as if he had been suddenly stung to madness, gleaming with a strange fierceness; a supernatural lustre, like that which flashes from the eye-balls of the panther, when crouched in a dark covert, and ready to dart upon his prey."

By the time Melville explored the theme of Indian-hating, it was thus a fundamental part of the nation's literature. Projecting violence onto the mirror of the Indian, the pioneer and the novelist alike risked a reversal of savagism, a containment of Indian violence by its inversion in the white imperial self. As Parkman wrote in *The Conspiracy of Pontiac*, "the chronicles of the American borders are filled with the deeds of men, who, having lost all by the merciless tomahawk, have lived for vengeance alone; and such men will never cease to exist so long as a hostile tribe remains within striking distance of an American settlement." The revenge of the Indian hater is central, for example, to Bennett's *The Forest Rose*, Samuel Young's *Tom Hanson, the Avenger* (1847), Samuel B. Hanson's *Tom Quick, the Indian Slayer* (1851), and James McHenry's historical narratives *The Wilderness; or, Braddock's Times* (1823) and *The Spectre of the Forest* (1823). In James Kirke Paulding's *The Dutchman's Fireside* (1831), Indian-hating forms part of the material that Paulding argues should constitute our national literature; and in his *Western Ho!* (1832), a novel based on Flint's work, the hunter Ambrose Bushfield is a Boone-like isolato whose experience has made him of one mind on Indians: "When [pioneers] plough their fields, they every day turn up the bones of their own colour and kin who have been scalped, and tortured, and whipped, and starved by these varmints, that are ten thousand times more bloodthirsty than tigers, and as cunning as 'possums." Bushfield's lament simply reverses the more common, and more accurate, Native American assertion that Euro-American plows were turning up the sacred bones and relics of *their* ancestors.

Easily the most famous fiction of Indian-hating was written by Robert Montgomery Bird (1806–54). Trained as a physician, Bird wrote several historical dramas before turning to novels such as *The Infidel; or, the Fall of Mexico* (1835) and *The Hawks of Hawk-Hollow* (1835), a revolutionary romance. But it is *Nick of the Woods; or, the Jibbenainosay* (1837), dramatized by Louisa Medina the following year, that fixed the bloodstained Indian hater in western mythology. Attacking the "dreams of poets and sentimentalists" who saw the Indian as a noble figure, Bird's novel took Boone as a model for the Janus-faced Nathan Slaughter, a Quaker who, once his family is massacred, leads a double life as pacifist and Indian-hunter. His vengeance never fully satisfied, he mutilates and scalps his victims, as he himself was once scalped. Considered a madman by other pioneers, Nick's acts of revenge seem indeed to exacerbate his insanity:

The bundle of scalps in his hand, the single one, yet reeking with blood, at his belt, and the axe of Wenonga, gory to the helve, and grasped with a hand not less blood-stained, were not more remarkable evidences of transformation than were manifested in his countenance, deportment, and expression. His eye beamed with a wild excitement, with exultation mingled with fury; his step was fierce, active, firm, and elastic, like that of a warrior leaping through the measures of the war-dance.

Nathan Slaughter's madness, like Bushfield's psychological reversal of the Indian's grievance, suggests that the celebration of revenge could reveal an undercurrent of white guilt, a paradoxical imbalance of emotions brought on by an ideology of conquest that harbored a powerful identification with that which was being destroyed. Because the literature of Indian-hating was an extreme case of the process of inversion by which white writers exchanged attributes, both heroic and savage, with those they identified as enemies, the hero often remained trapped in a self-reflexive theory of savagism.

The Orb of Civilization

By midcentury, the time of Parkman's seminal *Conspiracy of Pontiac*, the rhetoric of Indian-hating and the romantic incorporation of the American Indian hero had merged. The annexation of Texas and Mexican territories served at once to extend the official frontier, accelerate Removal, and increase warfare with the numerous tribes of the West. Proposals to treat with the Plains Indian tribes with a view to creating reservations for them date from 1849, following the creation of a new Department of the Interior, which oversaw the Indian Bureau. In 1850, Commissioner of Indian Affairs Orlando Brown recommended a policy of "concentration—the creation for each tribe of a reservation consisting of "a country adapted to agriculture, of limited extent and well-defined boundaries; within which all, with occasional exceptions, should be compelled constantly to remain until such time as their general improvement and good conduct may supercede the necessity of such restrictions." What would constitute such conduct and improvement was never self-evident, and the advance of the white agricultural frontier, fueled by the rapid construction of roads and railroads and important mineral discoveries in California, Colorado, and other interior areas, soon flooded the region with frontiersmen who had little respect for the fragile bargains struck between the federal government and tribal chiefs. The creation of reservations, with all its implications for the course of Native American culture and literature on into the twentieth century, was the logical outcome of the policy of Removal as the tragic experience of eastern tribes was repeated on the Plains and in the transmontane West.

By the 1850s the Euro-American cultural response to Native Americans was firmly in place. One can trace it clearly in the major historical and ethnological works of the period, or perhaps more effectively in the now less well known novels that nonetheless display the infusion of archetypal thought into popular culture. Two examples that superimpose past upon present, the originating configurations of myth upon currently volatile issues, serve to sum up the status of American Indians in the white mind in the decade before the Civil War. In *Mount Hope; or, Philip, King of the Wampanoags* (1850), Gideon Hollister sets out "to retrace some of the faded and now scarcely-visible features of those exterminating wars" of early settlement and to delineate historical figures who are now "almost as fabulous as the fictions of poets or the creations of an early mythology." Philip is compared to Caesar and Hannibal, but more conspicuously—in a figure of striking duality—to an eagle that never faltered "in its flight till it was quenched in the radiance of the orb of civilization, which it sought in vain to blot from the heavens." Hollister's imperial poetic style is everywhere driven by a concept of manifest destiny that by midcentury gave a new force to the incorporation of the Native American into national ideology.

In M. C. Hodge's *The Mestico; or, the Warpath and Its Incidents* (1850), the Creek Wars of 1836 are the backdrop for a simultaneous meditation on mixing and miscegenation, Removal, and the metaphoric value of the Native American. Hodge typically finds the Indian's pristine state romantically noble but sees his bad traits exaggerated and "swelled into fearful controlling influence" by white contact. Indians become vile, drunken, and rapacious when "artificial desires" are "grafted into the parent stem" by contact or interbreeding. A standard melodrama of native attacks and the captivity of a white heroine fuels the claim that "poetry and romance have given a charm to Indian character which stubborn facts, instead of enhancing, will dispel." The migrants crowding into Creek territory simply act out a natural process, just as the heroine's rescue and concluding marriage symbolize the land's restoration to peace and fecundity: "the fertile land that was wasting under their [the Creeks'] tillage now blooms under the industry of the whites." As much a minor and forgotten novel as Hollister's *Mount Hope*, Hodge's *The Mestico* contains in brief the multitude of themes that Euro-American literature derived from, and imposed upon, the events of Indian Removal.

Such novels overlapped the popular ethnographic material produced in abundance at midcentury by Schoolcraft and Catlin, among others, and they mirrored the fixed attitudes of conquest and Euro-American progress that almost every account of western exploration and development conveyed. The Mexican War, the Gold Rush, and the gradual demise of the theory of the Great American Desert opened for white settlement an enormous new territory and undermined the futile theory that removal of Native American tribes to the west of the Mississippi would protect them and halt border warfare. The increasingly complex but also ideologically paradigmatic view of American Indians found in historical documents and fiction by the 1850s testifies to the triumph of a psychopoetic image over a more disturbing and often brutal reality, to the need to contain in carefully controlled forms of discourse the dangerous energy of the imperial mind.

No More Auction Block for Me

Slavery and African American Culture

On the first anniversary of the founding of his famous antislavery magazine, the *Liberator*, William Lloyd Garrison invoked the "Spirit of Liberty" that was "thundering at castle-gates and prison-doors" throughout the world. Rather than celebrate the fires of democratic revolution that had spread from America in 1776 to revolutions in a number of European countries by the early 1830s, however, Garrison dwelt on the significant failure of the American Revolution—the problem of slavery. When liberty "gets the mastery over its enemy," Garrison inquired rhetorically, "will not its retaliation be terrible?" Only "timely repentance" could save the American nation's "blind, unrelenting, haughty, cruel, heaven-daring oppressors" from the fate of foreign despots and aristocracies. Because repentance on a national scale did not seem likely in the 1830s, Garrison put forth a paradoxical proposition: in order to avoid having to join in defending the South against slave insurrection, the North ought to dissolve the Union. Were this threat to "break the chain which blinds [the South] to the Union" carried out, however, Garrison predicted that "the scenes of St. Domingo would be witnessed throughout her borders."

Garrison was no doubt thinking of Nat Turner's slave rebellion in Southampton, Virginia, the previous year. The most successful slave uprising in American history, Turner's rebellion caused alarm in the South about a repetition of the massive democratic rebellion of slaves in San Domingo (Haiti) at the end of the eighteenth century and quickly became a touchstone of both antislavery and proslavery sentiment. But Garrison may also have had in mind the black abolitionist David Walker's fiery pamphlet, *Appeal . . . to the Coloured Citizens of the World,* which had appeared in 1828 and which some had held responsible for Turner's rebellion. Like many writers of his generation, Walker invoked the central paradox of American democracy that lay at the core of arguments over slavery:

Man, in all ages and all nations of the earth, is the same. Man is a peculiar creature—he is the image of God, though he may be subjected to the most wretched conditions upon earth, yet the spirit and feeling which constitute the creature, man, can never be entirely erased from his breast, because God who made him after his own image, planted it in his heart; he cannot get rid of it. The whites knowing this, they do not know what to do; they know that they have done us so much injury, they are afraid that we, being men, and not brutes, will retaliate, and woe will be to them; therefore, that dreadful fear, together with an avaricious spirit, and the natural love in them, to be called masters . . . bring them to the resolve that they will keep us in ignorance and wretchedness, as long as they possibly can, and make the best of their time, while it lasts.

Fearful of violent slave rebellion, the pacifist Garrison drew back from advocating outright "treachery to the people of the south," and the more radical Walker perceptively underlined the mechanisms of suppression that would keep slavery in place for another generation and racism long after.

Even so, the prediction of a "double rebellion," as Garrison called it, which both writers found stirring—the rebellion of the South against the U.S. government and of slaves against masters—was at least partially fulfilled. African American slaves did not rise in large-scale revolt against their masters, as had the slaves in San Domingo, but individually they did rebel, and the slave narratives are filled with instances of small-scale resistance and plots of escape, with impassioned orations about freedom, and with folktales and religious songs of resistance. Many blacks, moreover, joined both the abolitionist movement against southern slaveholding and the Union ranks in the Civil War. Ultimately it was the South that revolted against the Union, and the Civil War was officially designated "the War of the Rebellion." That very fact, however, made evident how closely allied had been the North and the South in maintaining the immoral institution of slavery in the name of preserving the political integrity of the new nation. The price of union was named by Garrison in 1844 when he announced the American Anti-Slavery Society's policy of "No Union with

Slaveholders" and declared that "the Union which grinds [slaves] to the dust rests upon us" as well, that "their shackles are fastened to our limbs."

Although he dissented from orthodoxy in calling for the dissolution of the Union at a time when most American writers and politicians were searching anxiously for ways to preserve it, Garrison's nonviolence was symbolic of the reluctance many white Americans felt about acting resolutely against the institution of slavery, which seemed to have the blessing of the founders and the protection of the Constitution, and which both augmented and concealed within the protection of law deeper forms of racism. On this issue, as on many others, the new generations, including free blacks and ex-slaves, were ambivalent about the meaning and the heroes of the Revolution. Whereas David Walker called for strenuous, violent resistance to bondage, Frederick Douglass, despite his own experience of slavery, would not espouse violence until the early 1850s, and even then he would remain a proponent of traditional American revolutionary idealism. The Revolution itself became in many instances a conservative constraint on reform impulses; in the case of slavery, defenders of the institution identified potential slave rebellion not with the achievement of liberty in the American Revolution but with the forces of license, madness, and primitive energy often attributed to the French Revolution. In defining their relationship to the past, the descendants of the Revolution thus embraced conflicting impulses and contradictions, which also mark the literature of the period. Just as the political and social documents of the antebellum period constitute some of its greatest and most imaginative writing, so the literary work in its most powerful forms is infused with directly engaged social and political issues—the greatest of all being the problem of African American enslavement, which produced a national ideology riddled with tension and ambiguities.

The "renaissance" that classic American literature of the mid-nineteenth century is often said to constitute occurred in an era (from the 1830s through the Civil War) in which the authority of the Founding Fathers was in question and the issue of slavery had compelled a return to the fraternally divisive energies of the revolutionary period. The Civil War restored union and may therefore be seen as essentially conservative and redemptive, just as the American Revolution itself came in a later generation to seem a return—a *revolution* rather than a *rebellion*—to freedoms suppressed in 1776 or betrayed early on in American colonial history by the trade in the "black cargo" of African slaves initiated soon after the Columbian voyages. Indeed, the rise of the ideal of liberty and the rise of slavery in America took place simultaneously from the seventeenth to the nineteenth century. In Virginia especially, slavery made free, white society more homogeneous, allowed the flourishing of commonwealth ideas about taxation, property, and representation, and thus brought Virginians into the political tradition of New England. As Nathaniel Hawthorne wrote in one of his few allusions to the problem of slavery, appearing in an essay entitled "Chiefly About War Matters" (1862), "the children of the Puritans" were connected to the Africans of Virginia in a singular way, since the "fated womb" of the Mayflower "sent forth a brood of Pilgrims on Plymouth Rock" in her first voyage and in a subsequent one "spawned slaves upon the Southern soil." First as colonies, later as an independent nation, America found its political freedom and economic prosperity entangled with the unpaid labor, and often the deaths, of millions of African slaves over the course of three centuries.

The links between liberty and slavery were all the more complicated in view of the rhetoric of enslavement that American colonists employed during the Revolution. A famous suppressed clause of the Declaration of Independence charged George III with "violating the most sacred rights of life and liberty" in the practice of the slave trade and, moreover, with instigating rebellion among American slaves, "thus paying off former crimes committed against the *liberties* of one people, with crimes he urges them to commit against the *lives* of another." Revolutionary pamphlets often cast Americans as slaves of king and parliament, suggesting at times that chattel slavery was but an extreme form of a more pervasive political oppression. As attempts to abolish slavery after the Revolution foundered upon questions of (human) property rights, vital economy, fear of insurrection and miscegenation, and the legacy of the founders, the tentative identification between colonists and slaves collapsed. Yet the irony of the comparison remained intact. Fixing on the more important dimension, that of American tyranny over slaves, Charles Ball's 1836 narrative *Slavery in the United States: A Narrative of the Life and Adventures of Charles Ball, a Black Man* (composed by Isaac Fisher) introduced the former slave's story with a trenchant observation:

Despotism within the confines of a plantation, is more absolute and irresistible than any that was ever wielded by a Roman emperor. The power of the latter, when no longer supportable, was terminated by revolt or personal violence, and often with impunity. But to the despotism of the master, there is scarcely any conceivable limit, and from its cruelty there is no refuge. His plantation is his empire, his labourers are his subjects, and revolt and violence, instead of abridging his power, are followed by inevitable and horrible punishment.

The very fact that some of the most influential Founding Fathers—among them Thomas Jefferson and George Washington—were slaveholders enhanced the doubleness at the heart of the American experiment and in the long run invited the two-edged sarcasm of Theodore Parker in his great speech on "The Nebraska Question" (1854). "The most valuable export of Virginia is her Slaves," Parker wrote, "enriched by 'the best blood of the old dominion;' the 'Mother of Presidents' is also the great Slave Breeder of America. Since she ceased to import bondsmen from Africa, her Slaves [have] become continually paler in the face; it is the 'effect of the climate'—and Democratic Institutions."

Parker's attack on the internal slave trade, on miscegenation, and on the irony of Virginia's revolutionary heritage highlights issues that had produced a political crisis by the 1850s. By then, both proslavery and antislavery sentiment had hardened into recalcitrant forms: the Compromise of 1850 (which seemed to many in the North a victory for the slaveholding South) and contention over the extension of slavery into western territories signaled a further crisis in the Union that was implicit in the flawed design of the revolutionary era but only became clear as the nation expanded. The 1830s, while the country was still transported by the enthusiastic nationalism of the previous decade, witnessed a surge in America's sense of democratic mission and the belief in its "manifest destiny" to settle the territory of the continent if not the entire hemisphere. But it remained to be seen whether the newly acquired territories would allow the extension of slavery and at what price, then, the Union could be preserved. Celebrating the centennial of Washington's birth in 1832, Senator Daniel Webster of Massachusetts reminded his audience that nothing was of greater importance than the "integrity of the Union" and warned that "disunion and dismemberment" would "sweep away, not only what we possess, but all our powers of regaining lost, or acquiring new possessions." The following year, the novelist and social activist Lydia Maria Child, taking a different point of view, argued in *An Appeal in Favor of that Class of Americans Called Africans* that Washington's farewell advice about the necessity of union no longer "operated like a spell upon the hearts and consciences of his countrymen." Although she was thankful that Mexico, at that point, prevented the annexation of Texas by the United States, she was nonetheless fearful that southern threats of secession had so eroded public reverence for union that all restraints upon the spread of slavery would soon be lost. Once Texas was acquired in 1845 and the cession of Mexican territory accomplished following war in 1848, the risk to the Union became all the greater.

Yet the South, like the North, claimed that its interests were authorized by the legacy of the Revolution. The spirit of American mission that legitimized war with Mexico and prompted self-congratulation that 1776 was the source of contemporary democratic revolutions in Europe also prompted patriotic defenses of moderation, and sometimes even "fire-eating" extremism, on the question of slavery. In his inaugural speech as president of the Confederacy, on Washington's birthday in 1862, Jefferson Davis underlined the symbolic significance of the date by attacking the *North* for its deviation from the rights and principles authorized by the founders and by calling upon divine Providence to guide the South in its quest to preserve liberty without union: "The experiment instituted by our Revolutionary fathers, of a voluntary union of sovereign States for the purposes specified in a solemn compact, [has] been perverted by those who, feeling power and forgetting right, [are] determined to respect no law but their own will. The Government [has] ceased to answer the ends for which it was ordained and established. . . . To show ourselves worthy of the inheritance bequeathed to us by the patriots of the Revolution," Davis concluded, the South "must emulate that heroic devotion" and be itself tested in "the crucible in which their patriotism was refined."

A belief in the divine mission of America could sanction antislavery ideology, then, but it could just as easily compel a devotion to union based on the preservation and expansion of slaveholding rights. The vexed relationship between the revolutionary tradition and slavery animated almost every significant political and cultural issue of the antebellum years, often in fact providing the grounds on which politics and literature met. For example, Nathaniel Hawthorne, in his presidential campaign biography of his college friend Franklin Pierce, celebrated Pierce's descent from a renowned revolutionary father and took note of his distinguished service in the Mexican War, which "struck an hereditary root in his breast" and linked him to the heroic past. He argued that Pierce's support of the Compromise of 1850 indicated his understanding that slavery could not be stopped without "tearing to pieces the Constitution . . . and severing into distracted fragments that common country which Providence brought into one nation, through a continued miracle of almost two hundred years, from the first settlement of the American wilderness until the Revolution." Hawthorne's *Life of Franklin Pierce* (1852) thus tied together union and slavery, sentimental politics and expansion, much as Pierce himself, in making his 1853 inauguration speech "within reach of the tomb of Washington," would invoke the providential guidance of "our fathers" and call for the protection of slavery and the acquisition of Cuba.

The American Revolution and its legacy in this way gave rise to strong sentiments both for and against slavery and to political clashes that not only divided the nation but also divided partisans in each section. Sociological and political writing became intertwined with literature on both sides of the question, and the writings produced by the two sections sometimes fed off each other, as extremists imagined conspiracies of abolitionist fanaticism or slave power directed against them. That such conspiracies were more often rhetorical than real did not mitigate their influence or their ability to crystallize the most deeply rooted doubts about the just course of American democracy in both the political and the cultural spheres.

Parricides Instead of Patriots

The abolitionist Thomas Wentworth Higginson wrote in an 1861 *Atlantic Monthly* essay that Nat Turner's rebellion became "a memory of terror, a symbol of wild retribution" in the South. Even though the rebellion was minor (about sixty whites were killed, but twice as many blacks, including the rebels, died in violent response) compared to much larger uprisings in Latin America and the Caribbean, it provoked fears that the terror of the Haitian revolution would spread to the United States. Following the flight of terrified planter refugees to America in the 1790s, San Domingo was often summoned up in arguments over the possibility of slave or free black insurrection, and it eventually became central to literary treatments of revolt such as Herman Melville's *Benito Cereno* and Martin Delany's *Blake*. It led to the demise of French power in the New World and thus provoked the Louisiana Purchase, which in turn resulted in the period's central question about the territorial expansion of slavery. Like a prism, therefore, San Domingo reflected all sides of the issue of slavery, as would Turner's revolt, with which it became inevitably linked.

In the wake of Turner's rebellion at Southampton, the Virginia House of Delegates undertook the most serious debate in its history on the question of slave emancipation. The delegates were almost evenly divided on the possibility of abolishing slavery in its American place of birth, with a significant number arguing that the bloody Turner rebellion was a sign of the need to dismantle the "peculiar institution" and a portent of larger revolts. At the same time, however, the proslavery side contended that emancipation would lead neither to the tranquil assimilation of freed slaves nor to the easy dispersal of them to the North or outside the borders of the United States. Instead, they feared widespread crime, economic and political dependency, and even a race war. Moreover, emancipation would be financially ruinous for many southerners. The defeat of abolition legislation coincided with the revival of the state's economy after a depression and the rapid increase throughout the South in the cultivation of cotton. The spread of the Cotton Kingdom into the Deep South during the 1820s to 1850s (resulting in a tenfold increase in production, to a peak of nearly five million bales per year, three-fourths of the world's cotton, by the outbreak of the Civil War) guaranteed the survival and expansion of slavery. Sentiment in favor of emancipation was submerged by the economic growth of a complex market that benefited large aristocratic planters, small frontiersmen, and northern manufacturers alike.

Within this context, the representation of Nat Turner's rebellion as an isolated act of fanaticism, instead of a legitimate if futile quest for freedom, can be seen as a strategic necessity. The publicity that surrounded the trial and execution of Turner, as well as his purported *Confessions* (1831), recorded by the attorney Thomas Gray, suggested a black viciousness that had to be held in check by the careful use of force by slaveholders. The legalistic form of the account of Turner's confessions, half autobiographical narrative and half court document, ambiguously participates in the suppression of ideas of rebellion and freedom. The emphasis lies, in Turner's recorded words, on his messianic and apocalyptic visions and, in Gray's editorial commentary, on the derangement of Turner and his "dreadful conspiracy" of "diabolical actors." By staging Turner as a "gloomy fanatic" lost "in the recesses of his own dark, bewildered, and overwrought mind" as he plotted and carried out his revolt in methodical, cold-blooded fashion, Gray attempted to reduce Turner's revolt to a unique example of deviation from the normally goodwilled, safe relationship of master and slave. But because the *Confessions* embodied the central paradox of southern representations of slaveholding—that the institution was one of affectionate paternalism *but* that bloody insurrection could break forth at the least relaxation of vigilance—they served both to sound an alarm and to suppress the justness of Turner's plot.

Although Gray's text situates him within a tradition of revolutionary archetypes and romantic artifice, there is little doubt that Turner was a legitimate millenarian visionary, and careful attention to the *Confessions* reveals how his voice controls its replication of the revolt in the realm of polemical resistance. The fact that Turner quickly became a heroic figure in black folk history underlines the degree to which his recorded words, despite Gray's legalistic framework, establish a vital link between African American religious practice and a formative tradition of revolutionary thought. That this was not lost on the slaveholding South is registered, among other places, in the account of the Turner aftermath given by Harriet Jacobs in her *Incidents in the Life of a Slave Girl* (1861). After Turner's capture had somewhat reduced anxiety among Virginia's slaveholders, Jacobs writes that

the slaves begged the privilege of again meeting at their little church in the woods, with their burying ground around it. It was built by the colored people, and they had no higher happiness than to meet there and sing hymns together, and pour out their hearts in spontaneous prayer. Their request was denied, and the church was demolished. They were permitted to attend the white churches, a certain portion of the galleries being appropriated to their use. . . . The slaveholders came to the conclusion that it would be well to give the slaves [just] enough of religious instruction to keep them from murdering their masters.

The increasing rigidity of southern opinion that came to prevail in succeeding decades was characterized with fierce precision by the professor of political law (and later president) at the College of William and Mary, Thomas R. Dew (1802–46), who likewise invoked the archetypes of revolutionary fanaticism in describing the grave risks of slave emancipation. Drawing on the example of Turner's rebellion, Dew's classic 1832 essay "Abolition of Negro Slavery" (expanded as *Review of the Debate in the Virginia Legislature of 1831–2*), argued against both emancipation and the colonization of freed slaves in Africa or other foreign territories. Pointing to the example of Haiti and comparing potentially freed slaves to a Frankenstein monster incapable of coping with liberty, Dew belittled analogies between the cause of American slaves and current revolutions in Poland and France. He contended that, incited by abolitionist propaganda which is "subversive of the rights of property and the order and tranquillity of society," emancipated blacks would become *"parricides* instead of *patriots.*" The "right of revolution" cannot exist for persons "totally unfit for freedom and self-government," Dew argued. In this case, revolution was certain to bring "relentless carnage and massacre" upon their former benefactors. If slaves were freed, "the melancholy tale of Southampton would not alone blacken the page of our history, and make the tender mother shed the tear of horror over her babe as she clasped it to her bosom; others of a deeper die would thicken upon us; those regions where the brightness of polished life has dawned and brightened into full day, would relapse into darkness, thick and full of horrors." Like Garrison on the antislavery side, Dew defined the most extreme form of southern polemics for the next thirty years. His gothic figures indicate a central strain in much proslavery and later racist thought: slavery was justified on the grounds that blacks were infants or beasts who could not cope with liberty and would, if set free, give vent to murderous animalistic passions.

The fear and abhorrence of blackness and blacks that lurked beneath the plantation myth were brought quickly to the surface in the racist tracts and fiction of the postwar era; but their appearance throughout the antebellum period suggests the ways in which the devices of the gothic novel, used by the North to expose the sufferings of slaves, could in contrast express anxieties about the mixing of races. More often, such devices revealed less a corrosive racism than the rationalization of a profitable labor system. A clear example is the long didactic poem *The Hireling and the Slave* (1856), by William J. Grayson (1788–1863), one of the most famous replies to *Uncle Tom's Cabin.* Grayson's poem includes a representation of the American slave's escape from the darkness of African superstition and primitivism that had become increasingly commonplace in proslavery argument in the decades before the war:

> In this new home, whate'er the negro's fate—
> More blessed his life than in his native state!
> No mummeries dupe, no Fetich charms affright,
> No rites obscene diffuse their moral blight;
> Idolatries, more hateful than the grave,
> With human sacrifice, no more enslave;
> No savage rule its hecatomb supplies
> Of slaves fore slaughter when a master dies:
> In sloth and error sunk for countless years

His race has lived, but light at last appears—
Celestial light: religion undefiled
Dawns in the heart of Congo's simple child.

The contradiction between infantilization ("simple child") and demonization ("human sacrifice") in views of Africans is characteristic of much proslavery theory. Grayson portrays Harriet Beecher Stowe as a literary scavenger who

Snuffs up pollution with a pious air,
Collects a rumor here, a slander there;
With hatred's ardor gathers Newgate spoils,
And trades for gold the garbage of her toils.

This appropriately classes Stowe with the Victorian urban novelists, since Grayson's main line of attack was to suggest, as did many of his southern colleagues, that wage labor in England and the North was more vicious than slavery:

No mobs of factious workmen gather here,
No strikes we dread, no lawless riots fear . . .
In useful tasks engaged, employed their time,
Untempted by the demagogue to crime,
Secure they toil, uncursed their peaceful life,
With labor's hungry broils and wasteful strife.
No want to goad, no faction to deplore,
The slave escapes the perils of the poor.

A journalist and congressman, Grayson also defended slavery in *Letters of Curtius* (1851), but he opposed secession in *Letter to Governor Seabrook* (1850), arguing that it would be economically disastrous and would only advance the cause of abolitionism.

In his thought and in his poem Grayson represents those arguments in political and social theory that emerged along with a distinctive southern literary culture and constituted what was in many respects the most significant southern writing on this question. The most famous congressional orators like Henry Clay, Robert Hayne, and John Calhoun produced speeches that argued with ornate eloquence that slavery was a benign labor system and a just social arrangement. In his efforts as secretary of war and of state, as vice-president, and as senator, in his secretly authored brief for the doctrine of Nullification, *South Carolina Exposition and Protest* (1828), and in his posthumous volumes *Disquisition on Government* and *Discussion on the Constitution and Government of the United States* (1851), Calhoun (1782–1850) in particular argued from a strong states' rights position and proposed various measures that would safeguard the vital interests of the southern minority from the despotic will of the majority and ensure that slavery could be extended to newly acquired territories. Running through Calhoun's thought is a correlation between liberty and order that is characteristic of proslavery thought in both the literary and the political arenas. Freedom, as Calhoun understood it, was only possible in a carefully regulated society that recognized some persons to be more suited to it than others, a society that "enlarges and secures the sphere of liberty to the greatest extent which the condition of the community will admit." Antislavery argument, in Calhoun's view, because it pressed governmental power beyond its proper limit, belonged to that illicit expansion of federal reach that "exposes liberty to danger and renders it insecure." For Calhoun, as for many of his white contemporaries, South and North, the institution of slavery did not contradict liberty but instead supported it.

Even though clearly articulated proslavery theory can be found among the political records of the South in the early decades of the century, Calhoun's work and Dew's "Abolition of Negro Slavery," following just a few years after the Nullification crisis, marked a point of departure for a surge of writing that eventually led to two important collections of documents: *The Pro-Slavery Argument* (1852) and *Cotton is King and Pro-Slavery Arguments*, edited by E. N. Elliott (1860). As these collections proved, the defense of slavery could take a variety of forms. In the book that gave Elliott's collection its name, *Cotton is King* (1855), the Cincinnati journalist David Christy argued that the markets and labor forces of the South, North, and Europe were bound together by King Cotton and that, despite the evils of slavery, little was to be gained and much to be lost by allowing abolitionist "quacks" to destroy the system: "KING COTTON is a profound statesman, and knows what measures best sustain his throne. He is an acute mental philosopher, acquainted with the secret springs of human action, and accurately perceives who will best promote his aims." Christy's remark is an excellent delineation of the strength of proslavery argument, which effectively kept most of the North, even through much of the Civil War, skeptical about emancipation.

The most sophisticated arguments for slavery, like those against it, tended to be economic and political in character and were advanced in the immense southern periodical literature by men like George Fitzhugh, William Harper, Hugh Swinton Legare, and James D. B. De Bow. But the most visceral proclamations appropriated the received scriptural truths of religion and tendentious theories of science. The elaborate biblical defense of slavery rested principally on three claims: that blacks were descended from Canaan, the son of Ham, whose father cursed him by saying "a servant unto servants shall he be to his brethren"; that Mosaic law authorized slavery; and that in the New Testament Paul commanded servants to obey their masters, and Christ himself uttered no specific condemnation of slavery. Representative of the many who argued that the Bible condoned slavery and offered no commanding proscription against it, the Virginian Baptist minister Thornton Stringfellow (1788–1869) contended in such works as *Scriptural and Statistical Views in Favor of Slavery* (1856) and *Slavery: Its Origin, Nature and History* (1860) that the South's guardianship of the black race in slavery was a moral obligation, as could be demonstrated by numerous scriptural passages on the subject. His best-known work, *A Brief Examination of Scripture Testimony on the Institution of Slavery* (1841; reprint, 1850), later included in Elliott's *Cotton Is King*, added the humanitarian argument that slavery had throughout history often rescued men from certain death after capture in battle:

> The same is true in the history of Africa, as far back as we can trace it. It is only sober truth to say, that the institution of slavery has saved from the sword more lives, including their increase, than all the souls who now inhabit this globe.
> The souls thus conquered and subjected to masters, who feared not God nor regarded men, in the days of Abraham, Job, and the Patriarchs, were surely brought under great obligations to the mercy of God, in allowing such men as these to purchase them, and keep them in their families.

Stringfellow in this way combined the scriptural defense of slavery with the equally widespread claim that the history of conquest had always included the humanitarian practice of enslavement, thus making it a cornerstone of all the great world civilizations.

The scientific argument for slavery on the basis of race, often more rigorous but no less dependent upon flights of faith grounded in racism, reached a climax of offensive theorizing in *The Moral and Intellectual Diversity of Races* (published in the United States in 1856) by the European race theorist Joseph Arthur de Gobineau. Some years earlier, similar arguments were advanced by the Alabama physician Josiah Nott (1804–73). Building on the scientific ethnology of Samuel Morton's influential *Crania Americana* (1839) and *Crania Aegyptiaca* (1844)—two works that distinguished supposed mental capacities on the basis of such physiological differences as skull size and shape but that were not themselves so blatantly racist in the conclusions derived from their data—Nott in turn promoted the polygenetic theory that the races of humankind had different origins and, because they are therefore predisposed to different laws of development, could be subjected to different ethical and political rules. In the massive *Types of Mankind* (1854), written in collaboration with the Egyptologist George R. Glidden, and in other volumes such as *Two Lectures on the Natural History of the Caucasian and Negro Races* (1844), Nott drew on a wide range of biblical, archeological, statistical, and ethnographic evidence to argue that blacks belonged to a separate species created by God at the beginning of time. Joining an old argument (appearing provisionally, for example, in the thought of Thomas Jefferson) that would be revived periodically by racists on into the twentieth century, Nott concluded that Negroes stood between Caucasians and apes in the hierarchy of nature and that the popular theory of "savagism" could be scientifically proved:

> The difference to an Anatomist, between the Bushman or Negro and the Caucasian, is greater than the difference in the skeletons of the Wolf, Dog, and Hyena, which are allowed to be distinct species. . . . Now can all these deep, radical and enduring differences [between races] be produced by climate and other causes assigned? It is incumbent upon those who contend for such an opinion, to show that some changes either *have* taken place, or that similar changes in the *human race* are *now in progress*. . . .
>
> We can carry back the history of the Negro (though imperfectly) for 4,000 years: we know that he had all the physical characteristics then which he has now, and we have good grounds for believing that he was morally and intellectually the same then as now. . . . Can any reasoning mind believe that the Negro and Indian have always been the victim of circumstances? No, nature has endowed them with an inferior organization, and all the powers of earth cannot elevate them above their destiny.
>
> Imperfect as the civilization of St. Domingo now is, if you were to abstract the white blood which exists amongst them they would sink at once into savagism.

Accompanied by an essay written by the famous Harvard zoologist Louis Agassiz, who had emigrated to the United States in 1846, *Types of Mankind* sold 3,500 copies in several months and went through ten editions by 1871. Subjecting blacks to the same scrutiny as Native Americans, Latinos, and Polynesians, Nott and Glidden, among other ethnologists, deduced from the theory of polygenesis a belief in the decline of racially inferior races and the missionary triumph of Anglo-Americans. Appearing in both books and in a voluminous northern and southern periodical literature from the 1820s through the post–Civil War period, proslavery argument and commentary on the "doom" of American Indian tribes joined hands with the search for humanity's origins in etymological evidence, Egyptian artifacts, Indian pictographs, and African and South Sea tribal practices—and even in the occasional fictive extravaganza uniting them all, such as Edgar Allan Poe's *The Narrative of Arthur Gordon Pym of Nantucket* (1838).

Nott's characterization of Haitian savagery corresponded to the rather paradoxical prevailing view of that country's slave revolution and subsequent independence. His contention that miscegenation created a "hybrid" race-species also accorded with the opinion of many that mixing the races would degrade the white race, perhaps eventually exterminating it. From the antebellum period until well into the next century, physiological expressions of racism made miscegenation a central theme. The most eloquent refutation of the theory that miscegenation would elevate the black race without harming the white came from New York physician John H. Van Evrie in *Negroes and Negro "Slavery"* (1861), which pointed out that the abolition of slavery would only increase the "awful perversion of the instincts of reproduction" that slaveholding miscegenation had already set loose. Uncertain that the South, or the nation, could ever "recover from the foul and horrible contamination of admixture with the blood of the negro," Van Evrie attacked what he characterized as the North's sentimental fascination with mulattoes, while lamenting the fact that the North ignored the degradation in poverty and prostitution of its own white women. Echoing the savage campaigns against Lincoln as a supporter of miscegenation, Van Evrie prophesied a near holocaust for the white race. Because he wrote in large part for a northern audience, his additional attack on all aristocratic class-based distinctions among whites, in both Europe and America, had a Jacksonian appeal that probably strengthened rather than contradicted his argument for the complete subjugation of blacks on the basis of their race. Reissued as *White Supremacy and Negro Subordination* after the war (1868), his book anticipated some modern racist literature in

racist literature some modern in arguing, for example, that because the sentiment of family is not "natural" to the African, the slave mother ceases to care
for her offspring once it is old enough to survive alone and soon "forgets it
altogether," since in the "affections corresponding with her intellectual nature,
there is no basis, or material, or space for such things."

Van Evrie's perverse but influential combination of liberal egalitarianism
and racism had elements in common with Free Soil doctrine, which sought to
protect labor and western territory from competition by both slavery and free
black labor. He appealed to those in both sections who believed not only that
blacks were inferior to whites but also that slavery (and here he produced a less
sophisticated version of Calhoun's arguments) had permitted the flourishing
of democracy among "*all those whom the almighty creator has himself made
equal.*" Van Evrie's claims corresponded as well to the famous metaphor of
the "mud-sill" advanced by South Carolina senator James Henry Hammond
in an 1858 speech to describe the necessity of a menial class on which to build
a social order—a "mud-sill" the South conveniently found among its slaves: a
"race inferior to her own, but eminently qualified in temper, vigor, in docility,
in capacity to stand the climate, to answer all her purposes. . . . We found them
slaves by the common 'consent of mankind,' which, according to Cicero, '*lex
naturae est.*' The highest proof of what is Nature's law."

So much does the idea of order and nature's supposedly self-evident "law"
permeate southern thought that one reviewer of *Uncle Tom's Cabin* quite correctly apprehended that its critique of social ills might reach beyond chattel
slavery. Requested by the editor of the *Southern Literary Messenger* to write a
review "as hot as hell fire, blasting and searing the reputation of the vile wretch
in petticoats who could write such a volume," George Frederick Holmes
responded:

If it was capable of proving anything at all, it would prove too much. It would demonstrate that all order, law, government, society was a flagrant and unjustifiable violation
of the rights and mockery of the feelings of man. . . . The fundamental position, then,
of these dangerous and dirty little volumes is a deadly blow to all the interests and
duties of humanity, and is utterly impotent to show any inherent vice in the institution
of slavery which does not also appertain to all other existing institutions whatever.

It was a matter, argued William Harper along the same lines, of choosing
between the comparative evils of different systems of labor and hierarchical

arrangement: "To say that there is evil in any institution, is only to say that it is human." Judge, senator, and state chancellor of Missouri and South Carolina, Harper (1790–1847) examined not just southern slaveholding but the institution of human bondage, "deeply founded in the nature of man," in his *Memoir on Slavery* (1838). He concluded that "the relation of Master and Slave, when there is no mischievous interference between them, is as the experience of all the world declares, naturally one of kindness." He asked, "is it not natural that a man should be attached to that which is *his own*, and which has contributed to his convenience, his enjoyment, or his vanity?" Harper followed Dew in believing that the denial of liberty to slaves means simply that they are relieved of the burdens "of self-government, and the evils springing from their own perverse wills." In this they participate, at the mud-sill, in the general hierarchy of social dependence that also includes, for example, women and children. "The virtues of a freeman would be the vices of slaves," Harper suggested. "To submit to a blow, would be degrading to a freeman, because he is the protector of himself. It is not degrading to a slave—neither is it to a priest or woman."

In demanding analogically whether one would "do a benefit to the horse or ox, by giving him a cultivated understanding or fine feelings," Harper anticipated Henry Hughes's *Treatise on Sociology* (1854), James D. B. De Bow's *The Interest in Slavery of the Southern Non-Slaveholder* (1860), and the most elaborate of all southern defenses of slavery, George Fitzhugh's *Cannibals All! or Slaves Without Masters* (1857), which carefully argued that the labor system and resulting social life of northern capitalism was less free and more inhumane than southern slavery. "It invades every recess of domestic life, infects its food, its clothing, its drink, its very atmosphere, and pursues the hireling, from the hovel to the poor-house, the prison and the grave." In this volume, in others such as *Sociology for the South; or the Failure of Free Society* (1854), and in frequent articles in the prominent proslavery journal *De Bow's Review*, Fitzhugh (1806–81) contended that, far from eliminating slavery, the modern world ought to extend it to certain classes of whites as well, thus eliminating the economic anarchy of Jeffersonian liberalism and protecting the lower classes from poverty and competitive exploitation. Liberty, he also argued, was in fact antagonistic to democracy, which proposes, "so far as is possible, to equalize advantages, by fairly dividing the burdens of life and rigidly enforcing the performance of every social duty by every member of society, according to his capacity and ability." Within the bounds of liberty authorized by Fitzhugh's construct, "the slave, when capable to do so, must work for the master; but the master, at all times, must provide for the slave. . . . The protection or support to which the slave is entitled [is] an ample consideration of itself for the sale of his liberty"—a larger consideration, Fitzhugh maintained, than that provided by capitalists of Europe and the North, who rightly "say that free labor is cheapest." Citing the fact that God had authorized slavery and that "human law cannot beget benevolence, affection, [or] maternal and paternal love," Fitzhugh summed up the hierarchical principles that supported slaveholding paternalism and distinguished it from the capitalistic struggle for survival:

Within the family circle, the law of love prevails, not that of selfishness.

But, besides wife and children, brothers and sisters, dogs, horses, birds and flowers—slaves, also, belong to the family circle. Does their common humanity, their abject weakness and dependence, their great value, their ministering to our wants in childhood, manhood, sickness, and old age, cut them off from that affection which everything else in the family elicits? No; the interests of master and slave are bound up together, and each in his appropriate sphere naturally endeavors to promote the happiness of the other.

The humble and obedient slave exercises more or less control over the most brutal and hard-hearted master. It is an invariable law of nature, that weakness and dependence are elements of strength, and generally sufficiently limit that universal despotism, observable throughout human and animal nature.

Built on the argument that free-market competition left many laborers with miserable lives, Fitzhugh's utopian vision of a "familial" slavery in which the slave's power over the master is exceeded only by the master's affection for the slave won the consent of none but those already converted to the proslavery view. Nonetheless, it served in a forceful way to borrow the abolitionists' central claims of morally superior benevolence and domestic affection.

As Fitzhugh proved, the paternalistic ideal espoused by so many southern novelists would have to be contradicted by more than sentimental fiction. Although their voices were seldom heard, however, there were those within the South who vigorously opposed the corruptions of slaveholding paternalism, none more eloquently perhaps than Mary Boykin Chesnut (1823–86), wife of a planter and Confederate official. In her diary of the years 1861–5, which was not written in full until the 1880s and was first published in 1905, Chesnut created a remarkable counterstatement to the image of the family advanced by slavery's apologists. Based on journals kept during different portions of her life and on her memory of the war years, the *Diary* is a fascinating personal account of plantation life, with astute observations on the politics of the day, the lives of slaves, and most particularly the effects on the family of the slaveholder of the brutal and morally corrupt institution of bondage and slave sexual abuse. A similar critique, describing the slaveholding South as tied to "the dominion of Satan," may be found in Charles W. Andrews's *Memoir of Mrs. Anne R. Page* (1844).

Among other such personal records of plantation life, Chesnut's is matched only by the detailed account of Edmund Ruffin's life and theories of southern society found in his *Diary*, unpublished until 1972. A successful agricultural scientist and staunch defender of slavery who personally fired the first shell against Fort Sumter, Ruffin (1794–1865) was also well known for his essays and his *Political Economy of Slavery* (1853), but he is best remembered for an avowed hatred of "the perfidious, malignant and vile Yankee race," whose victory prompted him to immediate suicide. Such extraordinary animus against the North was not widespread among prewar southerners, of course, but Ruffin's views represented a definite intensification in proslavery's embattled defense that accompanied renewed calls in the 1850s for the expansion of slavery. The more radical views of Van Evrie and Fitzhugh were developed within a context of southern thought that envisioned not just the survival of King Cotton but its extension to western territories or to lands beyond the continental borders. Whereas some southerners had imagined that the leveling forces of westward expansion would lead eventually to the demise of slavery, a different interpretation of expansion, which foresaw the Gulf of Mexico as the heart of a slaveholding region stretching across the Americas, continued in force during the same period and was buttressed by calls to reopen the legal African slave trade.

The southern dream of a Caribbean empire antedated the Mexican War, but the bounteous acquisition of land in the war, combined with longstanding designs on Cuba, Haiti, and other Latin American territories, served to inflame slaveholding interest once again during the 1850s. The proslavery colony established in Nicaragua in 1856–7 by the filibustering ideologue William Walker (1824–60) was only the most extreme realization of this vision. Although Walker claimed to be building a new nation according to principles of the American Revolution, the engine of his colony was to be black chattel slavery. In a variation of Fitzhugh's theories, Walker believed that the victory of a wage labor society in the United States (or in the Americas generally) would lead to a repetition of European political tyranny and economic failure; only a slave-based society, he wrote in *The War in Nicaragua* (1860), could give capital a firm basis and enable "the intellect of society to push boldly forward in the pursuit of new forms of civilization." The failure of Walker's venture (he was overthrown in 1857) did not diminish the appeal of his argument that slavery was justified both on the grounds of political economy and by reason of the fact that the whites, in enslaving Africans and bringing them to the New World, were teaching them "the arts of life" and bestowing upon them "the ineffable blessings of a true religion. Then only do the wisdom and excellence of the divine economy in the creation of the black race begin to appear with their full lustre."

Until the conclusion of the Civil War, proslavery groups such as the Knights of the Golden Circle continued to predict an American slave empire surrounding the Gulf of Mexico. Edward Pollard's *Black Diamonds Gathered in the Darkey Homes of the South* (1861), for example, claimed that southern expansion was not a sectional issue but one involving "the world's progress, and who shall be the founders of its greatest empire of industry." Eventually, he maintained, the seat of the southern empire would be in Central America; control of the West Indies, the isthmuses of Central America, and the production of the world's cotton and sugar would complete America's destiny:

What a splendid vision of empire! How sublime in its associations! How noble and inspiriting the idea, that upon the strange theater of tropical America, once, if we may believe the dimmer facts of history, crowned with magnificent empires and flashing cities and great temples, now covered with mute ruins, and trampled over by half-savages, the destiny of Southern civilization is to be consummated in a glory brighter even than that of old, the glory of an empire, controlling the commerce of the world, impregnable in its position, and representing in its internal structure the most harmonious of all systems of modern civilization.

At the same moment, however, the South was also capable of producing an intellectual point of view entirely inimical to an empire based on black slavery. Likely to have been ranked among the most important abolitionist writers except for the fact that he was a violent racist and thus gained little

sympathy among social reformers, North Carolina author Hinton Rowan
Helper (1829–1909) published a firsthand account of the California Gold
Rush, *Land of Gold: Reality Versus Fiction* (1855), before returning to the
South. Following lines of argument advanced by Daniel Reeves Goodloe
(1814–1902) in *Inquiry into the Causes Which Have Retarded the Accumulation
of Wealth and Increase of Population in the Southern States* (1844), Helper's
major work, *The Impending Crisis of the South: How to Meet It* (1857), proved
by statistical evidence that slavery retarded economic growth, but he proposed
unfeasible means to abolish it that involved economically pitting nonslavehold-
ers and planters against one another. Helper concluded with a brief account of
southern literature—one more casualty of slavery's degrading effect, in his
view—that represented at large the consequences of the peculiar institution:
"The truth is, slavery destroys, or vitiates, or pollutes, whatever it touches. No
interest of society escapes the influence of its clinging curse. It makes Southern
religion a stench in the nostrils of Christendom—it makes Southern politics a
libel upon all the principles of Republicanism—it makes Southern literature a
travesty upon the honorable profession of letters."

Helper overestimated the destructive effects of slavery on white southern
culture. In addition, his own theories of abolition were tainted by his insistence that blacks be deported, since in his view they could not—and should
not—find a place in U.S. society and economy. His views became even more
radical in the postwar years; he then joined the ranks of major Reconstruction
racists with such works as *Negroes in Negroland* (1868) and *Nojoque; A Question
for a Continent* (1867), in which he stated that his object was "to write the negro
out of America, and . . . to write him (and manifold millions of other black and
bi-colored caitiffs, little better than himself), out of existence." His anthropological account of inequality led Helper to predict an ultimate choice between
"deportation and fossilization." Although he received a political appointment
as consul to Buenos Aires under Lincoln (after Horace Greeley successfully
brought out *The Impending Crisis* in the form of a Republican campaign document), the president was resistant to Harper's fanaticism. However distorted
its reasoning, his argument against slavery was still the strongest to come from
the South. If it was burdened by racism, it only expressed in an ultimate form
the ambivalent views held by a significant number of northern abolitionists as
well—a fact corroborated by the rise of proscriptions against black political,
social, and economic freedom after the collapse of Reconstruction.

The Fairest Plant of Freedom

Despite the new stridency of its argument from the 1830s through the Civil War, the defense of southern slavery was not limited to political theorists or even, for that matter, to southerners. Figures whose work was primarily literary played an enormous role in the idealization of southern plantation life and the justification of slavery. One could even assert that the defense of human slavery was first and foremost an act of the imagination, since the portraits upon which it depended were often contrary to brutally evident realities. In a few cases, those who contributed significantly to the literary defense of the slaveholding South were distant from its daily life. Aside from those northerners who wanted first to protect the Union, many other literary and political figures were actively sympathetic to the southern cause. A central example is James Kirke Paulding (1778–1860) of New York, who had a varied career as a man of letters and in governmental service. His novel *Westward Ho!* (1832), which follows the migration of a Virginia planter to frontier Kentucky, depicts the disintegration of the planter ethic in a western setting. *Letters from the South* (1817; revised edition, 1835) collects a group of Paulding's travel sketches that picture an independent and romantic country life in Virginia distrustful of the industrial progress of the North but that seek to remind his northern audience that "we are a nation of brothers." In his major defense of slavery, *Slavery in the United States* (1836), Paulding voiced the increasingly common argument that the abolition of slavery was not worth the sacrifice of the Union. The slaves, he maintained, were better off than their "savage" brothers in Africa or the working peasantry of Europe; moreover, Paulding contended, they were accustomed to, and content in, their ceaseless "round of labor and relaxation." If slavery "be an evil, let those who cherish [it] bear it," he wrote, "but let not us, their kindred, neighbors, and countrymen, become instruments to scatter the firebrands of fanaticism among them, and lend a helping hand to insurrection and massacre." Like most northern moderates, Paulding framed an issue in terms that predicted dangers to the American democratic experiment: those who interfered with slavery were "laying the axe to the root of the fairest plant of freedom that adorns the New or the Old World."

The argument for slavery's compatibility with democratic ideals, as indicated above, was not in the least uncommon in the South, for proslavery thought erected elaborate philosophical and "scientific" demonstrations of the inferiority of blacks to justify their exclusion from democratic life. Nevertheless, the plantation myth generated by much southern literature (both before the Civil War and even more prominently in the later nineteenth century in the work of writers such as Thomas Nelson Page) often exploited aristocratic and feudal elements as the basis for Confederate tradition. Although the "cult of chivalry" that modern observers have sometimes identified as the essence of the Old South stems more from the conceptions of postwar writers and historians than from antebellum realities, it is still the case that the culture of the slave South was preoccupied with the value of tradition and ideals of personal and communal honor. The novels of Walter Scott were popular and influential even if the romantic feudal world they described—and which some planters imagined could be re-created in the Cotton Kingdom—was economically within reach of only a small fraction of the South's landowners. The spread of Jacksonian democracy after the 1830s eroded aristocratic privilege in the South as well as the North, a fact generally misunderstood and misrepresented by both radical abolitionists and more moderate northern writers, who sometimes portrayed the feudal planter with hundreds of slaves as the southern norm. "The Southern States of the Union," the historian Richard Hildreth remarked in *Despotism in America* (1854), "though certain democratic principles are to be found in their constitutions and their laws, are in no modern sense of the word entitled to the appellation of Democracies: They are Aristocracies; and aristocracies of the sternest and most odious kind." Altogether, the myth of the aristocratic plantation was in part a self-generated representation of idealized political order under threat by periodic economic depression and seemingly anarchic pressures of expansion, and in part the fantasy or the rhetorical ploy of antislavery forces.

The South's agrarian bias against the North, although it was not by any means univocal, grew in proportion to the attack upon it, and abolitionist oratory sometimes obscured the legitimate arguments the South made against the development of northern industry and wage labor. In addition to charting the decline of aristocratic tendencies in the South (rather than their increase), many southern writers advocated a closer economic and social relationship between the two sections. Others sought greater independence for the South but were certain it would come from a realistic combination of modernization and conservatism. In a long and diverse writing career, the economist, historical novelist, and University of Virginia professor George Tucker (1775–1861) argued in books such as *Political Economy for the People* (1859) that slavery was inefficient and discouraged the development of manufacturing, thus making the South more and more dependent upon the North. Although his *History of the United States* (1856–7) strongly favored states' rights, Tucker's *Letters From Virginia* (1816) criticized the Virginian aristocracy, and his *Life of Thomas Jefferson* (1837) portrayed Jefferson as a man of unshakable democratic principles. His best novel, *The Valley of the Shenandoah* (1824), was a domestic seduction tale set against the self-destructive decline of a prosperous Tidewater planter family. As in numerous northern novels of the period devoted to the reformation of industrial labor, the family in Tucker's novel, as in his political thought, was a figure for the economic health and independence of the South.

Also suspicious of the South's ability to sustain itself in aristocratic seclusion was the physician William Alexander Caruthers (1802–46), whose historical novels portrayed the South as a central, but not the only, contributor to American national character. *The Kentuckian in New York* (1834), an epistolary romance, sought to join the sections by criticizing both the North's moral and financial corruption and the South's degradation in slavery and self-indulgence. In *The Cavaliers of Virginia* (1835), a novel of Bacon's Rebellion, Caruthers's advocacy of western expansionism, which he believed owed much to the strength of Virginian Cavalier character, responded as much to contemporary concerns about manifest destiny as to the dramatized historical incident. Likewise, his romance based on the career of Virginia's Governor Spotswood, *The Knights of the Horseshoe* (1845), was influenced by the legend of Daniel Boone. It predicted a westward "march which would be renewed generation to generation, until in the course of a single century it would transcend the Rio del Norte, and which, perhaps, in half that time may traverse the utmost boundaries of Mexico." Because in Caruthers's view the harshness of slavery was determined largely by the region and class of the slaveholder (the Virginia planter might be benevolent but his South Carolina counterpart a crude tyrant), both western expansion and the leveling effects of Jacksonian forces entailed the eventual eradication of chattel slavery as the nation's various factions and characteristics merged in a single destiny.

John Pendleton Kennedy (1795–1870) denounced secession and wrote a volume supporting the Union in the Civil War entitled *Mr. Ambrose's Letters on the Rebellion* (1863). Earlier in his life, however, he wrote one of the most influential literary defenses of the South, a series of sketches of Virginia life entitled *Swallow Barn* (1832). Trained in law and politics, Kennedy served several terms in Congress and, as secretary of the navy under President Miliard Fillmore, was responsible for sending Matthew Perry to Japan. His political works include the *Memoirs of the Life of William Wirt* (1849), a biography of the famous Virginia statesman and writer; *A Defense of the Whigs* (1842); and *Quodlibet* (1840), a Whig satire of Jacksonian political demogoguery. Kennedy assisted Poe by helping him obtain a position with the *Southern Literary Messenger* and by awarding a prize to "MS. Found in a Bottle." His activity in important literary circles also brought him into contact with William Makepeace Thackeray, to whom he gave material the British writer would use in *The Virginians*. Kennedy's other works include two important historical novels. *Rob of the Bowl* (1838) chronicles the conflicts between Catholics and Protestants in colonial Maryland; *Horse-Shoe Robinson* (1835), a backwoods southern Revolutionary War romance reminiscent of Cooper's *The Spy* and other similar fiction of the 1820s and 1830s, depicts a colonial family fractured by the divided national and sectional loyalties unleashed by the Revolution.

It was the fictional essays of *Swallow Barn*, however, on which Kennedy's reputation as a writer rested. Influenced by the sketches of Irving and by Wirt's popular *Letters of the British Spy* (1803), a group of essays on southern life, Kennedy's volume employs the standard ruse of a northerner visiting the South who writes with mixed sympathy and mild satire in portraying the planter as an aristocratic country squire. *Swallow Barn* includes a few minor portraits of slave life, and Kennedy's general support of states' rights and the benevolent paternalism of the peculiar institution coincides with his contention that the abolition of slavery must come from within the South itself. Appearing in the wake of Nat Turner's uprising, the book was designed to restore calm and to reassure the South, as well as the North, that the great majority of Virginia's blacks, as in this description of slave children, were pacific and content: "Their predominant love of sunshine, and their lazy, listless, postures . . . might well afford a comparison to a set of terrapins luxuriating in the genial warmth of summer, on the logs of a mill-pond."

Unambiguous literary defense of the South and slavery is perhaps best reflected in the work of William Gilmore Simms, but the representatives of two distinct generations, Nathaniel Beverly Tucker (1784–1851) and John Esten Cooke (1830–86), prominently frame the argument for the southern Cavalier tradition. Son of the legal theorist St. George Tucker, whose *Dissertation on Slavery* (1796) outlined a plan for eventual emancipation, Tucker was himself a professor of law but also an early supporter of secession. His *Series of Lectures on the Science of Government* (1845), along with various essays in southern periodicals, prescribed a reactionary line. His first novel, *George Balcombe* (1836), an adventure and mystery story set in Virginia and Missouri, was thought by Poe to be one of the best American novels. But more important was *The Partisan Leader* (1836), a futuristic novel set in 1849, when Martin Van Buren has become a tyrannical dictator; the novel was reissued during the Civil War, and its prophecy of secession and sectional violence was viewed as uncanny. Cooke's career spanned the war and its aftermath, so that he participated in the cultural nostalgia for the Confederacy that flourished in the 1880s, but even in his youthful work he appears to be a prophet of the "Lost Cause." Brother of the poet and critic Philip Pendleton Cooke, he served as a staff officer for J. E. B. Stuart in the Confederate army and wrote important military biographies of Stonewall Jackson (1863) and Robert E. Lee (1871) and a number of war romances, such as *Surry of Eagle's Nest* (1866), *Hilt to Hilt* (1869), and *Hammer and Rapier* (1871). Although he continued to write fiction for several decades after the Civil War, his best-known fictional work remains the group of novels set in colonial Virginia written in the decade before the war began: *Leather Stocking and Silk* (1854), *The Virginia Comedians* (1854), and *Henry St. John, Gentleman* (1859). In all cases, the stories of romance and adventure are set against a backdrop of landholding gentility and slaveholding paternalism in which sectional differences are at once historical and resonant with contemporary tensions.

It is in the work of William Gilmore Simms (1806–70) that the use of the historical novel in defense of the South reached full maturity. Just as *The Yemassee* (1835), as noted earlier, depicted colonial South Carolina warfare against Indians but illuminated contemporary questions of Indian Removal, so Simms's series of Revolutionary War novels from *The Partisan* (1835) through *Eutaw* (1856) dramatized divided national and familial loyalties in ways that referred simultaneously to the history of American independence and the possibility of southern conflict with, or secession from, the Union. Along with other advocates of the Young America movement, Simms in the 1840s vigorously supported American expansionism and viewed democratic revolutions in Europe as an expression of the same ideals of liberty that gave the United

States a moral right to territorial destiny in the New World. The Revolution was for Simms therefore a sign not just of America's strength but of the nation's necessary resolve to resist internal destruction. Liberty in this view became more and more clearly identified with white, Anglo-Saxon, southern ideals, and slavery was explained as a benevolent alternative to the degraded wage slavery of northern industrialism.

Simms's varied and energetic career as a man of letters gave him considerable fame and made him an ardent spokesman for the South on the lecture platform and in numerous editorials and essays. His political theory stressed a stable, class-structured society in which democracy was not an invitation to mobility and disorder but a principle of coherence and control. In answer to the English writer Harriet Martineau's attack on slavery in *Society in America* (1837), Simms wrote in a much-cited essay in the *Southern Literary Messenger* (later reprinted in an 1838 pamphlet entitled *Slavery in America* and then again in the collection *The Pro-Slavery Argument*):

Democracy is not levelling—it is, properly defined, the harmony of the moral world. It insists upon inequalities, as its law declares, that all men should hold the place to which they are properly entitled. The definition of true liberty is, the undisturbed possession of that place in society to which our moral and intellectual merits entitle us. *He is a freeman, whatever his condition, who fills his proper place. He is a slave only, who is forced into a position in society below the claims of his intellect.*

To Simms, as to many of his contemporaries, South and North, such a theory of liberty and of intellect (however presumptively based on color) was not implausible. Harmony and hierarchical order—in terms of both class and race—were tied together, and any underlying pessimism about the final progress of humanity was subordinated to a view of permanent vertical rule within a democratic structure. The main question for Simms was whether, given the chaotic pressures of Jacksonian America, such a society could be made to work without at the same time destroying the democratic ideals that supported it.

The answer was that it could not. By the 1850s, moreover, the attack on the South was not simply one of political theory or of abolitionist lecturing but came in the form of Harriet Beecher Stowe's widely popular *Uncle Tom's Cabin*, which raised a fury of fictional replies in the South. Among them was one of Simms's important novels, *The Sword and the Distaff* (1853), soon revised as *Woodcraft* (1854). Set at the conclusion of the Revolution, the novel concerns the restoration to order of Captain Porgy's plantation after the destructive "civil war" between patriots and Loyalists. Among other incidents, the scenes depicting the relationship between Porgy and his trusted slave Tom are calculated defenses of slaveholding benevolence and, more particularly, answers to what Simms took to be the fabricated sufferings of Stowe's own Tom. Porgy says he will shoot Tom "in order to save him" from the hostile enemy (in allegorical terms, "abolitionist") forces that would carry him off, and he even tells Tom to kill himself to prevent capture. Likewise, Tom says to Porgy: "Ef I doesn't b'long to *you*, *you* b'longs to *me*! . . . so, maussa, don't you bodder me wid dis nonsense t'ing 'bout free paper any more. I's well off whar' I is I tell you." The purported "nonsense" of freedom, of course, speaks more pointedly to the 1850s than to the 1780s, and the ruin of the southern landscape, even in victory, appears to anticipate a new civil war on the horizon.

In 1856 Simms, speaking before a Buffalo audience in a speech about slavery in Kansas and alluding to Charles Sumner's notorious attack on South Carolina, foresaw the collapse of the Union but predicted the battered, ambiguous triumph of his home state, "a monument, more significant of ruin than all the wreck which grows around her—the trophy of a moral desolation." Simms's own South Carolina home would be burned twice (and his extensive personal library destroyed) during the war, once by accident and once by design during Sherman's march. With the deaths of his wife and two of his children, the war's toll on Simms was thus so heavy that it is remarkable that he continued to write in its aftermath, producing such volumes as *War Poetry of the South* (1866) and his eyewitness account of the destruction of Columbia, South Carolina. The prophetic character of *Woodcraft* was marred only by the fact that the North won the war, leaving the illusion of the paternalistic relationship of master and slave, which Simms thought of as an expression of democratic order held in place by the revolutionary heritage of the South, once and for all destroyed. It remained in memory and in myth, however, not least because of the effort of Simms over the course of his intellectual career to define a proslavery America free from the capricious and cruel behavior of bad masters and the inefficient political economy of a divided South.

Simms, Kennedy, Caruthers, Nathaniel Tucker, and Cooke all worked in the context of the increasingly strident proslavery writing that appeared after the early 1830s. The same can be said of the southerner Poe, who was decidedly reactionary in his domestic political views and whose *Narrative of Arthur*

Gordon Pym and short stories such as "Murders in the Rue Morgue" and "The System of Doctor Tarr and Professor Fether" hid fears of black rebellion and race contamination within baroque allegorical tales. Working in a similar vein, Oliver Bolokitten (pseudonym) produced a futuristic, scatological burlesque of an America plunged into miscegenation, *A Sojourn in the City of Amalgamation* (1835). Set in an unspecified year of the twentieth century, the book's new republic affords its citizens an industrial amalgamating process by which all men, women, and animals must be mentally and bodily purged of prejudice, and the wars of various colored particles of their physiologies brought under control. Like Poe's work, the novel was most effective because its attack on liberal, romantic ideals of race harmony exposed the sobering fears and hatreds that underlay both sides of the argument over racial equality and the correct means to achieve it. Among southern local-color and frontier sketches—such as Mexican War journalist and politician Thomas B. Thorpe's *The Mysteries of the Backwoods* (1843) and *The Hive and the Hunter* (1854), Joseph G. Baldwin's satire *The Flush Times of Alabama and Mississippi* (1853), and George Washington Harris's tall tales in *Sut Lovingood Yarns* (1867)—there is little mention of slavery as an institution. However, their depiction of southern characters prone to violent outburst and comic extravagance echoes the work of Simms and Caruthers (and adumbrates that of Twain and Faulkner) in showing that the aristocratic veneer of the South covered a wilder, often crude interior that thrived in a frontier environment economically energized and socially structured by slavery.

Although the great outpouring of southern domestic novels in support of slavery, many by women, did not begin until the 1850s, significant titles appeared earlier. Caroline Gilman's *Recollections of a Southern Matron* (1838) and the anonymous *Lionel Granby* (1835) depict the harmonious, comfortable life of slaves and masters; and the northerner Sarah J. Hale, later famous as the editor of *Godey's Lady's Book*, produced a book that would remain one of the most popular domestic defenses of plantation life, *Northwood; A Tale of New England* (1827). The cross-sectional romance of Hale's novel supports her view that the family is a model of social order and stability and the South an arena of benevolence and cultivated leisure that can moderate the North's contemplative greed and harshness of character. Reissued in 1852 with a preface condemning the abolitionist forces of disunion, *Northwood* argues that both the Bible and the Constitution regulate slavery (even if they did not specifically establish it), and that it is not "the tearing up of the whole system of slavery, as it were, by the roots, that will make the bondman free." Only careful religious instruction and gradual colonization can give freedom and a home to American slaves and at the same time rescue African blacks from degraded savagery. "The mission of American slavery is to Christianize Africa," she writes, a view elaborated at length in her novel devoted to the most extensive effort at African resettlement, *Liberia; or, Mr. Peyton's Experiment* (1853). In both novels, Hale joins the argument over women's role in the slavery question, strongly advocating the domestic ideology her magazine made famous: "'Constitutions' and 'compromises' are the appropriate work of men: women are conservators of moral power, which, eventually, as it is directed, preserves or destroys the work of the warrior, the statesman, and the patriot."

To the extent that they answer Harriet Beecher Stowe's representation of the slaveholding South, Hale's novels of the 1850s and Simms's *Woodcraft* belong to a large group of novels appearing in the decade after *Uncle Tom's Cabin* that raise strident, and often incredible, voices in defense of the plantation myth. The numerous direct replies to Stowe's novel (a number of them written by northerners sympathetic to the South) claimed that she had misconceived the benevolent paternalism of southern slaveholding, and they pointed out that Simon Legree was a northerner and thus an exception to the norm of kind southern masters. Like the proslavery essayists, the novelists also traded on the common argument that northern wage labor was far more vicious than chattel slavery. In Robert Criswell's *Uncle Tom's Cabin Contrasted with Buckingham Hall* (1852), the sedition of abolitionism is countered by the romanticized life of the decent planter, whereas northern labor and Jim Crow laws are exposed as corrupt and demeaning. Likewise, in John W. Page's *Uncle Robin, in His Cabin in Virginia, and Tom without One in Boston* (1853), it is argued that the miseries that this Tom encounters as a freeman in Boston would be multiplied exponentially if slavery were abolished; and in W. L. G. Smith's *Life at the South; or, "Uncle Tom's Cabin" As It Is* (1852), the escaped slave hero, after suffering illness, poverty, and homelessness in the North returns home to the Virginia plantation, back to "his master, father, home." The conjunction or virtual equation of these three terms succinctly indicates the main rhetorical lines of the southern paternalistic argument for slavery penned in scores of essays and dramatized in other novels such as *Cabin and Parlor, or Slaves and Masters* (1852), by J. Thornton Randolph (pseudonym of Philadelphia magazine editor Charles Peterson); Caroline Lee Hentz's *The Planter's Northern Bride* (1854), which asserts, in the face of "the burning lava of anarchy and servile war" threatened by abolitionism, that slaves are "the happiest *laboring class* on the face of the globe"; Thomas B. Thorpe's *The Master's House, A Tale of Southern Life* (1854), a strikingly more realistic and balanced account that hopes for an arrest in the decline of the cultivated, paternalistic power of a southern landed gentry; and Mrs. G. M. Flanders's *The Ebony Idol* (1860), whose title is suggestive of its virulent satire of the supposed abolitionist "worship" of African American life and race mixing.

Like *Uncle Tom's Cabin* itself, however, the novels that were most popular and effective tempered realism with inflammatory melodrama. In Caroline Rush's *North and South; or, Slavery and Its Contrasts* (1852), the northern heroine, driven into poverty and prostitution by her family's bankruptcy, becomes a "white slave," and her tale of urban suffering is pointedly contrasted to "the pampered, well-fed lazy negro children of the South." Because the familial feelings of whites are more refined than those of blacks, Rush argues, "the bondage of poverty [that] forces a lady to give up her child to the care of strangers is worse in the North," and the novelist stands on moral high ground in addressing her genteel, sentimental audience: "We shall see whether 'the broad-chested, powerful Negro' [i.e., Uncle Tom], or the fragile, delicate girl, with her pure white face, is most entitled to your sympathy and tears." Similarly, in Mary H. Eastman's *Aunt Phillis's Cabin* (1852), the deathbed scene of the old slave Phillis shows her telling her master *not* to free her children, who are well cared for on the plantation and will suffer in the North or in Liberia. Because the tearful scene also forecasts a reunion of slave and master in heaven, where "the distinctions of this world will be forgotten," it testified to the planters' need to rationalize slavery but at the same time to mitigate the sin they implicitly recognized to lie within it.

The argument for Christian conversion and colonization often rested on a corresponding recognition of the domestic sin of slaveholding linked to a Calvinistic fear of blackness associated with the African and with the "barbarism" and purportedly satanic practices of African tribal life. Among the many theoretical and fictional critiques of African primitivism, Mrs. Henry Rowe Schoolcraft's tale of gothic sentimentality and vicious racism, *The Black Gauntlet* (1860), is thus both extreme and representative. The wife of the famous ethnologist of American Indians, Mrs. Schoolcraft joined a number of vocal opponents of what she called Lincoln's "Ethiopian equality party" in castigating the notion of amalgamation (the "reign of the Anglo-Africans approaches," she warned) and defining Anglo-American Christian work as an expunging of the mark of Cain placed on blacks by their cannibalistic ancestry. Taking a leaf from her husband's writing on Native Americans, she advised that whites should keep blacks "in bondage until *compulsory labor* [has] tamed their beastliness, and civilization and Christianity [have] prepared them to return as missionaries of progress to their benighted black brethren." If it was less sophisticated than political oratory and economic theorizing, the proslavery novel, South and North, deployed economic rationalization, sentimentality, and racial fear in equal measures.

The Fatherland of the Race

Abraham Lincoln's interest in colonization was fueled by Free Soil objection to competition from slavery and from free black labor, but it sprang from long-standing northern, as well as southern, sentiment in favor of deporting freed slaves to Africa or colonies in Latin America, a view that had been advanced by Thomas Jefferson among others. The rise of legal opposition to the slave trade, culminating in its prohibition by congress in 1808, the passage of the more far-reaching Anti-Slave Trade Act in 1819, and the establishment of the American Colonization Society in 1816, made colonization the most powerful antislavery movement until the 1830s. At that time, the South's reactionary turn (sparked by Turner's revolt and by profits in the burgeoning internal slave trade, which supported an expansion of the cotton economy in the lower South) and fierce condemnation of colonization by William Lloyd Garrison and other antislavery leaders crippled the movement. Goaded by the protests of those blacks who opposed colonization, abolitionists increasingly recognized that the American Colonization Society, whatever its intentions, worked primarily in the service of proslavery and racist interests. The society's journal, the *African Repository*, also made clear its ultimate prejudices by including such documents as one that declared that African Americans, no matter what their proportion of African "blood," were subject to "a degradation inevitable and incurable" and argued that white prejudice could never be overcome in America.

Although the idea of colonization continued to be revived by both black and white leaders until the Civil War was over, the British colony of Sierra Leone, established in 1787, and the American colony of Liberia, established in 1822, were the only significant results of the movement's efforts. The first group of Liberian settlers, and those who later joined them voluntarily, were not so much exiles as models of black independence. The emigrants' difficult but challenging experience in West Africa was recorded in annual reports through-out the rest of the century, in letters and stories in the *African Respository*, and in volumes such as James Hall's *An Address to the Free People of Color* (1819, 1835), Matthew Carey's *Letters on the Colonization Society* (1828), James Lugenbeel's *Sketches of Liberia* (1850), and in a modern edition of their letters entitled *Slaves No More* (ed. Bell I. Wiley, 1980). Paul Cuffee, an American black who led a group of colonists to Sierra Leone in 1815, wrote about the colony in *A Brief Account of the Settlement and Present Condition of the Colony of Sierra Leone in Africa* (1812). In a different vein, Frederick Freeman's widely read *Yaradee; A Plea for Africa* (1836) contended that blacks had been depraved both by nature and by enslavement and that prejudice against them could be removed by "nothing short of divine power." Perhaps the text of most interest to come from the early phase of colonization was Ralph R. Gurley's *Life of Jehudi Ashmun* (1835), the biography of a white minister and colonial agent in Liberia, which gave a detailed picture of the colony and included Ashmun's own diary accounts of his spiritual trials and growth.

Despite the moderate success of Liberia, however, forced colonization on a large scale remained both impractical and immoral. When ideas of coloniza-tion were revived in the 1850s by black nationalists and by whites anxious about the results of emancipation, the project was even less plausible than it had been thirty years earlier. Abolitionism often undermined legitimate attempts at col-onization, but it did not stifle American interest in Africa, which reached its height later in the century when European imperialist exploration and settle-ment penetrated into the interior of the "dark continent" and when a signifi-cant number of historians, both black and white, began to recover Africa's past in detail.

American travel and adventure writing set in Africa, which likewise flour-ished in the late nineteenth century, was also popular even in the antebellum period. One of the books with the greatest readership, reprinted until the 1850s, was James Riley's *Sufferings in Africa* (1817), an account of his shipwreck and enslavement by Arabs. Finally ransomed by the British in Morocco, Riley painted a vivid, if Anglocentric, picture of his wanderings and ordeal in North Africa. His account of life as a white slave, which Lincoln read, provoked sympathy that could be displaced to abolitionist sentiment: "we were obliged to keep up with the camels, running over the stones, which were nearly as sharp as gun flints, and cutting our feet to the bone at every step. It was here that my fortitude and my reason failed me. . . . I searched for a stone, intending if I could find a loose one sufficiently large, to knock out my own brains with it." A work with similar appeal, antislavery leader Charles Sumner's 1843 volume *White Slavery in the Barbary States*, was one of several historical works that treated the Islamic–Christian conflict and consequent enslavements predating those of the New World, and it thus added a historically resonant international context, for example, to Melville's treatment of slavery in *Benito Cereno*.

Voyages of trade and adventure, often with commentary on Liberia, appeared in W. F. W. Owen's *Narrative of Voyages to Explore the Shores of Africa, Arabia, and Madagascar* (1833), William B. Hodgson's *Notes on Northern Africa, the Sahara, and the Soudan* (1844), J. A. Carnes's *Journal of a Voyage from Boston to the West Coast of Africa* (1852), and Charles W. Thomas's *Adventures and Observations on the West Coast of Africa* (1855). Even though the most important works on African exploration and economic enterprise would not appear until the zenith of the imperial age, antebellum writing about Africa borrowed from the energy of mission and conquest that motivated the Euro-American drive into the continental West and the Pacific. In both cases, the voyages and the works that became their records were predicated upon an explicit racial taxonomy and the belief that white Americans—or, in the case of Africa, emancipated African Americans—could introduce Christian and democratic civilization into a primitive world. Here, as in the case of writings about the Pacific, military and mercantile literature overlapped with the representation of American nationalism and ascendency. The U.S. naval operation against the slave trade was treated in Horatio Bridge's *Journal of an African Cruiser* (1845) and Andrew Hull Foote's *Africa and the American Flag* (1854); and the development of legitimate trade with Africa, which had existed alongside the trade in slaves, was recorded in such works as Edward Bold's *The Merchant's and Mariner's African Guide* (1823).

Perhaps the most revealing volume devoted to the United States and its relation to Africa was written by a former slave trader, Theophilus Conneau, who adopted the pen name Theodore Canot in publishing *Captain Canot; or, Twenty Years of an African Slaver* (1854). Conneau's work is finely detailed in its account of travel within Africa and the internal African slave trade, the perils and hardships of the middle passage, and the calculation of profit in human cargo transported illegally under the false flags of various ships. The record of his transport of slaves to the West Indies contains a highly personalized description of his successful career as a trader alongside events of mutiny and suicide. According to Conneau, his discipline was mild and his ship kept comparatively clean, but the tenor of his prose alone signals the true cost of trade in African slaves. Before shipping, newly purchased slaves were branded, shaved, and stripped, since "perfect nudity, during the whole voyage, is the only means of securing cleanliness and health." The moral resonance of Conneau's text is entirely in harmony with its utilitarian purpose:

In every well-conducted slaver, the captain, officers, and crew, are alert and vigilant to preserve the cargo. It is [in] their personal interest, as well as the interest of humanity, to do so. . . . At sundown, the process of stowing the slaves for the night is begun. The second mate and boatswain descend into the hold, whip in hand, and range the slaves in their regular places; those on the right side of the vessel facing forward, and lying in each other's lap, while those on the left are similarly stowed with their faces towards the stern. In this way each negro lies on his right side, which is considered preferable for the action of the heart. In allotting places, particular attention is paid to size, the taller being selected for the greatest breadth of the vessel, while the shorter and younger are lodged near the bows. When the cargo is large and the lower deck crammed, the super-numeraries are disposed of on deck, which is securely covered with boards to shield them from moisture. The *strict* discipline of nightly stowage is, of course, of the greatest importance in slavers, else every negro would accommodate himself as if he were a passenger.

Even though it was not written as an antislavery work, the effectiveness of Conneau's volume lay to a degree in its revelation of a mind and spirit hardened to suffering by an international economic web of legal and illegal trade in human flesh.

The renewal of interest in colonization in the 1850s was prompted in part by fears of emancipation and miscegenation that had been converted into ideals of Christian mission by writers as different in their intentions as Mrs. Henry Rowe Schoolcraft and Harriet Beecher Stowe. As in earlier decades, those with antislavery sympathies sometimes argued even more ingenuously for the benefits of colonization than did defenders of southern slavery. Like a number of authors in the decade before the Civil War, Jacob Dewees employed his adventure narrative *The Great Future of America and Africa* (1854) as a means to contend that colonization was the only path to black success and redemption. David Christy, antiabolitionist author of *Cotton is King*, rendered a complimentary picture of Liberia in *Ethiopia: Her Gloom and Glory* (1857), arguing that American blacks returned there with civilized and Christian principles to replace the brutishness and paganism of Africa. In thus "securing to Africa the benefits of her own labor," Christy believed, the new colonists both improved their ancestral land and recognized that "intellectually, morally, or politically, [blacks] can no more flourish in the midst of whites, than the tender sprout from the bursting acorn can have a rapid advance to maturity beneath the shade of the full-grown oak . . . its lordly superior." So too, Thomas Jefferson Bowen, a Southern Baptist missionary among the Yoruba who also wrote a grammar of their language, maintained in *Central Africa: Adventures and Missionary Labours in Several Countries in the Interior of Africa from 1849 to 1856* (1857) that God's evident purpose in allowing slavery had been to take the "millions of civilized negroes in America, better clothed and fed, and more virtuous and happy than the analogous classes of white people in some other countries," and use them to regenerate their homeland, "flowing back as a river of light and life upon the African continent."

From the beginning of the colonization movement, blacks as well as whites envisioned resettlement outside the borders of the United States, sometimes prophesying a millennial regeneration within the black community that would ultimately spread to the entire globe. J. Dennis Harris and James T. Holly, for example, pointed in the 1850s to the revolutionary success of Haiti as the forerunner of utopian Caribbean colonies. Holly's lecture, *A Vindication of the Capacity of the Negro Race for Self-Government and Civilized Progress, as Demonstrated by Historical Events of the Haytian Revolution* (1857), adopted a version of Bowen's argument in predicting that Haiti would become the "Eden of America, and the garden spot of the world": "Civilization and Christianity [are] passing from the East to the West . . . God, therefore in permitting the accursed slave traffic to transplant so many millions of the race, to the New World . . . indicates thereby, that we have a work now to do here in the Western World, which in his own good time shall shed its orient beams upon the Fatherland of the race [Africa]."

The providential view of slavery, which rested on a paradox inimical to modern liberalism, was thus hardly restricted to white intellectuals. In the more complex thought of Alexander Crummell, however, black American slavery was only the most obvious political dimension of a greater moral problem. Although his greatest fame and power as a spokesman for evangelical black nationalism would come later in the century, Crummell (1819–98) was second only to Frederick Douglass at midcentury in the breadth of his thought and influence. A black Episcopal priest and African missionary, Crummell believed that Africa was "the maimed and crippled arm of humanity" in need of regeneration by American blacks. He advanced his argument in such works as "The Relation and Duties of Free Colored Men in America to Africa" (1861) and *The Future of Africa* (1862), basing his call for black evangelism and African commerce on the hope that such trade could be made to rival "the market value of the flesh and blood they [white traders] had been so eager to crowd beneath their hatches." Christianity and the market would redeem Africa, Crummell avowed, but not necessarily pacifically: "for the establishment of a strong black civilization in central Africa, a strong and bloody hand must be used."

Crummell returned to the United States in 1873 and became a leading figure in the conservative wing of the black nationalist movement, as well as one of the founders in 1897 of the American Negro Academy. Born free, he did not share the view of Douglass and other black leaders that slavery alone was responsible for black degradation but argued that the need for racial uplift stemmed in part from the rudimentary state of civilization in Africa. "Darkness covers the land," he wrote of Africa in 1861, "and gross darkness the people. Great devils universally prevail. Confidence and security are destroyed. Licentiousness abounds everywhere. Moloch rules and reigns throughout the whole continent, and by the ordeal of Sassywood, Fetiches, human sacrifices, and devilworship, is devouring men, women, and little children." His estimate of Africa was sometimes hardly less scathing than that of European imperialists. Nevertheless, Crummell's call for evangelical colonization in the antebellum years was based on an idealized vision of African nationalism grounded in the recovery of an ancient racial "vigor," and throughout his career he espoused the need for a Pan-African territorial home and a mature role in world politics and economics for black people.

The increasing apprehension among blacks that they would never find freedom, much less equality, in America prompted calls for colonization that were not all missionary in spirit. The most prominent black political leaders in the antebellum period—Frederick Douglass, Martin Delany, and Henry Highland Garnet among them—held differing views on colonization at different points in their careers, though their sentiments in favor of it were usually based on a certain degree of Afrocentric nationalism. The shift in support for colonization from white missionaries (and proslavery advocates) to black nationalists that occurred from the 1820s to the 1850s is one index of the increasing frustration of abolitionists who thought that in condemning colonization they were striking an effective blow for the equality of freed African Americans.

Testimony of a Thousand Witnesses

William Lloyd Garrison's *Thoughts on African Colonization* (1832), which attacked colonization as futile and undemocratic, was a natural outgrowth of his embrace of more radical antislavery principles in the 1830s. Along with William Jay's *Inquiry into the Character and Tendency of the American Colonization Society* (1835), it worked to turn abolitionist sentiment away from colonization and toward the practical issue of freeing slaves to join the life of national democracy America was meant to offer. After working on the abolitionist newspaper *The Genius of Universal Emancipation*, edited by the Quaker and colonizationist Benjamin Lundy, Garrison (1805–79) launched his own more fiery journal, the *Liberator*, in 1831. His calls for "immediate emancipation" and eventually for disunion from the South made him the leader of the most extreme wing of antislavery, and his avowal of "perfectionism" (the religious social reform doctrine asserting that people could indeed be wholly freed from sin on earth) fixed slavery as the most degraded of evils infecting the world. However, his belief in the power of nonviolence and his general disregard of all institutional means of fighting slavery through the church, political campaigns, and social reform movements always threatened to leave him isolated from reality. Garrison's manipulation of the rhetoric of democratic liberty, noted at the outset of this chapter, was especially potent; for example, he entitled an 1860 collection of documents about violence and suppression in the South *The New "Reign of Terror" in the Slaveholding States*. His flair for melodramatic rhetoric fitted him for an age of oratory, and his excoriations of slavery appealed to humanitarian concerns bolstered by guilt.

Speaking of the imminent abolition of slavery in British colonies in 1832, he thundered:

What heart can conceive, what pen or tongue describe, the happiness which must flow from the consummation of this act? That cruel lash, which has torn so many tender bodies, and is dripping with innocent blood; that lash, which has driven so many human victims, like beasts, to their unrequited toil; that lash, whose sounds are heard from the rising of the sun to its decline, mingled with the shrieks of bleeding sufferers; that lash is soon to be cast away, never again to wound the flesh, or degrade those who are made in the image of God. And those fetters of iron, which have bound so many in ignominious servitude, and wasted their bodies, and borne them down to an unlikely grave, shall be shivered in pieces, as the lightning rends the pine. . . . O, how transforming the change! In contemplating it, my imagination overpowers the serenity of my soul, and makes language seem poor and despicable.

Garrison's thought and language indicate two converging strains in antislavery ideology. On the one hand, Garrison voiced the romanticist drive of antislavery protest, a belief in the moral primacy of common people, especially those who are oppressed, and the consequent expressive power of sympathy; on the other, he underscored antislavery's evangelical nature, derived from the spirit of revivalism that swept many religious groups in the first third of the century and entered into the panoply of social reform causes that appeared from the 1820s to the 1860s.

The evangelistic spirit and the language of sympathy, in lectures as in fiction and poetry, lent a particular power to the antislavery crusade, for its egalitarian principles coincided with what were thought to be easily perceived moral truths. Its characteristic early texts were therefore expressions of direct experience and straightforward calls for action. For example, John Rankin, who developed the underground railroad in Ohio (and rescued the woman who became the model for Eliza in *Uncle Tom's Cabin*), made a direct appeal for citizen participation in *Letters on Slavery* (1826). Despite problems of factionalism, antislavery's success depended on its adherence to simple principles that were independent of the abstruse doctrines of organized churches, most of whose leaders were less than forthcoming in support of antislavery and as a result were severely criticized by Garrison, Stowe, Douglass, and others.

Even in the early decades of the movement, clear articulations of black rights and bold challenges for immediate emancipation, by means of insurrection if necessary, appeared in antislavery writing, especially in that by

African Americans themselves. Although it counseled an ambiguous submission to suffering while awaiting deliverance at the hands of a coming savior, Robert Alexander Young's *Ethiopian Manifesto Issued in Defense of the Black Man's Rights in the Scale of Universal Freedom* (1829) was the first text of black nationalism produced by an African American. Far more striking and influential was the revolutionary pamphlet produced by the free black David Walker (1785?–1830). Entitled *Appeal . . . to the Coloured Citizens of the World*, Walker's 1828 pamphlet, cited earlier, was banned in the South because of its incendiary call for violent rebellion. In a carefully argued but blazing style, Walker replied directly to Thomas Jefferson's theory in *Notes on the State of Virginia* that the risk of miscegenation was a barrier to emancipation. Adopting the rhetoric of black messianism that runs through abolitionist and much later black nationalist thought, Walker attacked Christian doctrine that led blacks to submit to their bondage while prompting whites to ignore the certain judgment of the Almighty: "I call God—I call angels—I call men, to witness that your DESTRUCTION *is at hand*, and will be speedily consummated unless you REPENT." His important statement of black nationalist principles was not calculated to gain the favor of sympathetic whites, and it advocated an appropriation of principles of revolution that even Garrison would eschew:

But remember, Americans, that as miserable, wretched, degraded and abject as you have made us in [the] preceding, and in this generation, to support you and your families, that some of you [whites], on the continent of America, will yet curse the day that you were ever born. You want slaves, and want us for your slaves!!! My colour will yet, root some of you out of the very face of the earth!!!!! . . . I ask you candidly, [were] your sufferings under Great Britain, one hundredth part as cruel and tyrannical as you have rendered ours under you? Some of you, no doubt, believe that we will never throw off your murderous government. . . . If Satan has made you believe it, will he not deceive you?

Walker's *Appeal* anticipated the better-known jeremiads of black leaders like Douglass and Delany. Although Walker's fame was short-lived—he died two years after publication of his *Appeal* and was overshadowed by the figure of Garrison—his call increased black interest in antislavery even as it terrified slaveholders. As in the case of Garrison, radicalism here accomplished something short of its stated goals of violence and separatism, but its statement of principles and its ultimate effect on the consciousness of the nation were the true measure of its success.

More remarkable than Walker's rhetoric was that of Maria Stewart, a black evangelist from Boston whose *Productions of Mrs. Maria W. Stewart* (1835) included a group of meditations and public addresses directed especially at the "daughters of Africa." She placed herself squarely in the tradition of the jeremiad by invoking scripture and condemning the "foul and indelible" stain of American slavery for which the nation would be judged and punished:

Dark and dismal is the cloud that hangs over [America], for thy cruel wrongs and injuries to the fallen sons of Africa. The blood of her murdered ones cries to heaven for vengeance against thee. Thou art almost become drunken with the blood of her slain; thou hast enriched thyself through her toils and labours. . . . And thou hast caused the daughters of Africa to commit whoredoms and fornications. . . . O, ye great and mighty men of America, ye rich and powerful ones, many of you will call for the rocks and mountains to fall upon you, and to hide from the wrath of the Lamb, and from him that sitteth upon the throne; whilst many of the sable-skinned Africans you now despise, will shine in the kingdom of heaven as the stars forever and ever.

The "mighty men" of America were Stewart's particular target. Aligning slavery with a pervasive male dominance, Stewart told women that it was "no use for us to sit with our hands folded, hanging our heads like bulrushes, lamenting our wretched condition." Her message foreshadowed later black nationalist assertions of a separatist self-help ethic, but it did so in explicitly feminist terms: "How long shall the fair daughters of Africa be compelled to bury their minds and talents beneath a load of iron pots and kettles? . . . Shall [men] laugh us to scorn forever? Do you ask, what can we do? Unite and build a store of your own if you cannot procure a license. Fill one side with dry goods, and the other with groceries." Although white antislavery women like Stowe and Lydia Maria Child would receive more attention, Stewart's discourses are a significant chapter in antislavery writing and a striking early signpost in the literature of black feminism.

At the same time that Walker, Stewart, and Garrison embraced immediatism, more conservative religious and social groups, which typically advocated gradual measures and often maintained clearly hierarchical racial and sexual divisions, worked in a counterdirection. In the early years of relative harmony, the antislavery crusade gained numerous adherents, effectively petitioned politicians for action on civil rights, and drew on the energies of reform directed at the urban problems of prostitution, gambling, and temperance. It generated a number of important journals and newspapers, including the *Anti-Slavery Examiner*, the *Emancipator*, the *National Anti-Slavery Standard*, the *Liberty Almanac*, and the *Philanthropist*, and it withstood the scorn of the South and of many northerners, who repeatedly attacked its offices and leading speakers in mobs.

The more diffuse the movement became, however, the less coherent was its purpose. Garrison's adoption of religious perfectionism and his denunciation of all governmental authority and political processes attracted eccentrics and isolated him from the moderate majority. Lewis Tappan and Arthur Tappan, who had been instrumental in organizing and financing the American Anti-Slavery Society, were skeptical of, among other things, Garrison's support of women's direct participation in antislavery work, a controversy sparked by the 1837 lecture tour of Sarah Grimké and Angelina Grimké, southern Quaker sisters who had a great impact on the development of a feminist antislavery ethic. In 1840, a quarrel over Garrison's proposal to place a woman on the executive committee of the American Anti-Slavery Society created volatile dissension, which was exacerbated later in the year when the World Anti-Slavery Convention in London refused to admit women delegates from the United States. In the first case, Lewis Tappan split from Garrison and formed the American and Foreign Anti-Slavery Society; in the second, two of the delegates, Lucretia Mott and Elizabeth Cady Stanton, immediately resolved to launch a women's movement, and the 1848 Seneca Falls convention was the eventual result. The same resistance to their participation in the antislavery movement, ironically enough, was sometimes encountered by blacks in the North, who were more interested in action than in theory. Like women, blacks gradually gained an important place in the movement but at the cost of internecine fighting that retarded the effectiveness of the antislavery campaign.

Of particular interest in the shift of attitudes that spurred the alliance between revivalism and social reform, and in some respects provoked the convergence of the women's movement with antislavery, is theologian Lyman Beecher (1775–1863), the father of Harriet Beecher Stowe. A New England Presbyterian minister who was instrumental in revivalist preaching, Beecher moved west to Cincinnati in 1832 to preside over the Lane Theological Seminary, which became a center for moderate antislavery thought and activity. In many of his sermons and essays, collected in his *Works* (1852), as well as in his influential volume entitled *A Plea for the West* (1835), Beecher mixed anti-Catholicism and a reformed Calvinist theology in calling for religious and political freedom in America, the alternative to the "prison house" and "slavery" of despotic Europe. With respect to the enslavement of American blacks, however, Beecher recommended moderation—moral suasion rather than violent activism—and looked to colonization of freed blacks as the best solution to the race problem. One of his sons, Henry Ward Beecher (1818–87), became the most famous minister of his day. Although Henry was best known for his urban reform activities and self-improvement writings such as *Seven Lectures to Young Men* (1844), for his writings on religion, and for a notorious adultery scandal in later years, his *Star Papers* (1855) and other works supported the antislavery cause and his New York church publicly aided escaped slaves. Another Beecher son, Edward (1830–95), was also an active opponent of slavery. In his *Narrative of Riots at Alton* (Illinois) (1838), an account of the murder of the prominent antislavery editor Elijah Lovejoy, he argued that the "nation" itself had been murdered and that a "deluge of anarchy and blood" would follow if peaceable abolitionism were not allowed its voice.

Because Lyman Beecher's beliefs were based upon the Calvinist theology of Jonathan Edwards, which held that humanity was depraved and dependent upon God's grace for salvation, he promoted gradualist methods for achieving salvation and combating slavery that came to seem too tentative to his children and most of all to his students, a large number of whom deserted Lane to follow the revivalist Charles Grandison Finney in establishing Oberlin in 1833. One of the Lane students who resigned after the antislavery controversy, Theodore Dwight Weld (1803–95), wrote the work that probably had the greatest influence on Stowe's conception of *Uncle Tom's Cabin* as a polemic. *American Slavery As It Is: Testimony of a Thousand Witnesses* appeared anonymously in 1839 with a terse, appropriate epigraph from Ezekiel: "Behold the abominations that they do!" From over twenty-thousand southern newspapers that Weld examined between 1837 and 1839 the volume drew myriad examples of the treatment and conditions of slaves in the South, along with other first-hand testimony and narratives, many from slaveholders, detailing the punishment, random violence, and day-to-day degradation inflicted upon blacks.

Comparable to Weld's volume in popularity was the work of the Quaker John Greenleaf Whittier (1807–92), who wrote an American Anti-Slavery

Society pamphlet entitled *Justice and Expediency* (1833) but was best known for his antislavery and reform poetry and for a quasi-fictional slave narrative he ghostwrote, *Narrative of James Williams* (1838). Working in the Garrisonian tradition of immediatism, Whittier called for the day when the Declaration of Independence would be honored, "when under one common sun of political liberty the slave-holding portions of our republic shall no longer sit, like the Egyptians of old, themselves mantled in thick darkness, while all around them is glowing with the blessed light of freedom and equality." His work as an editor of antislavery publications led to other important essays, "What is Slavery?" and "Thomas Carlyle and the Slavery Question" among them; and his poems, taking such titles as "The Hunters of Men," "The Slave-Ships," and "To William Lloyd Garrison," reached a large popular audience. One of his most piercing, entitled "Ichabod," denounced Daniel Webster for his support of the Compromise of 1850:

> Of all we loved and honored, nought
>   Save power remains—
> A fallen angel's pride of thought,
>   Still strong in chains.
>
> All else is gone; from those great eyes
>   The soul has fled:
> When faith is lost, when honor dies,
>   The man is dead!

Throughout his poetry Whittier represents the South as an arena of cruelty and dissipation, its slaves driven by tyrants and its honorable character prostituted to greed and lust. As in much antislavery literature, of which *Uncle Tom's Cabin* is only the best-known example, the separation of families and the abuse of slave women are key features of the rhetoric of sentiment that ensured the popularity of Whittier's verse.

Daniel Webster's acquiescence in the Compromise of 1850 made him the symbol of New England's failure to actively resist the machinations of the "Slave Power" and brought into symbolic crisis the heritage of liberty, granted in the national Union by the Founding Fathers, that Webster had spent his political life celebrating. Other political figures who stood out in the antislavery fight include John Quincy Adams, whose impassioned campaign to repeal the gag rule that prevented antislavery petitions from being presented to Congress

from 1836 to 1844 was ultimately victorious, and who successfully defended
the rebel slaves from the *Amistad;* and Senator Charles Sumner, whose famous
1856 speech on "The Crime Against Kansas" resulted in his notorious assault
on the Senate floor at the hands of Preston Brooks. But Webster (1782–1852)
came to seem a tragic figure precisely because of his moderation and caution on the issue that, he correctly saw, might destroy the Union. Webster's
obsession with the unity and "harmony" of the Union permeated his thought
and speeches, notably in his 1830 reply to Robert Hayne's Senate speech on
Nullification, in which Webster called on the memory of the founders to help
suppress what he took to be southern divisiveness and factionalism. But the
issue that cast the most searching light on the paradoxes of union symbolized
by Webster's career was the Compromise of 1850.

Growing from desperate efforts to resolve the imbalance of sectional interests occasioned by the acquisition of western lands in the Mexican War and
California's subsequent adoption of a free-state constitution, the Compromise
was pivotal in the political and literary war over slavery. Not just the great
political writing of the 1850s but also the central works of literature—*Moby-
Dick, Uncle Tom's Cabin, Leaves of Grass,* and *My Bondage and My Freedom,* to
name the most obvious—all reflected the fragile structure of the Compromise,
its perilous balance of destructive national forces. The central provisions of
the Compromise admitted California to the Union as a free state and abolished
the slave trade in Washington, D.C., but at the same time organized the New
Mexico and Utah territories without prohibiting slavery and enacted a new
Fugitive Slave Law requiring northerners to aid in the return of escaped slaves
to their masters. In words that linked his own feeble body to the body politic of
the Union, the aged and dying John Calhoun rejected the proposals as destructive of the rights of the South: "The cry of 'Union, union, the glorious union!'
can no more prevent disunion than the cry of 'Health, health, glorious health!'
on the part of the physician, can save a patient lying dangerously ill."

Webster's famous speech of March 7, 1850, in defense of Henry Clay's
Compromise resolution invoked again the heritage of the revolutionary
fathers that he had made his hallmark in speeches dedicating the Bunker Hill
Monument, where he had advised his listeners standing "among the sepulchres of our fathers" to beware the day when "faction and dismemberment
[would] obliterate for ever all hopes of the founders of our republic and the
great inheritance of their children." Conciliating slave interests and calling

for an end to antislavery agitation, Webster's reply glowed with optimism that Melville and others would quickly satirize. "Instead of dwelling in these caverns of darkness," Webster advised, "let us come out into the light of day; let us enjoy the fresh air of Liberty and Union. . . . Let us make our generation one of the strongest and brightest links in that golden chain which is destined, I fondly believe, to grapple the people of all the states to this Constitution for ages to come." The government of the United States, Webster proclaimed, had so far been entirely "beneficent" and had "trodden down no man's liberty" or "crushed no State." Antislavery writers, conscious of the suppressed liberties of African Americans, were quick to counter Webster's views with different interpretations of the revolutionary paradigm. Contemptuously alluding to Webster's "noble words" at his 1843 Bunker Hill speech, "the spot so reddened with the blood of our fathers," Theodore Parker answered Webster that "the question is, not if slavery is going to cease, and soon to cease, but shall it end as it ended in Massachusetts, in New Hampshire, in Pennsylvania, in New York, or shall it end as in St. Domingo? Follow the counsel of Mr. Webster—it will end in fire and blood."

Webster and others appealed to the Founding Fathers, whose views on slavery, embodied in the Constitution, were open to both proslavery and antislavery interpretation. Politicians in the North and the South alike conceived of America as a "family" presided over by benevolent paternal figures whose enormous achievement induced anxiety in the following generations and made them reluctant to contravene their inherited wisdom or to disturb the delicate equilibrium of the Union. In courting the attacks of Parker and others, Webster made his own appeal to the Revolution ironic, even (as Emerson said of the Fugitive Slave Law) "suicidal." Conversely, William Gilmore Simms and others on the proslavery side feared the "suicide" of disunion and war that they thought abolitionism would bring on. Which course was most likely to destroy the fragile Union was the implied subject of every slavery debate. Although his views on slavery were close to those of Clay, and although it would take him the length of the Civil War to reconcile his attempted salvation of the Union with the destruction of slavery, Abraham Lincoln was finally not so paralyzed as Webster by the burden of the Founding Fathers. However, if Lincoln's warning in the famous Lyceum Address of 1838 that "as a nation of freemen we must live through all time or die by suicide" did not forecast abolition, it did predict a crisis over slavery. Setting the context for his ostensible subject, "the perpetuation of our political institutions," Lincoln spoke against the kind of mob violence that took Elijah Lovejoy's life, and he chose as another example the lynching of "Negroes suspected of conspiring to raise an insurrection." Lincoln's address, often seen to desecrate the founders and to betray a monumental desire for personal power, marked his initial turn away from the mesmerizing influence of the revolutionary past, which he characterized as a "forest of giant oaks" now "despoiled of its verdure" and reduced to "mutilated limbs." Two decades later, in preserving the Union while abolishing slavery, Lincoln, not Webster, became the nation's tragic savior. In doing so, Lincoln carried the full weight of the revolutionary burden that had immobilized generation after generation on the issue of slavery, and he unified the contradictory symbolic sacrifices Stowe had portrayed in her 1851 antislavery sketch "The Two Altars, or, Two Pictures in One," which ironically compared the sacrifices of a family for the revolutionary cause at Valley Forge to the 1850 sacrifice of a fugitive slave on the "altar of liberty."

The crisis over the Union permeated the writing of Melville and Whitman, among others, but with the exceptions of Whittier, Stowe, and Douglass, the central literary figures of the antebellum period did not devote the greater part of their energies to antislavery writing as such. Among poets, Whitman (in *Drum-Taps*, 1865), Melville (in *Battle-Pieces*, 1866), and Emily Dickinson in scattered allusive poems wrote of the war itself with great power, and Whitman's democratic poems of the 1850s contain a number of references to the tragedy of slaves in bondage, at auction, or as fugitives. In "Song of Myself," for example, Whitman's searching phenomenological consciousness incorporates the experience of a pursued slave:

> I am the hounded slave, I wince at the bite of dogs,
> Hell and despair are upon me, crack and again crack the marksmen,
> I clutch the rails of the fence, my gore drips, thinn'd with the ooze of my skin,
> I fall on weeds and stones,
> The riders spur their unwilling horses, haul close,
> Taunt my dizzy ears and beat me violently over the head with whipstocks.

Most antislavery poetry was less distinguished, concerned primarily with the expression of outraged sentiment rather than with complex states of literary feeling. James Russell Lowell's *Biglow Papers*, the first series of which (1848) constituted a satiric poem on the Mexican War, implicitly castigated the wholesale extension of slavery that he contended the war would authorize, and he wrote a number of editorials for abolitionist newspapers. Lowell issued a second series of the *Biglow Papers* in 1867, devoted in part to the war, but his poems on the specific issue of slavery, like those of Holmes and most of all like the mass of antislavery verse appearing in reform periodicals, tended to rely on stylized rhetoric, as in "On the Capture of Fugitive Slaves Near Washington":

> Out from the land of bondage 't is decreed our slaves shall go,
> And signs to us are offered, as erst to Pharaoh;
> If we are blind, their exodus, like Israel's of yore,
> Through a Red Sea is doomed to be, whose surges are of gore.

Longfellow's *Poems on Slavery* (1842), collecting such poems as "The Slave's Dream," on freedom in Africa, "The Slave in the Dismal Swamp," and "The Quadroon Girl," was next to Whittier's work the most comprehensive poetic statement of antislavery. In "The Warning," for instance, Longfellow combines the theme of crisis over the meaning of the American Revolution with the possibility of a slave uprising that will destroy America itself:

> There is a poor, blind Samson in this land
>   Shorn of his strength and bound in bonds of steel,
> Who may, in some grim revel, raise his hand,
>   And shake the pillars of this Commonweal,
> Till the vast Temple of our liberties
> A shapeless mass of wreck and rubbish lies.

The most effective statements against slavery, however, came from essayists, not only maverick radicals like Garrison and feminists like the Grimké sisters but also writers associated with the literary and philosophical circles of New England. The main figures of Transcendentalism, Emerson and Thoreau, remained on the periphery of the battle, however, contributing important statements but expressing here as elsewhere their deep skepticism of organized reform movements. Emerson circumspectly alluded to the issue of slavery in his early essays, and he gradually came to support the cause more openly, speaking out in such addresses as "Emancipation in the British West Indies" (1844) and "The Fugitive Slave Law" (1851). Thoreau attacked the Mexican War as a proslavery ruse in "Resistance to Civil Government" (1849; reprinted as "Civil Disobedience" in 1894), celebrated John Brown's assault on Harper's Ferry in "A Plea for Captain John Brown" (1859), and mockingly condemned Webster and the Compromise in "Slavery in Massachusetts" (1854):

I hear a good deal said about trampling this law under foot. Why, one need not go out of his way to do that. This law rises not to the level of the head or the reason; its natural habitat is in the dirt. It was born and bred, and has its life, only in the dust and mire, on a level with the feet; and he who walks with freedom, and does not with Hindoo mercy avoid treading on every venomous reptile, will inevitably tread on it, and so trample it under foot,—and Webster, its maker, with it, like the dirt-bug and its ball.

But slavery, like Indian Removal, often seemed for Thoreau to be a philosophical conundrum rather than an immediate political problem.

Of greater importance were the writings of William Ellery Channing (1780–1842), the Boston Unitarian minister who had a significant influence on Emerson, Parker, and those instrumental in the formation of the Transcendentalist Club. The Unitarian emphasis on reason and the power of individual spirituality led Channing first to a gradualist doctrine in *Slavery* (1835), in which he chided abolitionists for their fanaticism. But his *Remarks on the Slavery Question* (1839), a reply to Henry Clay on the question of the annexation of Texas, emphasized the "contamination" of the North by slavery. Our moral feeling is "palsied," he wrote, and our merchants, when they cast their eyes south, see "Cotton, Cotton, nothing but Cotton. This fills the horizon of the South. What care they for the poor human tools by which it is reared?" Channing also condemned the sexual abuse of slave women but at the same time accepted the thesis of African docility, which ensured that whites need fear no war of retribution if slaves were emancipated: "The iron has eaten into [the slave's] soul, and this is worse than eating into the flesh." In "Emancipation" (1840) and *Duty of the Free States* (1842), Channing approached the central views of Garrison in the 1840s, disunion and the individual's right to disavow connection to all abusive political authority: "There is a law of humanity more primitive and divine than the law of the land. [Man] has higher claims than those of the citizen. He has rights which date before all charters and communities; not conventional, not repealable, but as eternal as the powers and laws of his being."

Channing's utopian belief in the power of the individual will, common enough among the Transcendentalists and Garrisonians but nonetheless impractical, is not unrelated to his conception of African American character.

The racist belief in African simplicity and meekness (a critical issue in all the sentimental literature on slavery both before and after its great testament, *Uncle Tom's Cabin*) is earnestly laid out in *Slavery*: "The African is so affectionate, imitative, and docile that in favorable circumstances he catches much that is good; and accordingly the influence of a wise and kind master will be seen in the very countenance of his slaves." This, of course, is just what the leading proslavery thinkers pointed out in advocating benevolent paternalism as the only system under which African Americans could survive and prosper. It is also the view parodied in that most brilliant of all critiques both of slavery and of northern myopia about it, Melville's "Benito Cereno" (1855). Whereas Hawthorne's views can only be construed as moderately proslavery, and Poe's complex symbolic and psychological treatment of the issue erupted in racist trauma, and Stowe's great work perpetuated divisive conceptions of racial character, Melville continually drove right to the heart of America's crisis. In *Mardi* (1849), his allegorical assault on manifest destiny, Melville caricatured the slaveholding South and especially Calhoun as "a cadaverous, ghost-like man" named Nulli who wields a bloody whip and contends that although the ancestors of his slaves may have had souls, "their souls have been bred out of their descendents; as the instinct of scent is killed in pointers." At the same time, however, Melville was attuned to the extravagance and ineffectiveness of much antislavery rhetoric. In *Benito Cereno* he caricatured the northern romantic view, advanced by Channing and others, that masters were dissipated aristocrats and their slaves docile, imitative (but brutalized) creatures, yet he also played upon fears of slave rebellion spreading throughout the Americas.

Melville built his tale upon the actual story of Amasa Delano (recorded in his 1817 *Narrative of Voyages in the Northern and Southern Hemispheres*), a New England captain who in 1805 rescued the Spanish captain Benito Cereno's ship from a revolt by its cargo of slaves. In changing the name of Benito Cereno's ship from the *Tryal* to the *San Dominick*, Melville invoked the revolution in San Domingo, represented in the South as a still smoldering volcano of Jacobin horrors, and by an intricate web of allusions and historical references virtually recounted the history of New World slavery in his tale, including contemporary U.S. contention over annexation of potentially rich slave territories in Cuba and Latin America. The Spanish captain is mocked as the prototypical languid slaveholder, whereas Delano, unable until the last moments of the story to perceive the fact that a rebellion has occurred but has been hidden from his view by an intricate masquerade staged by the black slave leader, Babo, is ridiculed as a benevolent but complacent northerner, content to criticize slavery but shocked when it leads to violence and revolt. As a response to the Compromise, which in part defined American policy in the territory acquired in the Mexican War, *Benito Cereno* exploits the collision of domestic and international interests that had previously arisen in the cases of revolt aboard the slave ships the *Creole* and the *Amistad*. Instead of envisioning a civil war between North and South, it anticipates, as well it might have in 1855, a struggle among three forces: a Protestant, Puritan tradition of democratic liberty deriving from the American Revolution; a Hispanic, Catholic world of slaveholding and despotism based on the dying monarchical values of Europe; and a black world of rebellion driving a wedge between the others and threatening political upheaval throughout the slaveholding world.

During the first half of the nineteenth century, as was noted before, Haiti remained a touchstone for arguments about the consequence of slave liberation in the New World. Although the island republic had its defenders, the common opinion was that its record, like that of emancipated Jamaica, was largely one of economic sloth and political barbarism. *De Bow's Review*, the influential organ of southern interests, carried an essay in 1854 typical in its critique of Haitian commerce and government. For over thirty years, the essay claims, the "march of civilization" had been dead in Haiti, its social condition one of sustained indolence and immorality:

From its discovery by Columbus to the present reign of Solouque, the olive branch has withered under its pestilential breath; and when the atheistical philosophy of revolutionary France added fuel to the volcano of hellish passions which raged in its bosom, the horrors of the island became a narrative which frightened our childhood, and still curdles our blood to read. The triumphant negroes refined upon the tortures of the Inquisition in their treatment of prisoners taken in battle. They tore them with red-hot pincers—sawed them asunder between planks—roasted them by a slow fire—or tore out their eyes with red-hot corkscrews.

As in Melville's ambiguous antislavery tale, the conflation of Spanish and French rule, coupled with the allusion to the Inquisition, links anti-Catholic and anti-Jacobin sentiment. Indeed, the rhetoric of manifest destiny in the Caribbean was often a mix of the two, and *Benito Cereno* thus envisioned an explosive pattern of revolt that was interlocked with U.S. ambitions in the

West and Mexico. The New England captain Amasa Delano, whose sunny optimism recalls Webster's embrace of the Compromise, confronts aboard the *San Dominick* the allegorical play of threats apparently offered to the United States by the New World at midcentury: Spanish misrule and deterioration combined with potential black insurrection and liberation dramatically realized in the subtle, heroic character of Babo.

Melville's imaginary transformation of Delano's true story undermined the romantic fantasy of African docility that Stowe and others promoted, and it was predicated on a conflict between Anglo-Americans and Spanish of the kind Theodore Parker had spoken of in his 1854 speech on "The Nebraska Question." As the "children of a decomposing State, time-worn and debauched," argued Parker, Spanish colonies in America were doomed to failure. Yet he thought that America's rabid claims of manifest destiny, often designed to conciliate slaveholding interests, were equally destructive of the ideals of liberty, which were not governed in America by monarchy and theocracy but by the "Almighty Dollar." A Boston Unitarian who took up the Transcendentalist cause but had few qualms about the use of violence, later supporting John Brown's attack on Harper's Ferry, Parker (1810–60) became a passionate spokesman for antislavery and other reform causes in the 1840s. He compared Webster to the traitor Benedict Arnold and lamented the "prostitution of [his] kingly power of thought," dramatizing him as a great tragic figure who had fallen from being "the hero of Bunker Hill" to become "a keeper of slavery's dogs." In "A Letter on Slavery" (1847), Parker stated succinctly the case against paternalism that Melville's tale of rebellion corroborated: "the relation of master and slave begins in violence; it must be sustained by violence, the systematic violence of general laws, or the irregular violence of individual caprice." The very idea of slavery, wrote Parker, echoing a common figure later to appear in Stowe's subtitle to *Uncle Tom's Cabin*, "is to use a man as a thing."

During the 1840s and 1850s, Parker and Garrison were rivaled in their attacks on slavery only by Frederick Douglass and, among whites, by Wendell Phillips (1811–84), one of the movement's most effective lecturers. Recruited by Garrison, Phillips nonetheless disregarded the former's idealistic advocacy of nonviolence and anti-institutionalism. He was particularly adept at creating an image of the South as a living hell, boiling over with punishment, sexual abuse, and misery, and he understood that masses of common people could be brought into agitated action more easily than recalcitrant institutions such as the church, the press, and political parties. His most famous address, *The Philosophy of the Abolition Movement* (1853), was a summary of the antislavery crusade, giving credit to eminent people and works, interspersed with fiery rhetoric of the kind that was echoed during the same years in the lectures and writings of Douglass:

> The South is one great brothel, where half a million women are flogged to prostitution, or, worse still, are degraded to believe it honorable. The public squares of half our great cities echo to the wail of families torn asunder at the auction-block; [there is] no one of our rivers that has not closed over the negro seeking in death a refuge from a life too wretched to bear; thousands of fugitives skulk along our highways, afraid to tell their names, and trembling at the sight of a human being; free men are kidnapped in our streets to be plunged into the hell of slavery; and now and then one, as if by miracle, after long years, returns to make men aghast with his tale. The press says, "It is all right"; and the pulpit cries, "Amen." . . . The slave lifts up his imploring eyes, and sees in every face but ours the face of an enemy.

Phillips's allusion to the tale of the returned kidnapped slave was based on the fascinating narrative of Solomon Northup, and his piercing but clichéd rhetoric borrowed from countless short stories and magazine essays, as well as the kind of documentation collected in Weld's *Slavery As It Is*. Along with Weld and Phillips, William Goodell was similarly interested in exposing the codes and actual practices that lay behind the peculiar institution, and he did so in *Slavery and Anti-Slavery* (1852), a work dealing with both hemispheres, and a best-selling volume entitled *The American Slave Code* (1853), which was simply a compendium of laws governing slaveholding and manumission practices that made brutal reading in their own right. Both the fugitive slaves and the New England lecturers frequently cited southern laws that for all practical purposes damned themselves.

The number of antislavery writers who could base their work on at least marginal experience of the South was great, given the popularity of travel writing in the period, but relatively few with direct experience produced work of high literary quality or accuracy. The unusual case of Hinton Rowan Helper, a southern abolitionist but also a virulent racist, has been discussed above. The antislavery Transcendentalist Moncure Conway (1832–1907) came from a prominent Virginia slaveholding family. His *Autobiography*, not published until 1904, reveals in retrospect his conversion to an abolitionist perspective; and his spiritual essay *The Rejected Stone* (1861) praised the Civil War as a providential and revolutionary action ensuring that "the kingdoms of this world shall become the Kingdom of Christ forever." But the testimony of converted southerners like Conway or the Grimké sisters was relatively rare. With the important exception of fugitive slaves, only several novelists and a handful of travelers gave reliable firsthand accounts of the actual lives of slaves. Rather, the plantation itself was more often the subject. A typical travel work, C. G. Parsons's *Inside View of Slavery; Or, a Tour Among the Planters* (1855), with an introduction by Stowe, condemned the inefficiency of the slave economy and the brutal hardening of the master class. One of the most impressive works in its scope of observation and, at the time, the influence of its argument was the landscape architect Frederick Law Olmsted's *The Cotton Kingdom* (1861), a distillation of his three previous travel works, *A Journey in the Seaboard Slave States* (1856), *A Journey Through Texas* (1857), and *A Journey in the Back Country* (1860). Expressing the northern Free Soil sentiments of his day, Olmsted wrote with a keen eye for the details of plantation and more common life in the South. Yet he mistakenly portrayed slavery as a system in complete economic decay, with the majority of whites in the South nearly as degraded as the slaves of the few successful planters.

Much trenchant commentary on slavery came from foreign visitors to the United States. The relative success of British abolitionism, which had played a part in the end of slavery in the British West Indies in 1833, gave force to the attacks by Harriet Martineau in *Society in America* (1837) and *The Martyr Age in the United States* (1840), by Charles Dickens in *American Notes* (1842), by Frances Trollope in *Domestic Manners of the Americans* (1832) and in her fictional slave narrative *Jonathan Jefferson Whitlaw* (1841), and by Fanny Kemble in *Journal of a Residence on a Georgia Plantation, 1838–39* (1863). Among French commentators, the famous tour of Gustave de Beaumont and Alexis de Tocqueville (who collaborated on a volume concerning the ostensible reason for their tour, *On the Penitentiary System in the United States*) resulted in the former's romantic novel of a tragic mulatto, *Marie, or Slavery in the United States* (1835), which appeared in the same year as the latter's monumental *Democracy in America*. Tocqueville's forecast of the inevitable end of slavery came with predictions of despair and race hatred on both sides, and his assessment of the meaning of modern slavery in the Western world, like so many of his observations, struck to the heart of the questions of liberty and democratic liberalism that Europe had faced and America had brought to a new crisis:

From the moment when the Europeans took their slaves from a race different from their own, which many of them considered inferior to all other human races, and assimilation with whom they regarded with horror, they assumed that slavery would be eternal, for there is no intermediate state that can be durable between the excessive inequality created by slavery and the complete equality which is the natural result of independence.... They first violated every right of humanity by their treatment of the Negro and then taught him the value and inviolability of those rights. They have opened their ranks to their slaves, but when they tried to come in, they drove them out again with ignominy. Wishing to have servitude, they have nevertheless been drawn against their will or unconsciously toward liberty, without the courage to be either completely wicked or entirely just.

His Terrible Swift Sword

Despite the careful portrayals of the slaveholding South by Olmsted and others, truth and the representations of sentimental fiction often merged in the pictures drawn by antislavery writers. Still, if they were romantically heightened, they were seldom completely distorted, a fact that explains the great success of *Uncle Tom's Cabin* (1851), which uncovered a moral truth transcending statistical data and full of emotive power. Born in Litchfield, Connecticut, the seventh of Lyman Beecher's nine children by his first wife, Harriet Beecher Stowe (1811–96) aided her sister Catharine, a pioneer in women's education, at the Hartford Female Seminary and subsequently contributed to several of Catharine's important textbooks when they taught together in Cincinnati. Influenced by the increasingly vocal antislavery activity of her brothers and the family's friendships with important abolitionists such as James G. Birney, Salmon Chase, and Gamaliel Bailey (later the editor of the *National Era*, where *Uncle Tom's Cabin* would be serialized from 1851 to 1852), Stowe too turned against the ineffective and often abstract views of her father and her husband, Calvin Stowe, a Lane professor of religion, whom she married in 1836. Although her direct experience of the slave South consisted of a brief visit to Kentucky in 1833, Stowe's family and friends had regular contact with men and women active in the underground railroad, and Cincinnati in the 1830s was a hotbed of antislavery activity and stories of escaped slaves, some of which found their way into Stowe's masterpiece. By the time she resettled in Maine, when Calvin took a job at Bowdoin College in 1850, Stowe had written several antislavery sketches (among other New England and midwestern stories), and she was poised to respond once the controversial Compromise of 1850, with its hated Fugitive Slave Law, was passed.

The literature of antislavery controversy into which Stowe entered so dramatically had in the previous twenty years produced a number of significant documents, though few of them reached an audience more than a fraction the size of Stowe's. The great speeches of Garrison and Phillips, for example, the congressional efforts of Adams, and even Whittier's popular poetry had made little impression. In addition to Weld's *American Slavery As It Is*, Stowe's sources were scripture, hymns, the sermons and religious readings of her family library, and probably a handful of antislavery fictions and slave narratives. In her *Key to Uncle Tom's Cabin* (1853), a documentary work put together by Stowe to prove that her novel had a basis in real events, she noted parallels to her work in the lives and slave stories of Henry Bibb, William Wells Brown, Solomon Northup, Frederick Douglass, Josiah Henson, and Lewis Clarke; indeed, the last two men built careers on the dubious claims that they were the models for the characters of Uncle Tom and George Harris.

Among fictional works that may have influenced Stowe, the most famous were Whittier's ghostwritten *Narrative of James Williams*, noted above, which drew a picture of ruthless plantation cruelty that was condemned as spurious by southerners (the volume had been briefly promoted by the American Anti-Slavery Society as the preeminent slave narrative until it was revealed to have been largely fabricated by Williams); and Richard Hildreth's *The Slave; or, Memoirs of Archy Moore* (1836), which offered a number of potential parallels in plot and character that were, if anything, watered down and undermined by Stowe. The mixed-race Archy and his wife, Cassy, may lie behind Stowe's George and Eliza Harris, for example, but their lives end in tragic separation; and the black slave Tom, at first religious and obedient, becomes a fugitive rebel after witnessing the flogging death of his wife at the hands of an overseer. Tracked down by the overseer, Tom calmly murders him. Moreover, in Hildreth's novel, as in most authentic narratives, the Christianity and domesticity valued by Stowe are shown to be thoroughly corrupted by plantation life. What Stowe understood, however, was that her audience was less likely to be moved by the logic of revenge than by sentimental stereotypes: "There is no arguing with *pictures*," she wrote her editor, "and everybody is impressed by them, whether they mean to be or not."

The stereotypes that would become famous—Eliza crossing the ice, Eva's melodramatic death, Tom's martyrdom at the hands of Legree—were scenes calculated, and driven by the book's great narrative powers, to demand the reader's sympathetic response. When it appeared in book form in 1852, 50,000 copies were sold within eight weeks, 300,000 within a year, and 1 million in America and England combined by early 1853. It added an entirely new dimension to a crusade that had often bogged down in petty quarrels and useless theorizing. By giving flesh-and-blood reality to the inhuman system for which the Fugitive Slave Law now required the North, as well as the South, to be responsible, it became a touchstone for popular sentiment, which was already reaching new heights in the North in response to the Mexican War and the Compromise (and soon to be heightened even further by passage of the Kansas-Nebraska Act). Stowe was hardly the first to call attention to slavery's destruction of both black and white families, but her novel perfectly combined sentimental fiction and the antislavery polemic. In scene after scene, the fragmentation of black households and its corrosive moral effect on white consciousness are her focal points. When the slave Lucy's child is sold by the unfeeling slave trader Haley, for example, Stowe writes bitterly: "You can get used to such things, too, my friend; and it is the great object of recent efforts to make our whole northern community used to them, for the glory of the Union."

Stowe's powerful use of families and familial metaphors drew not only on the notion of sentiment attached to "union" by Webster, Lincoln, and others but also on the more radical elements of domestic ideology that challenged the traditional patriarchal authority of society. According to some antislavery activists—for instance, the black feminist Maria Stewart, noted above—patriarchal dominance was epitomized by the degradations of slavery. The more moderate domestic tradition in fiction and in social thought declared women the moral superiors of men but at the same time attributed to them specific characteristics of sensitivity, docility, and weakness—the same qualities, in fact, that romantic racialists (Stowe among them) attributed to blacks. Drawing to itself the faltering powers of the clergy, the domestic tradition separated the "woman's sphere" of homemaking and the moral instruction of children from the masculine world of commerce and politics. However, it also risked providing a new rationale for the subordination of women which was recognized and resisted by the era's more ardent feminists. *Uncle Tom's Cabin* is split between these two kinds of power—domestic "influence" and public activism—for if it acts out patterns of bondage and rebellion that included for Stowe not just slavery and the Calvinist dogma of her father but also the bondage of women within the domestic ideal, the novel is in each case ambivalent about the limits and means of such rebellion.

From the 1820s through the 1840s the domestic ideal became an issue in various social reform causes; and as the split in ranks over female partic-ipation at the 1840 antislavery conventions suggests, not only men but women themselves were divided over the proper limits of their role. Catharine Beecher, for example, eschewed women's direct involvement in politics. In her *Essay on Slavery and Abolitionism* (1837), she denounced abolitionist societies for their public stridency; and carefully separating the duties of men from those of women, she warned that woman's deviation from the place she is "appointed to fill by the dispensations of heaven" would deprive children of their proper moral instruction and subvert the cause of reform: "For the more intelligent a woman becomes, the more she can appreciate the wisdom of that ordinance that appointed her subordinate station, and the more her taste will conform to the graceful and dignified retirement and submission it involves."

Beecher's ire was directed in particular at Sarah and Angelina Grimké, whose speaking tour of 1837 had aroused such controversy that the Congre-gational clergy of New England felt compelled to attack their inappropri-ate involvement in political affairs in a pastoral letter that argued that when woman "assumes the place and tone of man . . . she yields the power which God has given her for her own protection, and her character becomes unnatu-ral." The "promiscuous conversation of females with regard to things which ought not to be named" (i.e., slavery and sexual abuse on the plantation) dis-turbs their modesty and opens the way "for degeneracy and ruin." In addi-tion to their offensive lectures, Angelina had published *Appeal to the Christian Women of the South* (1836), which counseled women to study the Bible and seek ways to change the laws governing slavery. The attack of the clergy and Catharine Beecher's critique of feminist activism brought forth replies from both Sarah, in *Letters on the Condition of Women and the Equality of the Sexes* (1838), and Angelina, now the wife of Theodore Weld, in *Letters to Catharine E. Beecher* (1838). The latter volume, a group of essays first published in Garrison's *Liberator*, argued that a woman's rights are "an integral part of her moral being" and that "the mere circumstance of sex does not give to man higher rights and responsibilities than to women." Along with Lucretia Mott, Elizabeth Cady Stanton, and Susan B. Anthony, the Grimké sisters were instrumental in allying the forces of antislavery and feminism and defining women's public sphere of action as an outgrowth of larger movements of democratic social reform.

The appeal for feminist activism in *Uncle Tom's Cabin* stops short of the steps proposed by the Grimkés, Mott, and Stanton. The influence of its principal female characters is largely restricted to the "woman's sphere" of Christian example and moral instruction. But the book itself, however much it conforms to sentimental models, was an act of risk and of tentative rebellion, insofar as it attacked patriarchal society and likened the victimization of slaves to the suppression of women. The great emotive power of the novel arises from its capacity to equate the stations of the two groups, which are linked by children, a third supposedly oppressed group. In this respect, *Uncle Tom's Cabin* plays upon the potential conversion of sentiment into action adumbrated by another abolitionist, Lydia Maria Child. Both women and blacks, Child wrote, "are characterized by affection more than intellect; both have a strong development of the religious sentiment; both are exceedingly adhesive in their attachments; both, comparatively speaking, have a tendency to submission; and hence, both have been kept in subjection by physical force, and considered rather in the light of property, than as individuals." Child's characterization, advanced in letters and in *An Appeal in Favor of That Class of Americans Called Africans* (1836), is given further dimension in her story "Black Anglo Saxons," in which a group of slaves discusses the alternatives of flight or violent rebellion, with the mulattoes endorsing bloodshed and the blacks arguing for mercy and docility. Racial divisions here correspond to sexual divisions, with feminine, maternal submission and blackness ranged against masculine, paternal aggression and whiteness, as they are in Stowe's novel. If the ethical influence of mothers and wives was entirely to succeed in Stowe's novel, a host of problems attributable to male "lust" and patriarchal governance in politics and the family would disappear, and slavery—in which the abuse of women is taken to its extreme, as a number of northerners (like Wendell Phillips) and some southerners (like Mary Chesnut) suggested in characterizing the plantation as a brothel—would give way to a Christian democratic unity.

Stowe's use of the figure of the household, ranging from the maternal perfection of the Quakers to the degeneracy of Legree's house of sin, draws on
the political rhetoric of union as a house threatened with division, a metaphor
made famous in Lincoln's use of the New Testament phrase in his 1858 speech
on the "House Divided" but in common use in the years before. In its gothic
exploration of licentious behavior Stowe's novel diverges from the constrained
role of influence advised by Catharine Beecher in her writings on abolitionism
and in her handbook on homemaking, *Treatise on Domestic Economy* (1841).
Although Stowe herself later contributed to a revised edition of the *Treatise*, it
seems unlikely that she intended to endorse Beecher's argument that woman's
role was to support Anglo-American manifest destiny by subordinating herself to man and contributing to the civil stability necessary to build "a glorious
temple, whose base shall be coextensive with the bounds of the earth, whose
summit shall pierce the skies, [and] whose splendor shall beam on all lands."
Stowe's critique imagined the house not as a separate sphere but as a model
of the political world, and her approach to moral influence more resembled
Margaret Fuller's, who wrote in *Woman in the Nineteenth Century* (1845), "you
see the men, how they are willing to sell shamelessly the happiness of countless
generations of fellow-creatures, the honor of their country, and their immortal
souls, for a money market and political power." In thus attacking the annexation of Texas and the extension of slavery it would promote, Fuller took a
stance similar to Stowe's: "Do you not feel within you that which can reprove
them, which can check, which can convince them? You would not speak in
vain; whether each in her own home, or banded in unison. . . . Let not slip the
occasion, but do something to lift off the curse incurred by Eve."

Bypassing the question of Original Sin and the Calvinist tradition of her
father, Stowe embraced the New Testament and interpreted literally the saving
power of Jesus, drawing out the feminine aspects of his character and depicting him, in essence, as a woman. Besides Tom, her central Christ figure is Eva:
a child, a female, a typological figuring of Christ descended not from Adam
but from Eve, and—as her full name Evangeline implies—the book's most
powerful evangelist. In Eva are united the ministerial leader of evangelistic
social reform and the prime actor of sentimental literature, the child. The
proliferation of children in antislavery literature and in books and journals
specifically directed at children, such as *The Child's Anti-Slavery Book* and *Anti-
Slavery Alphabet*, assumed that, instead of needing moral instruction, children

were perhaps best equipped to give it. Asexual and uncorrupted, the child, like Eva, was often imagined to be the "only true democrat." The antislavery tradition of "benevolence," which elevated feeling above reason and advocated the democratic extension of rights to the lowliest of society, sought to put into practice the radical doctrines of equality generated in the age of revolution by linking them to the evangelical power of conversion and portraying them in scenes of deliberately theatrical sentimentality. Eva's pious life and death are not simply ornamental melodrama. They construct a bridge between pathos and reform that is morally superior to the corruptions of the adult, masculine world—the world, Stowe suggests throughout, of organized religion, which has failed to speak and act against slavery. Subsuming the failed power of institutional religion into the realm of sentimental social reform, Eva's death belongs to the period's enormous literature of mourning and consolation but transcends its simple pieties as Stowe reconceives Christian man in the image of beatific child-woman.

In the character of Tom, which was to receive the greatest criticism of later generations of readers, Stowe sought to combine her ideals of feminine power and African meekness. A martyr but hardly a coward, Tom is murdered because he refuses to betray Cassy and Emmeline and to capitulate to Legree's demand that he renounce his religious beliefs. Yet the fate of Tom's character was to become, along with Eva's, the most frequently re-created figure of the popular minstrel and burlesque shows (which made *Uncle Tom's Cabin* even more famous than Stowe could) and to exemplify black humiliation in African American culture of the next century. Tom and the corrupt dramatic versions of the novel became indistinguishable to later audiences, but even in its own time the book produced a flood of imitation: drama, poetry, songs, engravings, and other consumable artifacts (card games, silverware, needlepoint, and the like) that capitalized on its most saccharine scenes. The traveling "Tom troupes" purged any radical messages from the blackface drama (performed almost exclusively by whites until later in the nineteenth century) and made it conform to the degraded entertainment of the minstrel's song and dance. On stage, Topsy sang "Topsy's Song: I Am but a Little Nigger Gal"; the famous minstrel performer T. D. Rice "jumped Jim Crow" in the role of Uncle Tom; Tom and Eva were reunited in cardboard heavens; and abolitionism itself was attacked in such songs as "Happy Are We, Darkies so Gay." The further exploitation of the work on stage and in film continued into the twentieth century, destroying the integrity of Stowe's vision and accomplishment, which had made *Uncle Tom's Cabin* perhaps the most influential novel in the later nineteenth century for both white and black authors. By the modern era, the book's stereotypes had overwhelmed its moral intentions, inspiring one black writer, Richard Wright, to ironically entitle his collection of stories about black life in the Jim Crow South *Uncle Tom's Children* (1940) and another, Ishmael Reed, to burlesque Stowe and the antislavery tradition in *Flight to Canada* (1976).

Even if one rescues Tom from history's manipulations, however, his character as drawn by Stowe remains problematic. His conspicuous nonviolence— in contrast to the examples of San Domingo and Turner's Southampton rebellion, and in contrast to the calls for violence by Douglass and other antislavery leaders, black and white—stranded his power in the realm of sentiment, which might lead to direct antislavery action but might also produce only a cathartic release of tension. Stowe's next novel, *Dred: A Tale of the Great Dismal Swamp* (1856), modeled its titular hero on Nat Turner (and even included a copy of his *Confessions* as an appendix) but concentrated on his religious delusions and failed to reenact his dangerous revolt. In *Uncle Tom's Cabin*, moreover, it is the mixed-race George Harris, goaded by his "white blood," who invokes the revolutionary fervor of the Founding Fathers and demands his rights. Even Garrison, the prime abolitionist voice of nonviolent tactics, who once nominated Jesus Christ for president, found in *Uncle Tom's Cabin* a reflection of his own confusion:

We are curious to know whether Mrs. Stowe is a believer in the duty of nonresistance for the white man, under all possible outrage and peril, as well as for the black man. . . . When [slaves] are spit upon and buffeted, outraged and oppressed, talk not then of a non-resisting Savior—it is fanaticism! . . . Talk not of servants being obedient to their masters—let the blood of the tyrants flow! How is this to be explained or reconciled? Is there one law of submission and non-resistance for the black man, and another law of rebellion and conflict for the white man? When it is the whites who are trodden in the dust, does Christ justify them in taking up arms to vindicate their rights? And when it is the blacks who are thus treated, does Christ require them to be patient, harmless, long-suffering, and forgiving? And are there two Christs?

Even as they support her argument on behalf of a feminized, maternal world view, both Tom's martyrdom and George Harris's advocacy of a colonization movement that will found a millennial Christian nation in Africa indicate Stowe's grave anxieties about black rebellion and about the ultimate effects of emancipation.

Lincoln's own comparable hesitations about emancipation did not prevent him from being attacked by racists, and he often had to defend himself from charges that he favored miscegenation. In response to the Emancipation Proclamation, one southern pamphleteer wrote *Uncle Tom's Drama*, a play in which white maidens with "quivering limbs" and "snow-white bosoms, that ever throbbed in angelic purity," suffered "untold outrage, woe and wrong" at the hands of "Black Ourang-Outangs," who dragged them down in order to "gratify their brutal instincts." Northern apprehensions about miscegenation produced equally repellent racist prophecies; but more often the North, as John Van Evrie and others charged, romanticized the mulatto and made slaveholding miscegenation the epitome of domestic tragedy. Typical examples include Joseph Holt Ingraham's *The Quadroone; or, St. Michael's Day* (1841), a historical romance of creole New Orleans, and Lydia Maria Child's "The Quadroons," included in *Fact and Fiction* (1846), in which the illegitimate daughter of the mixed-blood heroine is seized and sold as a slave. Novels written in the wake of Stowe's capitalized on both the risk of miscegenation and the destruction of families. In Van Buren Denslow's *Owned and Disowned; or, the Chattel Child* (1857), the planter's mulatto daughter, sold as a slave, is rescued and becomes an antislavery crusader; in Emily C. Pierson's *Jamie Parker, A Fugitive* (1851), the black hero is reunited with his family in the North; in Hezekiah Hosmer's *Adela, the Octoroon* (1860), the mulatto daughter of a benevolent planter is forced by an evil suitor to flee north; and in Mary H. [Langdon] Pike's *Ida May* (1854), a northern white girl is kidnapped and sold into slavery. Dion Boucicault's popular play *The Octoroon* (1859), based on Mayne Reid's novel *The Quadroon* (1856), ended in the heroine's tragic death but was inadvertently so farcical that it was easily parodied by the Christy Minstrels in *The Moctroon*.

Among the more interesting minor antislavery novels written in the 1850s are Elizabeth Roe's *Aunt Leanna* (1855), which follows a northern family to Kentucky, where they become slaveholders but work for emancipation and colonization (in order to stop the spread of black labor to Kansas and Nebraska); and Emily C. Pearson's *Cousin Franck's Household* (1853), which, although sympathetic to the South, dwells on the separation of slave families and their escapes to the North. Almost proslavery in his sympathies, Nehemiah Adams wrote in his novel *The Sable Cloud* (1861) that "a system which makes Uncle Toms out of African savages is not an unmixed evil." Adams's essays in *A South-Side View of Slavery* (1854) similarly adopted the racist view that under benevolent masters slaves were redeemed and blessed. Abolitionism, he maintained, was a hindrance to emancipation, especially after being goaded by *Uncle Tom's Cabin*, which "has entered like an alcoholic distillation into the veins and blood of very many people in the free States." Equally ambivalent, Bayard Rush Hall's *Frank Freeman's Barbershop* (1852) satirized both sides of the slavery controversy and ridiculed northern fascination with the mulatto theme: "Writers of *fiction kill off* the jet black—not knowing how to *work them* advantageously to the North."

Hall's complaint, its glib tone aside, was well founded, but he failed to grasp the importance of racial mixing (given the sentimental expectations of the popular audience) and its power to expose the operation of northern prejudices that were often as destructive of black aspirations as slavery. Black writers' handling of the questions of slaveholding miscegenation and life in the North will be considered in more detail below in the context of the rise of the slave narrative and black abolitionism. In particular, these writers responded to *Uncle Tom's Cabin* by both incorporating and subverting Stowe's vision. Like Frederick Douglass, most of them sought the end of slavery through political action and the end of race hatred through education and integration. Stowe, on the other hand, for all the great power of her novel, conceived of colonization in Africa as the answer to inevitable contention over labor and social issues. Only with extraordinary caution, in the last pages of her novel, did she seek sanction for the violent overthrow of slavery in the suppressed Calvinistic vengeance of her father's religion: "This is an age of the world when ... every nation that carries in its bosom great and unredressed injustice has in it the elements of [the] last convulsion. . . . Christians! every time you pray that the kingdom of Christ may come, can you forget that prophecy associates, in dread fellowship, the *day of vengeance* with the year of his redeemed?"

The "wrath of Almighty God," however it might make itself known, was Stowe's solution; and when the war came, she wrote that it was "God's will that this nation—the North as well as the South—should deeply and terribly suffer for the sin of consenting to and encouraging the great oppressions of the South." Like Lincoln, she thought that "the blood of the poor slave, that had cried for so many years from the ground in vain, should be answered by the blood of the sons from the best hearthstones through all the free States." Although the war was almost a decade away when *Uncle Tom's Cabin* appeared, her work anticipated its rhetoric as it had summed up and brought into new focus, intentionally or not, the rhetorics of antislavery polemic, of sentimental domesticity, and even of the narratives of fugitive slaves. No work exceeded the novel in its impact on the public (though it can hardly be said to have caused the Civil War, as Abraham Lincoln is supposed to have remarked upon meeting Stowe), and only Frederick Douglass and Harriet Jacobs now challenge Stowe's position as the leading antislavery writer.

In iconographic stature, Abraham Lincoln was to become the nation's white embodiment of the spirit of emancipation, even if his views on abolition were less than clear. In his great speeches and in the symbolic role of sacrificial victim his assassination on Good Friday imposed, it was Lincoln who inadvertently gave credence to Stowe's vision. Wary of emancipation, fearful about miscegenation and free black labor, and uncertainly favoring colonization, Lincoln (1809–65) still abolished slavery and saved the Union, doing so as though in accordance with a divine plan. His eloquent conception of the war as an act of judgment in his second inaugural speech in 1865 gave shape to his own rebellion against the Founding Fathers and to the North's participation in the national sacrifice:

If we shall suppose that American slavery is one of those offenses which, in the providence of God, must needs come, but which, having continued through His appointed time, He now wills to remove, and that He now gives to both North and South this terrible war, as the woe due to those by whom the offense came, shall we discern therein any departure from those divine attributes which the believers in a living God always ascribe to Him? . . . if God wills that it continue until all the wealth piled by the bondsman's two hundred and fifty years of unrequited toil shall be sunk, and until every drop of blood drawn with the lash shall be paid by another drawn by the sword, as was said three thousand years ago, so still it must be said, "The judgments of the Lord are true and righteous altogether."

Like Stowe and others, Lincoln came to imagine the Civil War as a purifying redemption of America's great sin, accomplished only through violent purgation. The popularity of the view was best indicated in Julia Ward Howe's

"The Battle Hymn of the Republic," first published in 1862, with its apocalyptic vision of God's judgment:

> Mine eyes have seen the glory of the coming of the Lord;
> He is trampling out the vintage where the grapes of wrath are stored;
> He hath loosed the fateful lightning of his terrible swift sword;
> His truth is marching on. . . .

Howe's hymn codified the New England Protestant interpretation of the war— a response appropriate to the psychological blockage and moral darkening that the conscious (or unconscious) contemplation of slavery could produce over a period of decades. Lincoln, it might be said, provided a political version of that response. As noted above, his Lyceum Address of 1838 foreshadowed the role he would play in overcoming the ambivalence of the Founding Fathers on the question of slavery and grounding the politics of union *and* African American liberation in an American revolutionary tradition. Not only would the whole of his career seem in retrospect to lead to his own sacrificial greatness, but his magnificent orations, surpassing in their poetic beauty and expression of central American values all spoken words in the period, would seem to have moved toward the vision of war announced in his 1865 inaugural speech.

His debates with Senator Stephen Douglas in 1858 and his Cooper Union speech of 1860, on the problem of slavery and the Constitution, show Lincoln at his political best. But his most significant speeches transcend the politics of the day even as they remain firmly rooted in them. Driven in part by the relative failures of his early political career, Lincoln developed a style of thought and speech that linked humility and an identification with common people to a lucid articulation of his own potential as a leader. The 1838 Lyceum speech, inviting comparison to Caesar or Napoleon, showed Lincoln imperfectly in control of his own ambitions: "Towering genius disdains a beaten path. It seeks regions hitherto unexplored. It sees no distinction in adding story to story upon the monuments of fame erected to the memory of others." The lull in his political fortunes before the 1850s seems to have tempered Lincoln's egotism with a degree of humor, melancholy, and poetry, and to have brought into focus the mature rhetorical brilliance that coincided with his rise to the role of providential savior of the Union.

The crisis over the Kansas-Nebraska Act in 1854 elevated Lincoln to a position of fresh power as he began directly to challenge the leadership of Stephen

Douglas; and his formal alliance with the Republican Party in 1856 set him on the road to immortality as the "great emancipator." Nonetheless, some of his most significant speeches are marked not by a forthright opposition to slavery or the South but by ambiguity and conciliation, an index of his foremost dedication not to the end of black bondage but to the preservation of the Union. For example, the famous House Divided speech, part of his debates with Douglas in the 1858 Senate race, borrowed a New Testament metaphor resonant with the nation's impending political splintering, yet it remained uncertain where Lincoln's analysis would lead. His detection of a proslavery conspiracy behind the Dred Scott decision did not clarify his central claim: "I believe this government cannot endure permanently half slave and half free. I do not expect the Union to be dissolved—I do not expect the house to fall—but I do expect it will cease to be divided. It will become all one thing, or all the other." Nevertheless, an earlier speech in reply to Douglas in 1857 attacked Douglas and, dwelling on the Dred Scott decision, argued that the position of both slaves and free blacks in America had deteriorated since the Revolution:

In those days, our Declaration of Independence was held sacred by all, and thought to include all; but now, to aid in making the bondage of the negro universal and eternal, it is assailed, and sneered at, and construed, and hawked at, and torn, till, if its framers could rise from their graves, they could not at all recognize it. All the powers of the earth seem rapidly combining against him [the Negro]. Mammon is after him; ambition follows, and philosophy follows, and the Theology of the day is fast joining the cry. They have him in his prison house; they have searched his person, and left no prying instrument with him. One after another they have closed the heavy iron doors upon him, and now they have him, as it were, bolted in with a lock of a hundred keys, which can never be unlocked without the concurrence of every key; the keys in the hands of a hundred different men, and they scattered to a hundred different and distant places.

Lincoln's wonderful elaboration of the metaphor of the locked prison house indicates a style in contrast with the brevity and precision of his more famous utterances such as the House Divided speech and the Gettysburg Address of 1863. In all cases, however, his remarkable use of repetition, subordination, and trope drives the moral truth of his argument with relentless and enchanting power. At the same time, his metaphors often revealed a moral tension within the concept of black freedom that was not peculiar to Lincoln alone but was indicative of northern ambivalence about social and economic forms of integration. In a further reply to Stephen Douglas (one that anticipated his later responses to false inflammatory charges that the Republican Party endorsed miscegenation), Lincoln remarked:

There is a natural disgust in the minds of nearly all white people at the idea of an indiscriminate amalgamation of the white and black races. . . . I protest against the counterfeit logic which concludes that, because I do not want a black woman for a slave I must necessarily want her as a wife. . . . In some respects she is certainly not my equal; but in her natural right to eat the bread she earns with her own hands without asking the leave of any one else, she is my equal, and the equal of all others.

Likewise, because he took the view that the founders had envisioned the "ultimate extinction" of slavery, he could adopt a moderate stand in the important Cooper Union speech of 1860:

Wrong as we think slavery is, we can yet afford to let it alone where it is, because that much is due to the necessity arising from its actual presence in the nation; but can we, while our votes will prevent it, allow it to spread into the national Territories, and to overrun us here in the free States? . . . Neither let us be slandered from our duty by false accusations against us, nor frightened from it by menaces of destruction to the government, nor of dungeons to ourselves. Let us have faith that right makes might, and in that faith let us to the end dare to do our duty as we understand it.

Both his ability to lead and his tragic stature were shored up by such conservative views, which withstood pressure from all sides at once. Dedication to the preservation of the Union at nearly any cost made Lincoln the complex figure he was and prompted his most moving and, at the same time, most troubled thoughts. His first inaugural speech in 1861 was perhaps the last moment (if one of false hopes) when he spoke both as the westerner and southerner he in fact was and as the northerner and easterner he had become, trying in vain to knit together the fragments of the now imperiled Union. Describing secession as anarchy, Lincoln appealed to the people of both sections not to "break our bonds of affection. The mystic chords of memory, stretching from every battlefield and patriot grave to every living heart and hearth-stone all over this broad land, will yet swell the chorus of the Union when again touched, as surely they will be, by the better angels of our nature." The speech is not necessarily one of Lincoln's greatest, but its concluding attempt to reconcile North and South presaged the practical statement of paradoxically unified sectional hopes he expressed in the second inaugural address: "Both [sides] read the same Bible, and pray to the same God; and each invokes His aid against the other. . . . The prayers of both could not be answered—that of neither has been answered fully."

Lincoln's assassination, foreseen in one of his own dreams, completed the role of tragic democratic king he had played. Whitman's poetic tribute to his death and the nation's mourning, "When Lilacs Last in the Dooryard Bloom'd," has remained the most famous literary response; but Emerson's eulogy perhaps strikes a more fitting measure of simplicity: "He is the true history of the American people in his time. Step by step he walked before them; slow with their slowness, quickening his march by theirs, the true representative of his continent; an entirely public man; father of his country, the pulse of twenty millions throbbing in his heart, the thought of their minds articulated by his tongue." Indeed, Lincoln's own eloquence might be judged to be at its height of effectiveness on those occasions when what he said was imbued most fully with his own flawed vision. His own hesitations on the question of immediate freedom for African Americans have come over time to seem more vexing; but the act of liberation, whatever the nuances of Lincoln's motivations and however much military pragmatism overshadowed idealism in his decision, remains a fact. One month before the final Emancipation Proclamation was issued on January 1, 1863, Lincoln spoke in his annual message to Congress of the meaning of emancipation, choosing words whose promise was made real by the course of the war itself—even though true freedom for African Americans lay far in the future:

Fellow-citizens, *we* cannot escape history. We of this Congress and this administration will be remembered in spite of ourselves. No personal significance or insignificance can spare one or another of us. The fiery trial through which we pass will light us down, in honor or dishonor, to the latest generation. We *say* we are for the Union. The world will not forget that we say this. We know how to save the Union. The world knows we do know how to save it. . . . In *giving* freedom to the *slave*, we *assure* freedom to the *free*—honorable alike in what we give and what we preserve. We shall nobly save or meanly lose the last, best hope on earth. Other means may succeed; this could not fail. This way is plain, peaceful, generous, just—a way which, if followed, the world will forever applaud, and God must forever bless.

Rather Die Freemen Than Live to Be Slaves

Lincoln's dedication to saving the Union rested upon his perilous balance of antagonistic sectional forces manifesting themselves throughout the major thought and writing of the decade before the Civil War. The Compromise of 1850, not unlike the dreamlike oratorical embodiment given it by Webster or the collusion of North and South to restrict the rights of blacks whether they were slaves or free, or to deport them from the country that had put them in bondage, represented a fragile consensus that could not hold. Exacerbated by unstoppable western expansion, the sectional crisis reached new pitches of danger with the passage of the Kansas-Nebraska Act in 1854 and the conflict in "Bleeding Kansas" two years later. Within this volatile context, the Supreme Court reached a verdict in *Dred Scott v. Sandford* (1857) declaring that Congress had no authority to prohibit slavery in federal territories (as it had in the 1820 Missouri Compromise) and that blacks, free or not, had no rights as citizens. Blacks, read Chief Justice Roger B. Taney's majority opinion, "were not intended to be included under the word 'citizens' in the Constitution, and can, therefore, claim none of the rights and privileges which that instrument provides for and secures to citizens of the United States." Taney's reasoning, open to attack on a number of grounds, barely concealed a rising southern assault on antislavery and dramatically clarified the essence of African American enslavement. As Lincoln said, the Dred Scott decision imprisoned the slave "with a lock of a hundred keys . . . scattered to a hundred different and distant places." Frederick Douglass was even less temperate. "This infamous decision of the Slaveholding wing of the Supreme Court," he said in a speech before the American Anti-Slavery Society soon after the decision, "maintains that slaves are property in the same sense that horses, sheep, and swine are property [and] that slavery may go in safety anywhere under the star-spangled banner." The true threat of rebellion, Douglass recognized, lay neither with the antislavery movement nor with black slaves but with the South, which he considered in revolt against the Constitution:

The sun in the sky is not more palpable to the sight than man's right to liberty is to the moral vision. To decide against this in the person of Dred Scott, or the humblest and most whip-scarred bondman in the land, is to decide against God. It is an open rebellion against God's government. It is an attempt to undo what God has done, to blot out the broad distinction instituted by the *Allwise* between men and things, and to change the image and superscription of the everliving God into a speechless piece of merchandise.

The arguments over slavery between North and South, whether in political oration or imaginative literature, tended at times to become lost in cloudy theorizing and dry economic statistics or to lose sight of their principal subject—black Americans held in slavery. *Dred Scott* brought the subject back into focus by declaring that the founders had not intended to include blacks under the heading of "citizen" and that the slave, in the most essential way, was property. In the literature of slavery the testimony of both slaves and free blacks has a particular priority not simply because blacks were the institution's victims whose writings highlight the multiplicitous response slavery provoked but more important because they wrote in commanding proof of the fact that they were, or should be, citizens, not speechless objects of the nation's economy.

Lectures, essays, newspaper editorials, fiction, plays, songs and autobiographical narratives all compose the literature of slavery written by African Americans. As noted above, David Walker's *Appeal* in 1828 constituted one of the strongest antislavery statements of the early period, and its resolute defiance set the standard for the best polemical work that was to follow. A number of slave narrators responded to, or took issue with, Harriet Beecher Stowe, just as she had appropriated some of the materials of the slave narrative in her novel. More specifically, black novelists wrote from a wealth of experience that Stowe was compelled to invent, often producing works that effectively bridged the gap between fiction and truthful narrative. Just as the authenticity of slave narratives was often questioned (and was later disputed as reliable evidence by some historians), blacks who sought to tell their stories in fiction or in autobiography had to compete with fabricated texts such as the narrative of James Williams's life; the Briton Peter Nielson's *The Life and Adventures of Zamba, An African Negro King* (1850), which follows Zamba's life from Africa to a South Carolina plantation, with scathing attacks on slavery and America; and Mattie Griffiths's *Autobiography of a Female Slave* (1857), a work published anonymously that claimed it was "not a wild romance to beguile your tears and cheat your fancy" but neither, on the other hand, was it a "truthful autobiography."

A striking example of the problems that have surrounded slave documents appears in Harriet Jacobs's *Incidents in the Life of a Slave Girl* (1861), which was "edited" by Lydia Maria Child and later taken to be substantially Child's work. Modern discovery of Jacobs's letters and other documents has revealed that she was born a slave in North Carolina around 1815 and that her narrative of her experiences as a slave and her life in the North following her escape is to a significant degree autobiographical. By 1849 she was active in the antislavery movement in Rochester, New York, and during the war she nursed black troops in Washington, D.C., where she remained until her death in 1897. Stowe refused a request from Jacobs to help compose her story, and Child's editing turned out to be only light stylistic work. Published under the pseudonym of Linda Brent, the main character, the story is Jacobs's own, and it testifies in moving detail to the sexual abuse of black women under slavery, supporting the abolitionist charge that slavery and sexual violation were inseparable, and the plantation an arena of erotic dissipation and male lust, a "cage of obscene birds" (in Jacobs's phrase) that scandalized the most intimate affections of the domestic ideal by revealing the painful hierarchy upon which it was built.

The sexual threats of her master drove Jacobs into hiding for nearly seven years in the hope that she would one day escape with her children. Aided by relatives and friends, some of them white, Jacobs lived confined in the tiny garret of her grandmother's house, imprisoned in a suffocating enclosure that resembled more than figuratively the excruciating middle passage of the slave trade:

The garret was only nine feet long and seven wide. The highest part was three feet high, and sloped down abruptly to the loose board floor. . . . The air was stifling; the darkness total. A bed had been spread on the floor. I could sleep quite comfortably on one side; but the slope was so sudden that I could not turn on the other without hitting the roof. The rats and mice ran over my bed; but I was weary, and I slept such sleep as the wretched may, when a tempest has passed over them. . . . It seemed horrible to sit or lie in a cramped position day after day, without one gleam of light. Yet I would have chosen this, rather than my lot as a slave, though white people considered it an easy one; and it was so compared with the fate of others.

From her ironic "loophole of retreat" (as she called the garret once she had bored peepholes in the wall), Jacobs witnessed plantation life, including the lives of her children, from a concealed position that becomes a metaphor for her equally cunning position as narrator of her own story.

As the passages about her long concealment suggest, Jacobs's narrative has the inventive power of a novel, employing a significant number of formal and plot elements common to gothic and sentimental fiction. Yet it is also marked constantly by the sharp edge of a personal polemic: "I can testify, from my own experience and observation, that slavery is a curse to the whites as well as the blacks. It makes the white fathers cruel and sensual; the sons violent and licentious; it contaminates the daughters, and makes the wives wretched." Gender allegiance sometimes overrides racial prejudice in *Incidents*, but Jacobs's only reliable help comes from black women, whereas her white mistress is shown to be a jealous accomplice in her husband's schemes to seduce the young slave girl. The text throughout weaves together a complex set of the central tropes of the literature of slavery—secrecy and concealment, writing and letters, violation and resistance—so as to draw together the lives of women on two opposing sides of the color line while at the same time keeping them firmly separated by the realities of the racial barrier. The realistic treatment of the lives of slaves and white women in the South is in part modulated by the narrative's awareness of its genteel northern audience, and her appeals to the conventions of domestic romance constantly move Jacobs's autobiography in a novelistic direction without for a moment undermining its credibility. The details of her life and the story's novelization operate in perfect conjunction, for her construction of an alternative social model for the life of the black female slave—necessitated by the fact, shocking to a middle-class audience, that she deliberately took a white lover and bore his illegitimate children in order to escape the harassment of her master—depends upon redefining the idea of home and women's political community according to the violence and racism that marked black life in the North as well as the South.

A comparable text whose full significance was only appreciated upon its rediscovery in the late twentieth century is Harriet E. Wilson's *Our Nig; or, Sketches from the Life of a Free Black* (1859), the first novel by an African-American woman. Because Wilson's novel focuses on the prejudice and poverty faced by free blacks in the North, it is likely that its obscurity for over a century after it was written grew in part from the fact that, like Harriet Jacobs's narrative, it directly challenged prevailing cultural codes. The northern literary audience was willing to accept tales of violence on the plantation but remained unresponsive to the facts of northern cruelty against blacks. Little is known of Wilson other than that she was born a free black in the North and lived primarily in New Hampshire and Massachusetts; it is likely, however, that the novel was based in part on her own experiences. As part of the book's long subtitle suggests—*Showing That Slavery's Shadows Fall Even There*, that is, in the North—its story transfers the cruelty of a heartless mistress (not unlike Stowe's Marie St. Clare) from the southern plantation to a New England household, where the servant-narrator, Frado, is a virtual slave. Daughter of a black laborer and a poor white woman, Frado also bears the burden of racial mixture. She is left pregnant and abandoned at the end by a black antislavery lecturer, and the story concludes without the happy marriage the sentimental plot of the novel might seem to call for. The novel thus fuses elements of northern domestic fiction with those of the slave narrative. By focusing on the plight of the lower class and free blacks in the North, it ironically reinforces the proslavery claim that northern laborers merited the sympathy of reformers as much as slaves did. Wilson, however, attacks the standard themes of the slavery argument in three ways: she overturns the proslavery arguments of Fitzhugh and others and exploits the racism that underlies Free Soil doctrine and daily life in the Jim Crow North; she overturns the tragic mulatto theme by erasing its exoticism and revealing the economic oppression it promotes; and she overturns the ideal of maternal domesticity by making the northern home a hell and its mother figure a relentless tyrant. Along with Jacobs's *Incidents*, Wilson's novel stands not so much as a reply to Stowe but a critique of Stowe's limitations and as a more scathing extension of the novel's political purpose.

Comparable in her literary achievement to Jacobs and Wilson, and far better known throughout the nineteenth century, was Frances Ellen Watkins Harper. Born free in Baltimore, Harper (1825–1911) would not write some of the poetry or the single novel for which she is best known, *Iola Leroy* (1892), until after the war; but in the antebellum period she was an active antislavery lecturer and the author of a popular book of *Poems* (1854) devoted to romantic but finely executed treatments of such topics as "Ethiopia," "The Fugitive's Wife," and, her most famous, "The Slave Auction":

> The sale began—young girls were there,
> Defenceless in their wretchedness,
> Whose stifled sobs of deep despair
> Revealed their anguish and distress.
> And mothers stood with streaming eyes,
> And saw their dearest children sold;
> Unheeded rose their bitter cries,
> While tyrants bartered them for gold. . . .

Standing between the autobiographical narratives, which recorded the flight from slavery into the promised land, and sentimental verse and fiction, which sometimes concealed racial protest behind a mask of maudlin style and theme, was Harper's long allegorical poem *Moses: A Story of the Nile* (1869). Seventy years before Zora Neale Hurston did so in prose, Harper rendered in typologically acute form a story of the black delivery from bondage—not in the valley of the Nile but the valley of the Mississippi. Her epic summed up the significance of an adopted biblical story that appears throughout African American culture and implicitly reminded her audience that some of the strongest models for the black Moses in the antislavery tradition were not men but women like Harriet Tubman and Sojourner Truth. The poem also spoke perceptively of the traces of slavery that would last decades beyond emancipation:

> If Slavery only laid its weight of chains
> Upon the weary, aching limbs, e'en then
> It were a curse; but when it frets through nerve
> And flesh and eats into the weary soul,
> Oh then it is a thing for every human
> Heart to loathe, and this was Israel's fate,
> For when the chains were shaken from their limbs,
> They failed to strike the impress from their souls.

The other fiction by African American writers in the period is less compelling or, like Martin Delany's *Blake*, is important most of all as political argument. Philadelphia author Frank J. Webb's novel *The Garies and Their Friends* (1857), published in England, is the story of mixed marriage and race prejudice in the North, particularly that between blacks and white immigrant groups. The best-known novel by a black man in the period was William Wells Brown's *Clotel: Or, the President's Daughter* (1853), which appeared in several subsequent revised editions. An escaped slave who went on to become one of the leading black abolitionists (later taking over Douglass's position in the Massachusetts Anti-Slavery Society and enjoying a very successful speaking tour of Europe), Brown (1816?–84) also wrote a narrative of his own life, a volume of poetry entitled *The Anti-Slavery Harp* (1848), and three minor plays that have not survived: *Miralda; or, The Beautiful Quadroon* (1855), a version of *Clotel; Experience; or, How to Give a Northern Man a Backbone* (1856); and *The Escape; or, A Leap for Freedom* (1858). As the titles of his literary works suggest, Brown frequently employed the theme of racial mixing, in particular the legend of Thomas Jefferson's slave children, as the central weapon in his attack on slavery. In his popular novel, Clotel is treated cruelly, used as a mistress, sold twice to harsh masters, separated from her daughter, jailed in the wake of Nat Turner's rebellion, and driven to suicide in the Potomac River: "Thus died Clotel, the daughter of Thomas Jefferson, a president of the United States; a man distinguished as the author of the Declaration of Independence, and one of the first statesmen of that country." The compromise with white ideals that the tragic mulatto theme necessitates is underscored in the words of one of the novel's minor nearly-white slave rebels, George (clearly modeled on Stowe's George Harris): "Did not the American revolutionists violate the laws when they struck for liberty?"

The comparison of rebel slaves to American patriots was commonplace in antislavery rhetoric, all the more effective because it could not be justly rebutted. As Brown wrote in 1855, in a published lecture on *St. Domingo: Its Revolutions and Its Patriots*, "the revolution that was commenced in 1776 would . . . be finished, and the glorious sentiment of the Declaration of Independence" realized, only when African-American slaves were liberated. Having "shed their [own] blood in the American Revolutionary war," Brown argued, slaves were now "only waiting the opportunity of wiping out their wrongs in the blood of their oppressors." "What to the American slave," asked Douglass in a famous 1852 address, "is your Fourth of July"—what but "a thin veil to cover up crimes which would disgrace a nation of savages." Surely, Brown and others suggested, there was a leader like Haiti's Toussaint L'Ouverture waiting to rise in revolt against the southern states, a "black Cromwell," as Theodore Parker wrote, ready to annihilate slavery just as theocracy, monarchy, and aristocracy had been (or were being) annihilated in Europe. Brown's historical works, *The Negro in the American Revolution* (1867) and *The Black Man: His Antecedents, His Genius, and His Achievements* (1863), argued for the place of blacks in the revolutionary and intellectual traditions that Euro-Americans considered their sole prerogative; and his lecture on San Domingo drew a withering comparison between the white father of American freedom and the black father of Haitian freedom:

Each was the leader of an oppressed and outraged people, each had a powerful enemy to contend with, and each succeeded in founding a government in the New World.

Toussaint's government made liberty its watchword, incorporated it in its constitution, abolished the slave-trade, and made freedom universal amongst the people. Washington's government incorporated slavery and the slave-trade, and enacted laws by which chains were fastened upon the limbs of millions of people. Toussaint liberated his countrymen; Washington enslaved a portion of his, and aided in giving strength and vitality to an institution that will one day rend asunder the UNION that he helped to form. Already the slave in his chains in the rice fields of Carolina and the cotton fields of Mississippi burns for revenge.

With the exceptions of David Walker, noted above, and Frederick Douglass, Brown's only rival as spokesman for the ideal of black liberty was the minister Henry Highland Garnet (1815–82), who along with Martin Delany was an important early spokesman for black nationalism. Garnet's *Address to the Slaves* (1848), first delivered as a lecture to a convention of black abolitionists in Buffalo in 1843, called for violent revolt: "Brethren, arise, arise! Strike for your lives and liberties. . . . *Rather die freeman than live to be slaves.* Remember that you are FOUR MILLIONS." The call to revolution shocked most white abolitionists and many black leaders as well, among them at this point Frederick Douglass, who still followed the Garrisonian principles of nonviolence; but it gave new momentum to a rising tide of black separatism and renewed interest in emigration, which Garnet came to support during the next decade. Inspired by the independence of Liberia in 1848, Garnet and others began to look to it as a future empire for American blacks. Unlike Alexander Crummell, whose messianic view of Africa was predicated upon raising it from primitive barbarism to a civilized Christian standard of life and faith, Garnet depicted in *The Past and the Present Condition, and the Destiny, of the Colored Race* (1848) a proud tradition of black ancestors and issued a jeremiad on behalf of the nation's voiceless slaves, who, like all slaves of the New World, had been torn from their common African heritage:

We should have likewise, days of bitter bread, and tabernacle in the wilderness, in which to remember our griefworn brothers and sisters. They are now pleading with millions of tongues against those who have despoiled them. They cry from gory fields—from pestilential rice swamps—from cane breaks, and forests—from plantations of cotton and tobacco—from the dark holds of slave ships, and from countless acres where the sugar cane, nods to the sighing winds. They lift up their voices from all the land over which the flag of our country floats. From the banks of our silver streams, and broad rivers, from our valleys and sloping hills, and mountain tops.

The silence that reigns in the region where the pale nations of the earth slumber, is solemn, and awful. But what think ye, when you are told that every rood of land in this Union is the grave of a murdered man, and their epitaphs are written upon the monuments of the nation's wealth?

A decade later, when Garnet had founded the African Civilization Society, one of his first adherents was Martin Delany (1812–85), who immediately attempted to purge the society of all white influence. Delany's distrust of whites' motives and his belief that blacks would never receive freedom and fair treatment in the United States made him a strong emigrationist, a position forcefully argued in *The Condition, Elevation, Emigration, and Destiny of the Colored People of the United States* (1852). The volume based its call for political separatism on the assumption that only blacks could, and would, correctly interpret their own historical experience and create a new moral state in another country, perhaps in the Caribbean or Latin America, an argument repeated in *Political Destiny of the Colored Race on the American Continent* (1854). Born a free man, Delany worked for years as an editor and lecturer in the antislavery cause and still found time to become a professional physician (despite being forced out of Harvard Medical School when white students protested his presence). Delany lived for a time in Canada, where in 1858 he discussed with John Brown the raid Brown would later undertake against Harper's Ferry. Although Delany always rejected the type of colonization sponsored in Liberia, he and Robert Campbell explored the Niger Valley in 1859 and published separate reports on their ventures as the basis of a never-realized plan to settle a colony with a select group of black Canadian emigrants. During the Civil War Delany was commissioned a major of black troops, and he later worked for the Freedman's Bureau and was active in Reconstruction politics in South Carolina.

Delany's most significant literary achievement, however, was not his writing on black nationalism but his novel, *Blake; or, The Huts of America*, which was serialized in part in the *Anglo-African Magazine* in 1859 and probably in full in the *Weekly Anglo-African* in 1861 (a complete text has not survived). In accordance with Delany's view of the United States as a virtual prison for blacks, his hero, Henry Blake combines the vision of Nat Turner with the commanding intelligence and authority of Toussaint. Identifying divine deliverance with violent revolution and associating the plotted insurrections of

Gabriel Prosser, Denmark Vesey, and Turner with the spirit of the American Revolution, Blake, a free man, spreads a plot for insurrection throughout the South after his wife, a slave who rejects the attentions of her owner–father, is sold to a planter in Cuba. Blake carries his plans for violent uprising to Cuba (where the unresolved action of the novel ends), and this plot device plays upon current contention over annexation of Cuba by the United States and fears among southerners that a conspiracy between Britain and Spain to grant freedom to slaves in Cuba (what was called the "Africanization of Cuba") would lead to revolt and carnage in the United States. The same year that *Blake* first appeared, for example, the *United States Magazine and Democratic Review*, long a proslavery organ of manifest destiny, published a lead essay promoting the acquisition of Cuba that implored the government to "rescue" Cuba from European despotism and anticipated the continued onward movement of "the ark of the Democratic covenant."

More directly than Melville's *Benito Cereno*, Delany's *Blake* illuminates an aspect of the slavery crisis that has been overshadowed by the civil conflagration that soon engulfed the United States. At the time, the Caribbean and Cuba in particular were at the center of arguments about expansion. New Spanish policies liberalizing slave laws, combined with the seizure in February 1854 of the American steamer *Black Warrior* on a violation of port regulations, accelerated both legal and extralegal maneuvering to obtain Cuba before it became, as a State Department agent wrote in March 1854, another "Black Empire" like Haiti, "whose example they would be prone to imitate" in destroying the wealth of the island and launching "a disastrous bloody war of the races." The height of imperialistic rhetoric came after the crisis had passed and attempts to force a purchase of Cuba had failed, in the notorious Ostend Manifesto of October 1854, which declared that Cuba belonged "naturally to that great family of States of which the Union is the providential nursery" and that the United States would be justified "in wresting it from Spain . . . upon the very same principle that would justify an individual in tearing down the burning house of his neighbor if there were no other means of preventing the flames from destroying his own home." The issue of Cuba, that is to say, was couched in the familial rhetoric that Lincoln would exploit, combining the domestic language of the revolutionary fathers and that of slaveholding paternalism.

The ironies of such patriotic designs upon Cuba are used to careful effect by Delany, who in his novel as in his essays connects the freedom of American slaves with black aspirations throughout the New World. Focusing on the same agony of sexual abuse and family separation that appears in the work of Stowe and Jacobs, for example, *Blake* answers the destruction of family not with tragedy and still less with sentiment but rather with an invocation of the suppressed power of the Age of Revolution. Delany borrowed a number of polemical poems from James M. Whitfield's *America and Other Poems* (1853), and the novel throughout has the character of political theater enlivened by prophetic warning. *Blake* remains an unfinished novel in several senses; yet its vital amalgamation of contemporary events with a romantic plot of rescue and an anatomy of rebellion makes it one of the more astute political novels of the mid-nineteenth century. Along with Garnet and Brown, Delany defined in his work a tradition of black nationalism that would only in the following century stand out from under the imposing shadow of Frederick Douglass and achieve the recognition it deserved.

Delany did not share with Douglass or with the majority of the leading black abolitionists the experience of slavery or the intellectual initiation of the slave narrative, often the first important writing (or lecturing) undertaken by the escaped slave. As a group, the narratives are of enormous diversity, ranging from simple stories dictated to white sympathizers in the North to elaborately reported and richly detailed accounts of life in, and flight from, slavery. The authors variously employed the conventions of Euro-American sentimental fiction, political polemic, slave songs, the remnants of African folklore, and personal testimony in creating a unique and compelling genre of American literature. Only with the modern historical and literary recognition of the great richness of African American life, during slavery and after, did a more complete record and more complex theoretical interpretations of black cultural forms begin to appear. In the decades after the Civil War, published slave narratives of the earlier nineteenth century were complemented, and given a more reliable context, by projects in oral history, by the increasing collection of folktales and songs by ethnographers, and most important by black writers who began more assiduously to recover the culture of African American slavery, recognizing both its African sources and its unique American elements as they incorporated it into contemporary intellectual history, drama, fiction, and poetry. It is from that point forward that one can begin to see more clearly the continuity between antebellum black texts and African cultural survivals and the rise of black literature and arts on through the twentieth century.

African Americans were involved in most antislavery societies, but they were often expected to play subordinate roles or, like white women, to form auxiliaries to the main group. Black antislavery newspapers and magazines included the *Colored American*, the *Mirror of Liberty*, and *Freedom's Journal*, but the best known was Douglass's *North Star* (later renamed *Frederick Douglass's Paper*). As Douglass complained, however, blacks failed to support such journals with the same energy that they devoted to the underground railroad, where women like Harriet Tubman and men like David Ruggles (and whites like Levi Coffin) became legends for their heroic assistance to escaped slaves, a story recorded in great documentary detail by William Still in *The Underground Railroad* (1872). Tubman in particular was admired for her courage in returning to the South to aid in further escapes, and her anecdotal account of the underground railroad was recorded by Sarah H. Bradford in *Scenes in the Life of Harriet Tubman* (1869) and *Harriet Tubman: The Moses of Her People* (1886). Black writers also produced antislavery verse, the most notable being George M. Horton's volume *The Hope of Liberty* (1829), the first book of poetry by a black author since Phillis Wheatley. More important, African Americans were enormously effective as speakers on the antislavery circuit, though they often found themselves dominated and manipulated by white colleagues. By the 1840s Douglass, William Wells Brown, Tubman, William and Ellen Craft, and Sojourner Truth were among those lecturing in the North. Sojourner Truth's life story was transcribed by Olive Gilbert in 1850 in the *Narrative of Sojourner Truth*, but she gained lasting fame for a speech at an 1851 women's rights convention in Ohio in which she demanded:

Look at my arm! I have ploughed and planted and gathered into barns, and no man could head me—and ain't I a woman? I could work as much and eat as much as a man—when I could get it—and bear the lash as well! And ain't I a woman? I have born thirteen children, and seen most of 'em sold into slavery, and when I cried out with my mother's grief, none but Jesus heard me—and ain't I a woman?

Because of Sojourner Truth's effectiveness as a speaker, her words would have a celebrated life in the history of feminism. As Douglass would reveal in a famous episode of his autobiography, though, whatever his or her rhetorical power, the black speaker was likely to be subordinated to the white and was often expected to play the role of an exhibit or, at the most, to recount a saga of suffering on the plantation to audience after audience while leaving the discussion of politics and morality to Garrison, Phillips, or another white polemicist.

The fact that autobiography and antislavery rhetoric were often merged on the lecture platform accounts in part for the rhetorical form of many slave narratives. The centrality of the years immediately preceding and following the Civil War to the published record of slave narratives obscures the fact that important examples appeared before the antebellum period, among them *The Interesting Narrative of the Life of Olaudah Equiano, or Gustavus Vassa, the African* (1789) and *Narrative of the Life and Adventures of Venture, A Native of Africa* (1798). The majority, however, were published in the several decades after 1840, with many more being recorded later in the nineteenth century and in twentieth-century collections such as the enormous Federal Writers' Project compilation of oral remembrances, later edited by George Rawick and published as *The American Slave: A Composite Autobiography* (1972–8). In the years before the Civil War, the slave narratives sold well and were in large part responsible for the North's popular view of life under slavery, with the result noted before that autobiography and fiction in important cases came to resemble one another. With a few exceptions, the narratives were authentic, whether or not they carried the frequent caption "Written By Himself," and whether or not the writing was entirely the escaped slave's own. Some, like *Narrative of Lunsford Lane* (1842), reproduced fugitive slave ads or bills of sale for members of the slave family, for "such of my readers as are not accustomed to trade in human beings"; or like *Narrative of Moses Grandy* (1844), they mockingly recorded the prices of friends and relatives. Others enthralled their audiences (in print as on the lecture platform) with bizarre adventures of escape. The *Narrative of Henry "Box" Brown* (1851), in addition to its provocative attack on the cruelty of the plantation system, told the unusual story of the slave who had himself enclosed in a crate and shipped by railroad to freedom in the North. William and Ellen Craft, in *Running a Thousand Miles for Freedom* (1860), told the tale of their inventive 1848 escape from Georgia, she with her light skin posing as a young southern gentleman and he posing as her servant.

Such intricate deceptions were less common than simple flight, but they revealed in magnified form a central fact of slave life the narratives bring forth—that the slaves were required for their own survival in some cases and for their sense of self-esteem and communal dignity in all cases to adopt roles and to wear masks that, however benevolent their white masters, were not often penetrated by those outside the African American community itself. The southern claims of slave contentment and the northern racist claims of African docility failed to take account of the fact, recognized easily on the evidence of the narratives and borne out by later historical research, that slaves had good reason to disguise their feelings, as well as their plans, and did so with great ingenuity. Questions of identity and voice are consequently of enormous importance in the slave narratives, and the best of the narratives are of special literary interest because they both preserve a sense of true black identity and communal life and at the same time reveal the protagonist's talents for fabrication, acting, and subtle deceit.

The narratives typically register the cruelty of slave masters in vivid detail (those who sought to escape were perhaps the most mistreated, but their narratives tell the story as well of the many who suffered even more brutality without chance of escape). The *Narrative of Adventures and Escape of Moses Roper, from American Slavery* (1839), for example, tells of an instance in which Roper's fingers were placed in a vise and his toes hammered on an anvil because he would not reveal the name of a slave who helped him remove his chains. John Brown's *Slave Life in Georgia* (1855) told of being subjected to sunstroke experiments, including blistering his skin to see how deep the "black" went. Both the narratives and documentary sources such as Weld's *American Slavery As It Is* and Stowe's *Key to Uncle Tom's Cabin* recount numerous instances of murder and brutality by slaveowners that pass without any legal sanction. The very popular *Slavery in the United States: A Narrative of the Life and Adventures of Charles Ball, a Black Man* (1836), which went through six editions by 1859 (the last entitled *Fifty Years in Chains*), told of Ball's separation from his parents, and later his wife and children, and included representative descriptions of whippings of himself and other slaves:

[Billy] shrank his body close to the trunk of the tree, around which his arms and his legs were lashed, drew his shoulders up to his head like a dying man, and trembled, or rather shivered, in all his members. The blood flowed from the commencement [of the whipping], and in a few minutes lay in small puddles at the root of the tree. I saw flakes of flesh as long as my finger fall out of the gashes in his back; and I believe he was insensible during all the time that he was receiving the last two hundred [out of five hundred] lashes. . . . The gentlemen who had done the whipping, eight or ten in number, being joined by their friends, then came under the tree and drank punch until their dinner was made ready, under a booth of green boughs at a short distance.

Such incidents appear in many of the narratives, giving rise to the suspicion that some of the popularity of the narratives derived from the white audience's voyeurism. Even so, whipping came to be the single defining emblem of southern slaveholding. Escaped slaves exhibited their scars on the lecture platform, and narrators like Douglass rhapsodized about the whip itself and its power to contaminate all, both white and black, with a corrupting lust for power: "Everybody, in the south, wants the privilege of whipping somebody else. . . . The whip is all in all."

The record of such cruelty became a stock device in the narratives without ever losing its powerful appeal or seeming fabricated. Whatever melodrama fired the episodes of rape, whipping, or humiliation, the slave narratives corroborated other evidence of violence and mistreatment and made the lives of their authors and protagonists representative of the thousands of stories that remained untold. Harriet Beecher Stowe's appropriation of slave narrative testimony was for good reason most effective in its revelation of violence against families, both physical and emotional. If the slave narratives generally lacked her stagecraft, though, they straightforwardly told of human pain. As he wrote in *Narrative of the Life and Adventures of Henry Bibb* (1849), Bibb "was compelled to stand and see my wife shamefully scourged and abused by her master," and his separation from his daughter, still in slavery, made him thankful that "she was the first and shall be the last slave that ever I will father, for chains and slavery on this earth." The protagonist of the *Narrative of Moses Grandy* was held at bay with a pistol while his wife was dragged away; and William Grimes wrote in *Life of William Grimes, Runaway Slave* (1855) of the common situation in which blacks themselves were turned into brutal overseers and forced to whip their friends and family. Such degradation appears throughout the narratives, and it is all the more striking in the best narratives, like those of Ball, Douglass, Brown, and Northup, which portray it against a detailed backdrop of slave life and situate their polemics within a dramatic human context that ranges from gothic horror, inflicted at near random, to the orderly and efficient operation of the slave system. The general poverty of conditions—of food, clothing, shelter, medical care, and instruction—emerged clearly in the narratives. The multiple violations of slaves' lives by emotional and physical abuse, even if they were occasionally exaggerated by abolition-ists, cast a damning light upon the proslavery claim that blacks were mere animals—the men beasts of burden unable to cope with freedom and the women vessels of lust and reproduction—who could be reduced to their bodily functions. When a slave accused of stealing meat is drowned in the *Narrative of William W. Brown, A Fugitive Slave* (1847), Brown remarks how the body is left to be picked up the next day: along came "a cart, which takes up the trash of our streets . . . and the body was thrown in, and in a few minutes more was covered over with dirt which they were removing from the streets." What the northern audience learned from the slave narratives—in contrast to the claims of southern essayists and accommodating northern travelers and novelists who portrayed the plantation in idyllic terms—was that the effect, if not the goal, of slavery was often to reduce blacks to the least human dimension.

A few of the most successful narratives owed their popularity to the charismatic personalities or unusual careers of their protagonists. Elizabeth Keckley's *Behind the Scenes* (1868) told of her rise from slavery to become a White House dressmaker for Mary Todd Lincoln, and *A Sketch of the Life of Okah Tubbee* (1848) portrayed the life of a manumitted Natchez slave turned traveling musician who dressed in Indian clothing and claimed to be descended from Choctaw chiefs. Perhaps the best known of slave narrators until the twentieth century was Josiah Henson, a Methodist Episcopal min-ister whose own 1849 narrative (*Life of Josiah Henson*, written by Samuel A. Eliot) presented a simple but effective record of his conversion, his sufferings, and his family's escape to Canada, where he became the leader of Dawn, a suc-cessful black communal settlement. Henson's fame, however, came from his assertion, now discredited by scholarship, that he was the model for Stowe's Uncle Tom. By manipulation of, and acquiescence in, a legend that grew of its own accord (and eventually had Stowe's own participation), Henson made a career for himself by playing this part in subsequent versions of his autobiography, which appeared under titles such as *Truth Stranger than Fiction: Father Henson's Story of his Own Life* (1858). As with most other developments in the legend of Uncle Tom, however, Henson's posturing served mainly to drain Tom of his interest as a character as well as to obscure the significance of Henson's own life story.

Henson's narrative is one of many that are important as much for their por-traits of life as freemen, whether North or South, as for their accounts of life under slavery. James W. C. Pennington's popular autobiography, *The Fugitive Blacksmith* (1849), recounts his escape, conversion, and the beginnings of his career as a minister, concluding with a letter to his former master begging him to release his slaves and be reconciled to God. Pennington's life is more notable, however, for the fact that he received an honorary doctorate from the University of Heidelberg but was denied admission to the classrooms of Yale, being permitted only to stand outside the doors to listen to lectures. Educated only after his escape from slavery, Pennington worked actively for antislavery and wrote a children's book entitled *A Text Book of the Origin and History of the Colored People* (1841). Interestingly, Pennington maintained that in many respects mild slavery was the worst form, because of its more subtle dehumanizing effects, and he condemned the institution most of all for forcing slaves to be deceitful and for denying them education, attitudes that were reinforced by his experience of prejudice against free blacks in the North.

Again like Douglass, most escaped slaves not only feared constantly that they would be captured or kidnapped and returned to slavery but also faced Jim Crow laws and suspicion or hatred almost everywhere in the northern United States outside of antislavery circles (and in some cases certainly within them as well). The same was often true of those blacks born free. The *Life of James Mars* (1864) tells of a Connecticut man who, though born after the abolition of slavery in that state in 1788, had to remain in servitude under its terms until 1825. In his *Autobiography* (1984), written in the 1890s, James Thomas tells of his years among free blacks in Nashville, his life in Kansas and Missouri on the eve of the Civil War, and his eventual success as a businessman and property owner in St. Louis. Similarly, William Johnson, known as the "Barber of Natchez," wrote in a diary of 1835–51 (published in 1951) of his work as a farmer and a barber in a volatile Mississippi world of duels, romance, racism, and corrupt politics. One of the most famous antislavery orators, Samuel Ringgold Ward, escaped slavery to become a minister in the North, yet his *Autobiography of a Fugitive Negro* (1855) not only gives us a full picture of his abolitionist activities but is highly critical of the northern churches' complicity in slavery. After Austin Steward (1794–1860) moved to frontier New York with his master and eventually gained his freedom by hiring himself out, he became a successful grocer and an antislavery activist, and later organized the Canadian black settlement of Wilberforce. Like Benjamin Drew's *Northside View of Slavery* (1856), a collection of African-Canadian narratives that is structured by the irony that black Americans could only become free Americans by leaving the country altogether, Steward's volume, *Twenty-Two Years a Slave, and Forty Years a Freeman* (1857), takes its strength from exposing the fact that exile was the only route to black liberty. His story begins in slavery but dwells on prejudice against free blacks and the immoral implications of the Fugitive Slave Law for men and women of conscience in the North. If Steward's lot was not as grim as that of the heroine in *Our Nig*, the irony that Frederick Douglass pointed to in his treatment aboard a Massachusetts train (in *My Bondage and My Freedom*) was nevertheless typical of such black experience in the North: "At the same time that they excluded a free colored man from their cars, this same company allowed slaves, in company with their masters and mistresses, to ride unmolested."

Perhaps the most vicious irony of black life in antebellum America, however, fell upon those free blacks, like Solomon Northup, who were kidnapped and sold into slavery. Northup's *Twelve Years a Slave* (1853) describes his captivity and eventual redemption from a Louisiana plantation (when, after nine years, he finally obtains pen and ink to write the North for help). The narrative includes some of the most remarkable and detailed descriptions of the daily routine of the slave, the elaborate marketing techniques that accompany the slave auction, and the slaves' development of an African American culture that separates them from the brutality of their masters. Stowe included Northup's letter about his enslavement in her *Key to Uncle Tom's Cabin*, and he joined other blacks who wrote in the wake of her novel in both attacking proslavery apologists and implicitly criticizing the limits of understanding evident in the writings of men and women like Stowe:

Men may write fictions portraying lowly life as it is, or as it is not—may expatiate with owlish gravity upon the bliss of ignorance—discourse flippantly from arm chairs of the pleasures of slave life; but let them toil with him in the field—sleep with him in the cabin—feed with him on husks—let them behold him scourged, hunted, trampled on. . . . Let them know the *heart* of the poor slave—learn his secret thoughts—thoughts he dare not utter in the hearing of the white man . . . and they will find that ninety-nine out of every hundred are intelligent enough to understand their situation, and to cherish in their bosoms the love of freedom, as passionately as themselves.

Because Northup's narrative also takes advantage of his double perspective of a free man and a slave, it provides a special instance of the masking that slaves maintained was necessary to their daily survival and their development of a history, a consciousness, and an artistic culture of their own.

What also emerged from the slave narrative's bleak picture of plantation life or prejudice in the North, in fact, was a sense of the strength and independent spirit of survival, alongside forthright counteractions of slavery and racism, among a people who were building a world neither strictly American nor African but uniquely syncretic, a world destined to grow into its own distinct form and to have an important impact on American religion, art, social thought, and politics in coming years. The slave narratives in many cases not only provide a fragmentary record of early black culture but also form a bridge between the traditions of oral storytelling and the formal written narratives of Euro-American culture.

In their creation of selves responsive to the demands of an often liminal existence between cultures—an existence that could depend on both spiritual strength and cunning—the narrators sometimes resemble the trickster figures of African American folklore, whose tales were increasingly collected by the turn of the century and later recorded in literary form, for example, by Joel Chandler Harris in his several volumes of Uncle Remus stories, by Charles Chesnutt in *The Conjure Woman*, and by Zora Neale Hurston in *Mules and Men*. As in other forms of self-expression and communication that flourished under slavery, the trickster tales of Brer Rabbit and Brer Fox, to name only the best-known of animal tales, and the stories of Old Master and John could provide psychological relief or a realistic articulation of power in the hostile world of bondage. Often, moreover, the tales became embellished in such a way as to extend their allegorical commentary into the postwar period. For example, in one of the Master-John tales recorded by Hurston, one among countless variations on the widespread "Philly-Me-York" tale, Master pretends to leave town on a trip to a northern city but returns in disguise to catch John throwing a dance for his fellow slaves in the "big house," drinking and eating Master's stores, and killing his hogs. Master plans to hang John, but John tricks him in turn by having a friend sit in the hanging tree with a box of matches when John begins to pray to God for help. The tale concludes:

"Now John," said Massa, "have you got any last words to say?"
"Yes sir, Ah want to pray."
"Pray and damn quick. I'm clean out of patience with you, John."

So John knelt down. "O Lord, here Ah am at de foot of de persimmon tree. If you're gointer destroy Old Massa tonight, with his wife and chillun and everything he got, lemme see it lightnin'."

Jack up the tree, struck a match. Old Massa caught hold of John and said: "John, don't pray no more."

John said: "Oh yes, turn me loose so Ah can pray. O Lord, here Ah am tonight callin' on Thee and Thee alone. If you are gointer destroy Ole Massa tonight, his wife and chillun all he got, Ah want to see it lightnin' again."

Jack struck another match and Ole Massa started to run. He give John his freedom and a heap of land and stock. He run so fast it took a express train running at the rate of ninety miles an hour and six months to bring him back, and that's how come [blacks] got they freedom today.

As this brief example suggests, layers of tall tale and grotesque irony are the main operative mechanisms of the African American folktale. Inverting the disguised roles of domination and submission so that the weak but cunning "slave" figure, whether John or Brer Rabbit, gets the better of, or even destroys, his "master," the folktales of slavery that would get set down in countless variations in subsequent decades constitute one of the strongest artistic legacies of African American slavery.

The Rhythmic Cry of the Slave

Perhaps the most important feature of antebellum black life in America—the element that merged divergent geographical and chronological experiences, linked slave to free black life, and became the central vehicle for the survival and growth of distinctive African American cultural forms—was religion. African-American religion united evangelical Protestantism with surviving elements of African religion to create the African Methodist Episcopal Church, various formalized Baptist churches, and many noninstitutional worship groups. In the form of prayer, song, or worship, religion was an important part of slave life whether it was imposed as a means of control by the masters or developed in communal worship among the slaves. Religion was crucial to the narratives of both free blacks and slaves, in the latter case because the slave's escape often conformed to the biblical archetype of delivery from bondage. Frederick Douglass was only one of many narrators who recounted their experiences of religious conversion and periods of despair over the inability of organized religion, especially the Christian churches, to do anything about slavery. The *Narrative of the Life of Reverend Noah Davis* (1859), for example, gives a history of Davis's ministerial life in Baltimore and his frustrating attempts to purchase his children's freedom. In a representative pattern of the slave conversion narrative, the *Life of John Thompson, A Fugitive Slave* (1856) records a tale of family separation and escape, after which Thompson becomes literate and learns to read the Word of God before eventually departing for Africa. William Wells Brown dedicated his narrative to the Ohio man who aided him and from whom he took his name in words that drew an analogy between his experience and Christ's command to Christian duty: "Thirteen years ago, I came to your door, a weary fugitive from chains and stripes. I was a stranger, and you took me in. I was hungry, and you fed me. Naked was I, and you clothed me." Two free black women evangelists, Jarena Lee and Zilpha Elaw, recorded their stories before the Civil War; and several more, including Julia Foote and Amanda Smith, wrote autobiographies in later years. Smith's 1893 account of her career in the African Methodist Episcopal Church followed her evangelical activities in England and India; and her rise to deaconess, despite the pronounced opposition of male preachers, is all the more striking against the backdrop of her childhood experience of slavery. In the transport of her own conversion experience, the young Amanda Smith ran to a mirror to see whether her color had changed.

The Christian doctrine presented to slaves by their white masters typically emphasized a regime of submissiveness and docility derived from New Testament scripture. But the slaves' own worship and black preaching of the nineteenth century were more often centered on Old Testament stories of judgment and those passages from scripture that spoke of the liberation of enslaved peoples from bondage. Frances Harper's post–Civil War poem *Moses: A Story of the Nile*, noted above, is the clearest literary example of the archetype that would be repeated throughout African American culture well beyond slavery. The black minister was often a leading figure of the community not just for his ability to guide the community's faith or carry its spiritual burden but also to a degree for his role as an embodiment of surviving African customs or beliefs that remained hidden from, or misunderstood by, observing slaveholders or plantation visitors. The powerful preacher could unify African Americans who may have come from very different African traditions, and like storytellers or musicians, he could preserve cultural materials that might seem pagan or meaningless to Euro-Americans. Even though many plantations and white communities provided regular Sunday services for slaves, slave narrators and historians have shown that covert black services—often employing call and response, more emotive or rhythmically expressive music and dance, or aspects of African spiritualism—were crucial to the life of the slave community and the form of the black church beyond slavery. Black plantation music, for example, carried strong traces of African life in the practice of *juba* patting, or jubilee beating, a rhythmic inheritance of African drumming transferred to hands, voice, fiddle, or new percussive instruments. Partly through the medium of slave religion, African folktales—of animal spirits, trickster figures, powerful ancestors, and the like—survived in transfigured form, as did the complex rhythms of African music, which evolved into new folk practice and combined with the Christianity taught to slaves to form the music of the spiritual.

Black spirituals were a combination of white Protestant music, African influences, and indigenous creation by the slaves themselves, and have been praised worldwide as the foundation of America's most distinctive music. The songs of the slaves had a variety of modes and meanings, some of them encoded with fragmentary African folk forms and beliefs, but one primary theme was the longing for escape from slavery, both physical and spiritual. As Thomas Wentworth Higginson wrote in an 1867 essay on black spirituals, slaves "could sing themselves, as had their fathers before them, out of the contemplation of their own low estate, into the sublime scenery of the Apocalypse." The first important collection was William Francis Allen's *Slave Songs of the United States* (1867), though over the course of the late nineteenth century, numerous collections of black spirituals appeared, the most famous based on the performances of black choral groups such as those at Fisk University and Hampton Institute. But it would remain for W. E. B. Du Bois, whose classic text *The Souls of Black Folks* (1903) folded the spirituals into the fabric of its argument on behalf of African American culture and civil rights, to make the strongest claim for the "sorrow songs": "The Negro folksong—the rhythmic cry of the slave—stands to-day not simply as the sole American music, but as the most beautiful expression of human experience born this side of the seas ... the singular spiritual heritage of the nation and the greatest gift of the Negro people."

The spirituals and the secular work songs of African American slaves (and the two forms often merged, as would gospel and blues in the next century) are in crucial respects the core of black oral culture. Marked by an inventiveness and improvisation that would remain characteristic of much black American music and literature, the songs celebrate a kind of individual performance that is most valuable in its contribution to a communal heritage constantly augmented as it is passed among groups and generations. Only in musical form can one feel the full power of the spirituals, especially those with the greatest melodic lines such as "Swing Low, Sweet Chariot," "Roll, Jordan, Roll," "Nobody Knows the Trouble I've Seen," and "Sometimes I Feel Like a Motherless Child." As in the case of the oral tradition of the folktales, both communal effort and improvisation are central to the legacy of the African American spirituals. Although the most common songs were those handed down and continually elaborated for the accompaniment of work—field hollers, boat songs, harvest songs, market cries, and songs for marching to work—the more intricate songs typically had a spiritual or allegorical character superimposed upon a narrative about the experience of slavery. For example, "My Lord, What a Mourning" also exists in variants that spell "mourning" as "morning," an index of both the metaphoric complexity and the moral ambivalence in the spirituals' adaptation of Christian eschatology to the circumstance of bondage:

> My Lord, what a mourning,
> My Lord, what a mourning,
> My Lord, what a mourning,
> When the stars begin to fall.
>
> You'll hear the trumpets sound
> To wake the nations underground,
> Looking to my God's right hand
> When the stars begin to fall.

One simple but powerful spiritual recorded by Allen and appearing in many variations thereafter, "Many Thousand Gone," was ascribed to the slaves' reaction to emancipation, yet its common theme of liberation (whether through death, escape, or emancipation), its iteration of slavery's round of labor and punishment, and its commemoration of those who have gone before suggest an earlier origin:

> No more auction block for me,
> No more, no more;

No more auction block for me,
Many thousand gone.

No more peck of corn for me,
No more, no more;
No more peak of corn for me,
Many thousand gone.

No more driver's lash for me,
No more, no more;
No more driver's lash for me,
Many thousand gone.

Sometimes the elements of secular work or activity were combined with religious themes, as in the drummer boy's song recorded by Higginson, who served with a black regiment during the war:

O! we're gwine to de Ferry,
    De bell done ringing;
Gwine to de landing,
    De bell done ringing;
Trust, believer,
    De bell done ringing;
Satan's behind me,
    De bell done ringing;
'Tis a misty morning,
    De bell done ringing;
O! de road am sandy,
    De bell done ringing!

Several of the narratives published in the antebellum period (and many collected in later oral testimony) include examples of the slave songs. William Wells Brown, for example, records a song sung by slaves about to be sold further south:

O, gracious Lord! when shall it be,
That we poor souls shall all be free;
Lord, break them slavery powers—
Will you go along with me?
Lord break them slavery powers,
Go sound the jubilee!

Dear Lord, dear Lord, when slavery'll cease,
Then we poor souls will have our peace;—
There's a better day a coming,
Will you go along with me?
There's a better day a coming,
Go sound the jubilee!

Slave songs often employed biblical imagery to prophesy spiritual or actual escape, and double meanings were an integral part of most songs. A British journalist who toured the southern states in 1856 preserved a chanted song, sung with extemporaneous variations, from a South Carolina prayer meeting:

In that morning, true believers,
                                    In that morning,
We will sit aside of Jesus
                                    In that morning,
If you should go fore I go,
                                    In that morning,
You will sit aside of Jesus
                                    In that morning,
True believers, where your tickets
                                    In that morning,
Master Jesus got your tickets
                                    In that morning.

The most famous song to survive from the slave experience, "Go Down, Moses," reappeared in numerous versions and became an integral part of literary expressions of black life for writers from Frances Harper to William Faulkner. First printed in the *National Anti-Slavery Standard* in 1861, the hymn drew an explicit analogy between the bondage of the Israelites in Egypt and that of blacks in the South:

When Israel was in Egypt's land,
    O let my people go!
Oppressed so hard they could not stand,
    O let my people go!

O go down, Moses
    Away down to Egypt's land,
    And tell King Pharaoh
    To let my people go!

No more shall they in bondage toil,
   O let my people go!
Let them come out of Egypt's spoil,
   O let my people go!

"Go Down, Moses" and songs like it had a widespread currency throughout the slave community before being written down, sometimes because of their potential to carry covert messages of subversion or resistance. Whether or not one can plausibly argue, as a later commentator would, that "Steal Away" was actually written by Nat Turner, it is an example of the coded call to flight—to freedom in the North or in Canada, or allegorically in a return to Africa—that is latent in a number of the spirituals:

Steal away, steal away,
Steal away to Jesus!
Steal away, steal away home,
I ain't got long to stay here.

My Lord, He calls me,
He calls me by the thunder,
The trumpet sounds within my soul,
I ain't got long to stay here.

Likewise, Sarah Bradford's narrative of Harriet Tubman reveals that she employed songs as coded messages, as in the stanza that was said to indicate to slaves that it was not then safe to attempt an escape:

Moses go down in Egypt,
Till ole Pharo' let me go;
Hadn't been for Adam's fall,
Shouldn't hab to die at all.

Along with slave narratives, antislavery publications, and magazine articles appearing on into the twentieth century, collections such as William Allen's *Slave Songs of the United States* and numerous subsequent volumes preserved these songs that would become the foundation of modern black culture. The survival of African elements in slave folklore and the creation of a distinct culture were a source of individual and family solace and an incipient form of nationalistic self-preservation that can be reflected in only fragmented ways in the written documents of the antebellum period. Such elements, especially in religious music, offered a means not only of expressing but also of combating the dehumanizing effects of slavery. Yet more than that, they were the first form of a rich and powerful African American artistic expression later to appear in the black choral music, blues, and jazz destined to have profound effects on America's intellectual life and performing arts.

The Rights of Rebellion

According to Frederick Douglass, the slave songs had afforded him, as a boy, his "first glimmering conceptions of the dehumanizing character of slavery," because they revealed the pain beneath the superficial contentment of the slaves: "the songs of the slaves represent the sorrows, rather than the joys, of his heart; and he is relieved by them, only as an aching heart is relieved by tears." But the slave songs, whether spirituals, folk songs, or work songs, spoke at the same time of strength, dignity, and wit in the face of sorrow. They spoke too of protest, as in the example that Douglass himself offered as "not a bad summary of the palpable injustice and fraud of slavery":

> We raise de wheat,
> Dey gib us corn;
> We bake de bread,
> Dey gib us de cruss;
> We sif de meal,
> Dey gib us de huss;
> We peal de meat,
> Dey gib us de skin,
> And dat's de way
> Dey take us in.
> We skim de pot,
> Dey gib us the liquor,
> And say dat's good enough for the nigger.

Particularly in the revised versions of his famous autobiography, Frederick Douglass (1817–95) offered one of the most various and comprehensive portraits of the lives of African American slaves and of the culture they created. Douglass's fame, however, derives primarily from his vigorous career as an antislavery lecturer and editor and from his continued importance as a spokesman for blacks in political and social matters after the Civil War, when his career included positions as marshal and recorder of deeds for the District of Columbia, as well as U.S. minister to Haiti.

Born into slavery on a large Maryland plantation, Douglass escaped in 1838 to Massachusetts, where he became a follower of William Lloyd Garrison and a brilliant public speaker. After publishing *Narrative of the Life of Frederick Douglass* in 1845, which exposed him as a fugitive, he spent several years as an extremely popular antislavery lecturer in England and Ireland before returning to buy his freedom from his former owner. Douglass broke with Garrison over a number of issues: his unwillingness to accept Garrison's argument that the Constitution was necessarily a proslavery document and that conventional political activities were useless in combating slavery; Garrison's opposition to Douglass's founding of his own antislavery newspaper, the *North Star*, in 1847; and Garrison's probable jealousy of Douglass's success as a speaker and a writer. As Douglass wrote in the revised version of his narrative, *My Bondage and My Freedom* (1855), he quickly had begun to resent the limited role that Garrison and others expected him to play at antislavery lectures: "I was generally introduced as a '*chattel*'—a '*thing*'—a piece of southern '*property*'—the chairman assuring the audience that *it* could speak." He was told to keep "a *little* of the plantation" in his speech and to tell his story without elaboration, leaving the philosophy to the white speakers like Garrison, who would then take Douglass as their "text" for commentary. As his writings imply, Douglass not only found this stifling but also considered it a new form of enslavement, in its own way as harsh as the physical abuse he had escaped in the South.

Despite Douglass's more forcefully articulated stance of independence in *My Bondage and My Freedom*, the central themes of his whole career are present in the 1845 *Narrative*, and some modern critics have found it to be the most authentic of Douglass's writings because it was the closest to his firsthand experience of slavery. Obvious from the outset is Douglass's splendid control of his language, in part a self-conscious reflection on the book's recurring idea of literacy as the key to freedom. Forbidden by his master to continue learning to read, for example, Douglass recalls: "It was a new and special revelation, explaining dark and mysterious things, with which my youthful understanding had struggled, but struggled in vain. I now understand what had been to me a most perplexing difficulty—to wit, the white man's power to enslave the black man. It was a grand achievement, and I prized it highly. From that moment, I understood the pathway from slavery to freedom." More so than many other slave narrators, Douglass was aware of his ability and his need to create a paradigmatic story. His narrative stands out above others because in addition to telling his own life story, it offers an almost mythic embodiment of the acts of speech and self-making denied by law to slaves. Douglass's *Narrative* sums up the purpose of testimony by former slaves, namely, to dramatize the spiritual survival of the black family and community within the cauldron of plantation slavery and to explore the means by which power and dehumanization were united in slavery to prohibit African Americans from gaining control of those cultural signs that lend full dignity to life. Although they indicate a degree of conflict between the oral tradition of black folk life and the dominant culture, speaking and writing are both modes of discovery in the *Narrative*. As avenues to "mastery" of himself, they allow Douglass to fashion an "autobiography" in which the freed slave is in effect created as a man in the act of narration, whether before an audience or in print.

Even though it lacks some of the direct simplicity of the earlier *Narrative, My Bondage and My Freedom* bridges the two halves of Douglass's life, provides much more detail about his life in the North, and amplifies certain episodes in his life as a slave. It is not the simple story that his white advisers asked him to state on the lecture platform but an energetic, complex antislavery polemic that inquires deeply into the meaning of American freedom and the meaning of America for slaves and free blacks. The revisions constitute the first of several recastings of his life that appear in Douglass's thought and work, and they represent an extension of the lesson that lies at the heart of his life's story, as it does those of many of the escaped slaves—that literacy is the primary means to power. Just as the language of the "self-made man" comes to dominate his autobiographical writing in the postwar period, so in *My Bondage and My Freedom* the language of revolution and liberty is prominent. Both in the autobiography and in his 1853 short story "The Heroic Slave," which was based on a revolt aboard the slave ship *Creole* led by the slave Madison Washington, Douglass appropriated the ideals of democratic revolution to the cause of the black slave. As Madison Washington, the *black* Virginia patriot, says, "we have done that which you applaud your fathers for doing, and if we are murderers, *so were they*."

One of his most famous addresses, a speech on the meaning of the Fourth of July for blacks, invoked revolutionary rights but at the same time distanced the black man from the legacy of the white fathers. This is "the birthday of your National Independence, and of your political freedom," Douglass told his largely white Rochester audience in 1852. "This, to you, is what the Passover was to the emancipated people of God." For the American slave, Douglass charged, the Fourth of July was a sham and a mockery, "a thin veil to cover up crimes which would disgrace a nation of savages." Renouncing Garrisonian nonviolence, Douglass by the 1850s believed armed slave insurrection a just answer to black bondage. Whereas the proslavery arguments of Dew and others held that slaves would be "parricides" instead of "patriots," Douglass argued that they could be both at once. Or, as he wrote in *My Bondage and My Freedom*, the slaveholder every day violates the "just and inalienable rights of man," thereby "silently whetting the knife of vengeance for his own throat. He never lisps a syllable in commendation of the fathers of this republic, nor denounces any attempted oppression of himself, without . . . asserting the rights of rebellion for his own slaves."

Both "The Heroic Slave" and the reconceived argument for violent rebellion that came to mark Douglass's work in the 1850s can be understood, moreover, as a response to the widely popular example of Stowe's Uncle Tom. Douglass had from the outset of his career been skeptical of the church's commitment to abolitionism, and he wrote in a blistering appendix to the 1845 *Narrative*: "Revivals of religion and revivals in the slave-trade go hand in hand together. . . . The clanking of fetters and the rattling of chains in the prison, and the pious psalm and solemn prayer in church, may be heard at the same time. The dealers in the bodies and souls of men erect their stand in the presence of the pulpit, and they mutually help each other." After Douglass had renounced the pacifist principles of Garrison and called for violent resistance by slaves, the central incident in his own life as a slave, his fight with the slave-breaker Covey, was heightened in the revised autobiography in order to provide a contrast to Uncle Tom's capitulation to Legree:

I was a changed being after that fight. I was *nothing* before; I WAS A MAN NOW. It recalled to life my crushed self-respect and my self-confidence, and inspired me with renewed determination to be A FREEMAN. . . . He only can understand the effect of this combat on my spirit, who has himself incurred something, hazarded something, in repelling the unjust and cruel aggressions of a tyrant. . . . It was a resurrection from the dark and pestiferous tomb of slavery, to the heaven of comparative freedom. . . . I had reached the point where I was *not afraid to die*. This spirit made me a freeman in *fact*, while I remained a slave in *form*. When a slave cannot be flogged he is more than half free. . . . While slaves prefer their lives, with flogging, to instant death, they will always find Christians enough, like unto Covey, to accommodate that preference.

Douglass's response to Stowe can be judged as well in his recasting of his attack on the corruption of the family under slavery. When he remarks that "scenes of sacred tenderness, around the deathbed, never forgotten, and which often arrest the vicious and confirm the virtuous during life, must be looked for among the free," Douglass suggests the limitations of Stowe's vision even as he gives further ammunition to her attack on the destruction of the slave family. The issues of family and revolution are joined in Douglass's characteristic invocation of the revolutionary "fathers" that he must substitute for the white master-father he never knew and the unacceptable surrogates like his second master Hugh Auld or later Garrison. In Douglass's rhetoric the family was destroyed by slavery, but if reconstituted as part of the ideal democratic state, it could also become a weapon against slavery.

Douglass's lectures often satirized the purported paternalism of slavery and held up the slave codes themselves in counterpoint. He could do so all the more effectively because he knew, as his farewell speech in England had put it, that "the whip, the chain, the gag, the thumb-screw, the blood-hound, the stocks, and all the other bloody paraphernalia of the slave system are indispensably necessary to the relation of master and slave. The slave must be subjected, or he ceases to be a slave." In *My Bondage and My Freedom* the greater attention allotted to incidents of whipping is not simply a matter of gothic ornamentation but becomes a symbol of Douglass's more precisely characterized portrait of the institution of slavery. One need not consent to the much debated thesis that, in its dehumanization of slaves and inducement in them of an imitative pattern of behavioral bondage, the plantation resembled the concentration camp, the prison, or other "total institutions" in order to be struck by Douglass's new account of Colonel Lloyd's immense plantation in *My Bondage and My Freedom*. He not only gives a much fuller picture of slave life in the revised account, but the greater detail and the emphasis on the plantation's self-sufficient, dark seclusion, maintained by diverse labor and transbay trade on Lloyd's own vessels, create of this deceptively abundant, "Eden-like" garden world a veritable heart of darkness. Both the size of Lloyd's plantation and his prominent position as Maryland's three-time governor and two-time senator allow Douglass to expand his own story into a national archetype. In this era of reform movements and utopian communal projects, the plantation (in the proslavery argument) posed as a pastoral asylum in which state control and paternal coersion alike worked to the slave's benefit but did so by imprisoning him in a corrupt "family," one he might, like Douglass, belong to by blood but not by law.

Douglass's great success with the *North Star* (he changed its name to *Frederick Douglass's Paper* in 1851) was crucial to the expansion of his thought and of his capacity to reach a large audience. It made him to a great extent independent of Garrison and other white abolitionists and may be said to have created in him a Benjamin Franklin-like character of self-promotion and improvement, a side of his mature personality that is most evident in the later version of his autobiography, *Life and Times of Frederick Douglass* (published in 1881 and revised yet again in 1892). Douglass encouraged the participation of women in the antislavery movement and advocated their suffrage rights (the motto of *North Star* was "Right is of no sex—Truth is of no color"), and his campaign both before and after the war is perhaps more properly understood as one of human rights rather than simply black rights. His many volumes of speeches and editorial writings constitute probably the most complete social and political record left by any one individual of the struggle for black freedom in the nineteenth century. Lincoln sought Douglass's advice on several occasions, though the president moved more slowly on the issues of black troops and emancipation than Douglass would have liked. The distance between the two men, as well as the figurative status of blacks in the postwar period, may be judged by Douglass's remarks at the dedication of the Freedman's Lincoln Monument in 1876. President Ulysses S. Grant and his cabinet, the Supreme Court justices, and other dignitaries were in attendance as Douglass declared that "when the foul reproach of ingratitude is hurled at us, and it is attempted to scourge us beyond the range of human brotherhood, we may calmly point to the monument we have this day erected to the memory of Abraham Lincoln." But this concluding conciliatory apostrophe held suspended a tone more critical of Lincoln's policies that marked much of his address. Truth compelled him to admit, he said, that Lincoln, in his habits and prejudices, "was a white man." "You," Douglass addressed his mostly white audience, "are the children of Abraham Lincoln. We are at best only his step-children; children by adoption, children by the forces of circumstance and necessity."

Douglass's public services as marshal for the District of Columbia and later as consul general to Haiti were in part political rewards for his allegiance to the Republican Party. But such roles indicated as well that Douglass was recognized beyond the circle of white antebellum figures whose paternalism he had found to be so binding. Although it recorded the failure of Reconstruction and the escalating degradation of black civil rights in the last decades of the century, his *Life and Times* emphasized black economic success and cultural achievement through "self-reliance, self-respect, industry, perseverance, and economy." Given this emphasis, it is hardly a surprise that Booker T. Washington would consider himself Douglass's logical heir. During these years of his life, as well as earlier, however, Douglass's autobiographical self-presentation does not tell the whole story. The 1892 *Life and Times* concluded by declaring that the consulship in Haiti and Douglass's subsequent appointment to represent Haiti at the World's Columbian Exposition of 1893 in Chicago were "the crowning honors to my long career and a fitting and happy close to my whole public life," but the true lesson of Douglass's appearance at the exposition must be found elsewhere. Except for exhibits devoted to African (not African American) life, blacks were excluded from any official role in the exposition. As Douglass wrote in his introduction to a pamphlet by black Americans protesting this cultural ignorance and injustice, "when it is asked why we are excluded from the World's Columbian Exposition, the answer is Slavery."

Whereas Lincoln himself and his generation overcame the burden of the Founding Fathers and the problem of slavery, Douglass and his generation continued to face the harsh legacy of enslavement. Race prejudice and violence had not been destroyed, but neither had African American culture. By the end of Douglass's career, when the mantle of leadership had passed to Washington, Du Bois, Ida B. Wells, and others, black literature and art were on the verge of an extraordinary renaissance, one that remained rooted in the oral culture, poetry, fiction, song, and autobiography of antebellum African American slave life.

A Note on Sources

The quotation from Mariano Vallejo's *Recuerdos históricos y personales tocante a la Alta California* that opens the first chapter is taken from the translation by Earl R. Hewitt held in the Bancroft Library at the University of California, Berkeley. The version of "El corrido de Gregorio Cortez" is taken from Américo Paredes, *With His Pistol in His Hand: A Border Ballad and Its Hero* (Austin: University of Texas Press, 1958). For quoted material in the section on American Indian oral tradition and oratory, I am indebted to a number of secondary works. Some quotations appear in more than one of the following sources, in varying translations, or in antebellum works cited in the text; the modern collections cited here reprint or adapt material from nineteenth- or early twentieth-century sources. The oratory of Red Jacket and Speckled Snake appears in Samuel G. Drake, *Biography and History of the Indians of North America* (Boston: B. B. Mussey, 1851); the account of White Antelope's lyric appears in George Bird Grinnell, *The Fighting Cheyenne* (1915; rpt. Norman: University of Oklahoma Press, 1956); the Pawnee creation story appears in Natalie Curtis Burlin, *The Indian's Book* (New York: Harper and Brothers, 1923); the song of the black bear, appearing first in Pliny Earle Goddard, *Navajo Texts: Anthropological Papers of the American Museum of Natural History* (vol. 34, New York, 1933), the song of the maize, appearing first in Francis LaFléshe, *The Osage Tribe: The Rite of Vigil* (39th Annual Report of the Bureau of American Ethnology, Washington, 1925), and the Mescalero Apache puberty song, appearing first in Pliny Earle Goddard, *Gotal: A Mescalero Apache Ceremony* (New York: Stechert, 1909), are included in Margot Astrov, ed., *The Winged Serpent* (New York: John Day, 1946; rpt. by Capricorn Books as *American Indian Prose and Poetry* in 1962 and again by Beacon Press as *The Winged Serpent: American Indian Prose and Poetry* in 1992); the oratory of Ten Bears, Petalesharo, Hinmaton Yalakit, and Little Crow appears in W. C. Vanderwerth, ed., *Indian Oratory* (Norman: University of Oklahoma Press, 1971); the oration of Seathl (Seattle) and the death song of Red Bird appear in Thomas E. Sanders and Walter W. Peek, eds., *Literature of the American Indian* (New York: Glencoe, 1973); and the Cherokee and Luiseno creation stories, as well as the Navajo night chant, appear in Gloria Levitas, Frank Vivelo, and Jaqueline Vivelo, eds., *American Indian Prose and Poetry: We Wait in the Darkness* (New York: G. P. Putnam's Sons, 1974).

I benefited from a number of secondary sources, but I would like to single out the following: Henry Nash Smith, *Virgin Land: The American West as Symbol and Myth* (Cambridge, Mass.: Harvard University Press, 1950); Roy Harvey Pearce, *Savagism and Civilization: A Study of the Indian and the American Mind*, rev. ed. (Baltimore: Johns Hopkins University Press, 1967); William H. Goetzmann, *Exploration and Empire: The Explorer and the Scientist in the Winning of the American West* (New York: Norton, 1966); Richard Slotkin, *Regeneration Through Violence: The Mythology of the American Frontier, 1600–1860* (Middletown, Conn.: Wesleyan University Press, 1973); Eugene D. Genovese, *Roll, Jordan, Roll: The World the Slaves Made* (New York: Random House, 1974); and Reginald Horsman, *Race and Manifest Destiny: The Origins of American Racial Anglo-Saxonism* (Cambridge, Mass.: Harvard University Press, 1981). In addition, a very selective bibliography of further secondary sources, some of which appeared after the initial publication of this book, would include:

Aaron, Daniel. *The Unwritten War: American Writers and the Civil War*. New York: Oxford University Press, 1973.

Allen, Paula Gunn. *The Sacred Hoop: Recovering the Feminine in American Indian Traditions*. Boston: Beacon Press, 1986.

Andrews, William L. *To Tell a Free Story: The First Century of Afro-American Autobiography, 1760–1865*. Urbana: University of Illinois Press, 1988.

Bercovitch, Sacvan. *The American Jeremiad*. Madison: University of Wisconsin, 1978.

Blassingame, John. *The Slave Community: Plantation Life in the Antebellum South*. Rev. ed. New York: Oxford University Press, 1979.

Carby, Hazel V. *Reconstructing Womanhood: The Emergence of the Afro-American Woman Novelist*. New York: Oxford University Press, 1987.

Crane, Gregg D. *Race, Citizenship, and Law in American Literature*. New York: Cambridge University Press, 2002.

Davis, David Brion. *Slavery and Human Progress*. New York: Oxford University Press, 1984.

Dippie, Brian W. *The Vanishing American: White Attitudes and U.S. Indian Policy*. Middletown, Conn.: Wesleyan University Press, 1982.

Drinnon, Richard. *Facing West: The Metaphysics of Indian-Hating and Empire Building*. Minneapolis: University of Minnesota Press, 1980.

Epstein, Dena J. *Sinful Tunes and Spirituals: Black Folk Music to the Civil War*. Urbana: University of Illinois Press, 1977.

Ernest, John. *Resistance and Reformation in Nineteenth-Century African American Literature*. Jackson: University Press of Mississippi, 1995.

Fisher, Philip. *Hard Facts: Setting and Form in the American Novel*. New York: Oxford University Press, 1985.

Forgie, George. *Patricide in the House Divided: A Psychological Interpretation of Lincoln and His Age*. New York: Norton, 1979.

Foster, Frances Smith. *Witnessing Slavery: The Development of Antebellum Slave Narratives*. Westport, Conn.: Greenwood Press, 1979.

Fredrickson, George M. *The Black Image in the White Mind: The Debate on Afro-American Character and Destiny, 1817–1914*. New York: Harper and Row, 1971.

Furnas, J. C. *Goodbye to Uncle Tom*. New York, William Sloane, 1956.

Fussell, Edwin. *Frontier: American Literature and the American West*. Princeton: Princeton University Press, 1965.

Harrison, Brady. *Agent of Empire: William Walker and the Imperial Self in American Literature*. Athens: University of Georgia Press, 2004.

Hartman, Saidiya V. *Scenes of Subjection: Terror, Slavery, and Self-Making in Nineteenth-Century America*. New York: Oxford University Press, 1997.

Johannsen, Robert W. *To the Halls of the Montezumas: The Mexican War in the American Imagination*. New York: Oxford University Press, 1985.

Kolodny, Annette. *The Lay of the Land: Metaphor as Experience and History in American Life and Letters*. Chapel Hill: University of North Carolina Press, 1975.

Krupat, Arnold. *For Those Who Come After: A Study of Native American Autobiography*. Berkeley: University of California Press, 1985.

Levin, David. *History as Romantic Art: Bancroft, Prescott, Motley and Parkman*. New York: Harcourt, Brace, and World, 1963.

Levine, Lawrence W. *Black Culture and Black Consciousness: Afro-American Folk Thought From Slavery to Freedom*. New York: Oxford University Press, 1977.

Levine, Robert S. *Martin Delany, Frederick Douglass, and the Politics of Representative Identity*. Chapel Hill: University of North Carolina Press, 1997.

Limon, Jose E. *Mexican Ballads, Chicano Poems: History and Influence in Mexican-American Social Poetry*. Berkeley: University of California Press, 1992.

Lincoln, Kenneth. *Native American Renaissance*. Berkeley: University of California Press, 1983.

Lott, Eric. *Love and Theft: Blackface Minstrelsy and the American Working Class*. New York: Oxford University Press, 1993.

Lovell, John, Jr. *Black Song: The Forge and the Flame*. New York: Macmillan, 1974.

Marx, Leo. *The Machine in the Garden: Technology and the Pastoral Ideal in America*. New York: Oxford University Press, 1964.

Mitchell, Lee Clark. *Witnesses to a Vanishing America: The Nineteenth-Century Response*. Princeton: Princeton University Press, 1985.

Merk, Frederick. *Manifest Destiny and Mission in American History*. New York: Alfred A. Knopf, 1963.

Moses, Wilson J. *The Golden Age of Black Nationalism, 1850–1925*. Camden, Conn.: Archon Press, 1978.

Nelson, Dana D. *The Word in Black and White: Reading "Race" in American Literature, 1638–1867*. New York: Oxford University Press, 1994.

Nichols, Charles H. *Many Thousands Gone: The Ex-Slaves' Account of Their Bondage and Freedom*. Leiden: Brill, 1963.

Padilla, Genaro. *My History, Not Yours: The Formation of Mexican American Autobiography*. Madison: University of Wisconsin Press, 1994.

Pitt, Leonard. *The Decline of the Californios: A Social History of the Spanish-Speaking Californians, 1846–1890*. Berkeley: University of California Press, 1966.

Reynolds, David S. *Beneath the American Renaissance: The Subversive Imagination in the Age of Emerson and Melville*. New York: Alfred A. Knopf, 1988.

Rogin, Michael Paul. *Fathers and Children: Andrew Jackson and the Subjugation of the American Indian*. New York: Alfred A. Knopf, 1975.

Saldivar, Ramon. *Chicano Narrative: The Dialectics of Difference*. Madison: University of Wisconsin Press, 1990.

Samuels, Shirley. *Facing America: Iconography and the Civil War*. New York: Oxford University Press, 2004.

Scheckel, Susan. *The Insistence of the Indian: Race and Nationalism in Nineteenth-Century American Culture*. Princeton: Princeton University Press, 1998.

Sheehan, Bernard. *Seeds of Extinction: Jeffersonian Philanthropy and the American Indian*. New York: W. W. Norton, 1974.

Sollors, Werner. *Beyond Ethnicity: Consent and Descent in American Culture*. New York: Oxford University Press, 1986.

Stepto, Robert B. *From Behind the Veil: A Study of Afro-American Narrative*. Urbana: University of Illinois Press, 1979.

Streeby, Shelley. *American Sensations: Class, Empire, and the Production of Popular Culture*. Berkeley: University of California Press, 2002.

Stuckey, Sterling. *Slave Culture: Nationalist Theory and the Foundations of Black America*. New York: Oxford University Press, 1987.

Takaki, Ronald T. *Iron Cages: Race and Culture in Nineteenth-Century America*. New York: Alfred A. Knopf, 1979.

Taylor, William R. *Cavalier and Yankee: The Old South and the American National Character*. New York: Doubleday, 1963.

Tompkins, Jane. *Sensational Designs: The Cultural Work of American Fiction, 1790–1860*. New York: Oxford University Press, 1985.

Tuveson, Ernest. *Redeemer Nation: The Idea of America's Millennial Role*. Chicago: University of Chicago Press, 1971.

Van DeBurg, William L. *Slavery and Race in American Popular Culture*. Madison: University of Wisconsin Press, 1984.

Walters, Ronald G. *The Antislavery Appeal: American Abolitionism after 1830*. Baltimore: Johns Hopkins University Press, 1976.

Weaver, Jace. *That the People Might Live: Native American Literatures and Native American Community*. New York: Oxford University Press, 1997.

Weinstein, Cindy. *Family, Kinship, and Sympathy in Nineteenth-Century American Literature*. New York: Cambridge University Press, 2004.

Wilson, Edmund. *Patriotic Gore: Studies in the Literature of the Civil War*. New York: Oxford University Press, 1962.

Acknowledgments

For assistance with this book in its original appearance as part of the *Cambridge History of American Literature*, I would like to acknowledge a Humanities Research Fellowship provided by the University of California, Berkeley, and the help of the staff at the Bancroft Library at Berkeley. For his advice on the whole I am grateful to Sacvan Bercovitch, and for comments on other portions of the manuscript I would like to thank Paula Gunn Allen, Richard Bridgman, Norman Grabo, and Kenneth Lincoln. In addition, I would like to acknowledge the indispensable help of Andrew Brown, Cyrus Patell, Julie Greenblatt, and T. Susan Chang.

For her welcome interest in publishing a new edition with the University Press of Mississippi, I am grateful to Seetha Srinivasan, and I likewise wish to thank Walter Biggins and Shane Gong for their assistance.

Parts of the material on African American slavery had their origin in a paper presented at the English Institute in 1983 and published as "Slavery, Revolution, and the American Renaissance," in Walter Benn Michaels and Donald Pease, eds., *The American Renaissance Reconsidered* (Baltimore: The Johns Hopkins University Press, 1985), pp. 1–33, and a few passages were incorporated into my book *To Wake the Nations: Race in the Making of American Literature* (Cambridge, Mass.: Harvard University Press, 1993). A section of the material on American Indians appeared as "The Indian Gallery: Antebellum Literature and the Containment of the American Indian," in Beverley Voloshin, ed., *American Literature, Culture, and Ideology: Essays in Memory of Henry Nash Smith* (New York: Peter Lang, 1990), pp. 37–64.

Index